STRANGE
BUT TRUE
TALES OF CAR
COLLECTING

STRANGE
BUT TRUE
TALES OF CAR
COLLECTING

Drowned Bugattis, Buried Belvederes,
Felonious Ferraris, and other Wild Stories
of Automotive Misadventure

By Keith Martin and
Linda Clark

First published in 2013 by Motorbooks, an imprint of MBI Publishing Company, 400 First Avenue North, Suite 400, Minneapolis, MN 55401 USA

Motorbooks titles are also available at discounts in bulk quantity for industrial or sales-promotional use. For details, write to Special Sales Manager at MBI Publishing Company, 400 First Avenue North, Suite 400, Minneapolis, MN 55401 USA. To find out more about our books, visit us online at www.motorbooks.com.

Editor: Jordan Wiklund
Design Manager: Brad Springer
Design and layout: Diana Boger
Cover Design: Jason Gabbert

On the front cover: This Bugatti Brescia Type 22 spent over 70 years underwater in Lake Maggiore, Switzerland.
On the back cover: The original Chitty Bang Bang; Pontiac's experimental "ghost car;" and a buried Belvedere whose time capsule was not quite waterproof.
On the spine: The wheel of a super rare 1963 Aston Martin DB4; the vehicle was finally found in storage after more than 30 years.

Library of Congress Cataloging-in-Publication Data

Martin, Keith, 1950-
  Strange but true tales of car collecting : drowned Bugattis, buried Belvederes, felonious Ferraris, and other wild stories of automotive misadventure / by Keith Martin and the staff and writers of Sports Car Market.
      pages cm
  ISBN 978-0-7603-4400-2 (hardcover/jacket)
  1. Automobiles--Collectors and collecting--Anecdotes. 2. Automobiles--History--Anecdotes. 3. Curiosities and wonders--Anecdotes. 4. Automobiles--Collectors and collecting--Biography--Anecdotes. I. Sports car market. II. Title.
  TL7.A1M364 2013
  629.222075--dc23
                              2013009405

Printed in China

10 9 8 7 6 5 4 3 2

CONTENTS

SECTION № 2 WRECKS & RUINS

SECTION № 3 STRANGER THAN FICTION

ACKNOWLEDGMENTS

MANY THANKS go to this book's lead writer, Linda Clark, and all the scribbling gearheads that also contributed, including Tom Cotter, Miles Collier, John Draneas, Tony Piff, Erin Olson, Mike Sheehan, Steve Ahlgrim, Colin Comer, Dale Novak, and Simon Kidston. This book would not have been possible without the help of Gooding & Co., RM Auctions, The Associated Press, Jay Leno, John Apen, Lance Miller, Jeff Stites, and David Tomaro. Finally, we couldn't have even dreamed of this book without the unbelievable—but true—antics of car lovers all over the world for the past century.

—Chester Allen
Executive Editor,
Sports Car Market

INTRODUCTION

A STRANGE, WONDERFUL WORLD

I'VE LOVED CARS for as long as I can remember, and this collection of strange tales often didn't seem so strange to me. I'm a little worried about that.

Okay, my will doesn't stipulate that I am to be buried in the 1964 Ferrari 330 America I once owned, I can't imagine buying truckloads of rare car parts and then hiding them away, and I would not pay $70,000 for Steve McQueen's sunglasses.

But our culture's love affair with cars is an entirely different passion than any other. I can't imagine a stamp collector wanting to take his treasures along to the grave, or coin collectors neatly displaying their shiny possessions on a golf course.

But car collectors are constantly finding, restoring, showing, touring, and rallying their prized possessions. In the pre-Internet era, having a car gave you instant freedom. And even today, getting behind the wheel of a classic 1965 Mustang convertible with "Surfer Girl" playing on the one-speaker AM radio can take you back to a simpler time. But our passion for old cars has led us to do some strange things:

Who would sink a 1925 Bugatti into a deep lake to avoid taxes?

Who would lovingly restore a 1957 Plymouth Belvedere that spent decades submerged in a water-filled vault in Tulsa, Oklahoma?

Why does famous comedian Jay Leno prowl Los Angeles neighborhoods in search of yet another Duesenberg?

Who would buy a car that floats—most of the time—just to drive across a lake as water sloshes perilously near the edge of the doors?

Why would anyone pay $16.4 million for a Ferrari that was once wrecked and twice burned?

The answer to all these questions is simple: gearheads love cars, and we'll go to great lengths—sometimes to the edge of madness and beyond—to follow our dreams.

This collection of 33 tales sometimes takes us over that edge, but it's a fun ride. I hope you enjoy the work of Linda Clark and other *Sports Car Market* writers, and the masterful editing of *SCM* Executive Editor Chester Allen. Now I have to go find a correct windshield-washer squirter for my 1967 Alfa Romeo GTV. Sounds crazy? It may be. But wait until you turn the page...

—Keith Martin

Founder & Publisher,

Sports Car Market magazine

"Imagine opening the door to your late uncle's small unassuming suburban garage and finding a rare car inside that's worth $4 million.

That's what happened to an English engineer in 2007, when he unlocked the door of the garage left to him and seven other relatives by his 89-year-old uncle, Dr. Harold Carr. The garage was in Gosforth, an affluent suburb of Newcastle, and the car was a Bugatti Type 57S Atalante coupe."

FAME &
FORTUNE

THE $16.4 MILLION FERRARI

BY SIMON KIDSTON

When its owner believed the aging Ferrari was worth more in cash than as a car, he doused the interior in gasoline and set it on fire. The fire—the car's second—totaled the vehicle beyond repair.

A TRIP TO HELL AND BACK
NETS $16.4 MILLION

ONLY 34 FERRARI 250 TESTA ROSSA race cars were built, and now they're among the most valuable cars on the planet.

At one time, though, these old racers were considered almost worthless, especially when you consider the wild, violent story of 0666TR, the prototype for the series.

The 0666TR made its debut at the Nürburgring 1,000 km, coming sixth in qualifying and tenth overall in the race. Later, between September and October 1957, it was stripped of its envelope body and refinished by Scaglietti in the now famous pontoon-fender style.

The 0666TR then raced in the Venezuelan Grand Prix, coming in third overall, before being transported to Argentina for the first race of the 1958 season, the Buenos Aires 1,000 km, where it finished second overall. The Targa Florio was the last race for 0666TR as a Scuderia Ferrari team car, where it was equipped with six Solex twin-choke carburetors. It was in fourth place when it had to leave the race.

In June 1958 the car was sold to Luigi Chinetti and delivered to him at Le Mans to be driven by Dan Gurney and Bruce Kessler. Late into the race, hurdling through the rain, Kessler collided with a privately entered D-type Jaguar. A fire erupted, and the Testa Rossa was out of the race.

Its story was not over, however. The burned car received a fresh pontoon-fender body from Scaglietti. In 1959 Chinetti sold the car to Rod Carveth, a Californian who entered it for the 12 Hours of Sebring, where it did not finish. The car also did not finish the Nürburgring 1,000 km. The car was entered at the 1959 Le Mans race, but it broke down on the Mulsanne straight. At Laguna Seca, Phil Hill drove 0666TR, but it didn't qualify. In 1962 Carveth sold the car. The car's new owner was a Buick dealer who used it as his personal street car, and after the original engine finally gave out, it was removed and traded away.

Then the unthinkable occurred. When its owner believed the aging Ferrari was worth more in cash than as a car, he doused the interior in gasoline and set it on fire. The fire—the car's second—totaled the vehicle beyond repair.

LEGACY OF THE TESTA ROSSA

In 1970 Charles Betz and Fred Peters took a flyer on the Testa Rossa. Over the next decade, 0666TR was restored to concours condition and an engine from another Testa Rossa was installed.

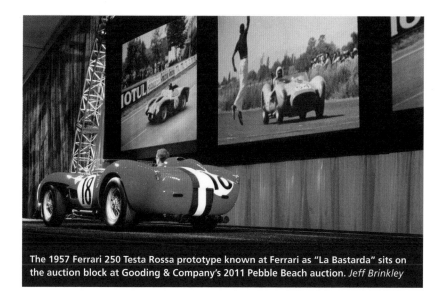

The 1957 Ferrari 250 Testa Rossa prototype known at Ferrari as "La Bastarda" sits on the auction block at Gooding & Company's 2011 Pebble Beach auction. *Jeff Brinkley*

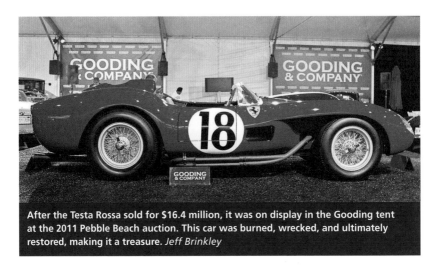

After the Testa Rossa sold for $16.4 million, it was on display in the Gooding tent at the 2011 Pebble Beach auction. This car was burned, wrecked, and ultimately restored, making it a treasure. *Jeff Brinkley*

In the late 1980s 0666TR began winning concours. Almost 20 years later in 2002, Betz and Peters sold it to a top collector, who restored it to its original Ferrari Racing Team appearance and specifications, including the reinstallation of the original engine.

The car entered the 2006 Pebble Beach Concours d'Elegance and won its class. But that wasn't all—like a phantom racer from the past, the car won more top awards at other venues.

In 2011 the car sold for a stunning, world-record $16.4 million at Gooding & Company's Pebble Beach auction. This price is still the highest amount ever paid for a motor car at auction.

How did a crashed, twice-burned, and then restored car go from near-junkyard status to the most expensive car ever bought at auction?

The 250 Testa Rossa is Ferrari's most celebrated sports-racing model, a legend in car collecting circles and one of the most valuable cars in the world.

Introduced in 1957 in anticipation of the upcoming 3-liter limit in the World Sports Car Championship, it stole a march on rivals Jaguar and Maserati, who had been pinning their hopes on "big bangers" such as the D-type and 450S, and achieved success everywhere it raced, from Europe and South America to the all-important SCCA races contested by Ferrari's wealthy U.S. privateer clients, earning the company healthy profits.

Named Testa Rossa (pronounced "ross-ah," not "rose-ah," meaning "redhead") after its red cam covers, 34 of these cars were built from 1957 until 1962. No two were identical, but works TRs were generally right-hand drive. The early ones were wet-sumped, and the 1958 cars had so-called pontoon-fender bodywork by Scaglietti, which was intended to help cool the front brakes. From 1959 the cars reverted to a full-fender envelope style made by Fantuzzi, as Scaglietti was busy clothing Ferrari GT cars.

From 1959 onward production was devoted to works cars, which featured disc brakes and separate gearboxes with rear differentials. All except the last TR (0808) had 3-liter motors largely derived from the production 250 GT.

Our subject car, 0666TR, is the first of two prototypes, both of which ran as works cars. As with all prototypes, some buyers prefer the recognition of the standard model, and others enjoy owning something different. I exchanged opinions with many experts and fellow TR owners before and after the auction as to the value of this car and its historical significance, and I heard both ends of the spectrum.

"A friend of mine would pay eight to ten million," said one owner, "as it's not a standard TR chassis, and I doubt much of the original bodywork survives." This, of course, was a reference to not one but two fires that the car endured during its early years. The auction catalog mentioned both fires but omitted that in the first incident, the driver of the other car perished. Although the catalog alluded to post-fire photographs, they were not published.

Other TR owners were more upbeat, confiding that they had received approaches north of $20 million for their cars and that the auction estimate seemed reasonable

The 1957 Ferrari Testa Rossa before Gooding & Company's 2011 Pebble Beach Auction. *Gooding & Company*

No traces remain of the car's rough days as a burnt-out, run-down wreck. *Gooding & Company*

It's hard to believe that this restored 250 Testa Rossa prototype was once a destitute, unloved car. *Gooding & Company*

for 0666. It's a fine example of British understatement to say that on the evening of August 20, 2011—in the middle of a worldwide economic storm—there was widespread interest in the fate that awaited this very high-profile Ferrari under the auctioneer's gavel.

They needn't have worried. A new collector—just starting out at 73 years old, but his line of business keeps him young—kicked off proceedings with a $10 million bid.

Rapid salvos ensued: $11 million, $11.5 million, $11.8 million. At $12.4 million, the auctioneer announced the reserve had been met, and it became a two-horse race between an absentee bidder and a telephone bidder in mostly $100,000 increments. When the mystery phone bidder prevailed, the hammer fell as cheers erupted all around the auction.

I consulted many sources to paint an accurate picture of this car. David Gooding, owner of Gooding & Company, opined that the 250 TR is undervalued compared with its close sister, the 250 GTO—a sentiment echoed by many (most vocally by TR owners who don't also have a GTO). Given time this will seem a good buy. Gooding believed that 0666's history was more illustrious than most, and when shown the post-fire photographs, bidders had remarked the damage wasn't as bad as expected.

I asked the seller, whose collection probably counts as one of the top ten in the world, why he had decided to part with a car in which he had invested so much. "I find my Maserati 300S easier to handle," he confided. "Plus I've just bought a house on Maui!" He also felt that after a restoration costing close to half a million dollars, he was concerned about spoiling the TR in historic racing. Ultimately he'd done pretty much what he wanted to with the car, and it was time to move on.

To get to the bottom of the controversy about the fires, I went to Maranello and met with friends at Ferrari Classiche. "Chassis 0666? Of course we remember it. We called it 'La Bastarda!' A very interesting car with two fathers: the front chassis is similar to a 500 TRC, the rear is like a later-works 250 TR, and you can still see all the little modifications that we tried out on it in period, all documented by various memos in our archive."

Was the chassis replaced after the Le Mans accident? "Definitely not. Only the upper part of the car was damaged. Look, it's all here on the microfilm, everything."

Lastly, I consulted a well-known Ferrari historian. How many 250 TRs does he think have their original bodywork? "Perhaps sixty percent, but it's hard to say, as for years nobody bothered to track such information." Let's face it, these bodies were cigarette-paper thin and were intended to last a few race seasons—not decades.

And what, in his opinion, would the very best 250 TR be worth? "That would be one of the Le Mans winners. They almost never come up, so I'd have to say twenty-five million dollars."

Hard auction results are available, as three Testa Rossas have crossed the block in the past decade. Chassis 0714 TR, a customer car, led a less eventful life but also

This photo shows the classic pontoon styling of this car. Only 34 vehicles of this type were built between 1956 and 1961. *Gooding & Company*

achieved far less on the track. Chassis 0808 is a Le Mans winner, but it spent years as a coupe before reverting to its original, quirky 1962 body style. Chassis 0738 TR had neither history nor originality on its side. A better comparison would be 0724 TR, a customer pontoon-fender TR with a modest history—it spent 49 ½ years in the same hands until it was sold privately this March for 4,400 times what the seller had paid originally—the price of a new MGA at the time!

So let's bring all those strands together and consider our verdict. Did the new owner of 0666 TR get caught up in the classic Monterey euphoria and overpay, or was this a shrewd investment?

On the one hand, we have a unique factory prototype with a front-line international racing history. The majority of 250 TRs were customer cars destined for weekend outings around airfields serving as SCCA circuits. This one roared around Le Mans, the Targa Florio and the 'Ring, and it was piloted by all-time heroes.

On the other hand, it led a hard life as a race car and later as an old hack. The chassis number 0666 is prophetic, as it's been to hell and back. Ultimately, though, it's been cherished for the past 40 years, restored without regard to expense for a highly respected collector whose passion, expertise, and motivation are beyond reproach, and the Ferrari factory has given it their unquestioned blessing.

Auctions are a roll of the dice that not all sellers want to risk, but in this case the gamble paid off. The car was well sold at auction and well bought for posterity.

THE O'QUINN COLLECTION

BY JOHN DRANEAS AND GREG RILEY

O'Quinn thought nothing of paying world-record prices for some of the world's rarest autos if he wanted them. He had a voracious auction appetite, and he often bought multiple high-end cars in a single weekend.

THE LEGAL BATTLE
OVER A BILLIONAIRE'S
MILLION-DOLLAR CARS

HERE'S A CAR STORY with all the ingredients of a soap opera: a billionaire dies in a car crash, and his longtime girlfriend is left out of his will. He owned hundreds of cars worth millions of dollars, but he also owed millions of dollars. To cap it off, all this turned into a high-stakes courtroom battle just before the sale of some of the cars at a high-profile auction.

The girlfriend claimed her boyfriend bought the cars as gifts for her, so they belonged to her. No matter that none of them were titled in her name—in fact, they were still held by "open titles" in the name of previous owners and were never reregistered.

The estate countered. *Just because your boyfriend said he was buying the cars for you*, the estate argued, *doesn't make them your cars*. He paid for them with his money and retained possession and control of them, so they were still *his* cars.

Houston lawyer John O'Quinn was a larger-than-life man who rose from poverty to become one of the top class-action attorneys in the world.

JOHN O'QUINN'S PASSIONS

Billionaire Houston attorney John O'Quinn burst upon the collector car scene in 2003. O'Quinn was an auto mechanic's son born into near poverty in a hardscrabble area of Houston. By all accounts, he was a workaholic who obtained verdicts for his clients worth billions of dollars, most notably as a leader of the huge tobacco company class-action lawsuit, and he made a fortune for himself along the way.

Forbes magazine once described O'Quinn as "the lawyer from hell." He was certainly a polarizing figure. Some saw him as a saint, whereas others described him—and his legal tactics—as despicable.

O'Quinn's automotive passions began as a young man when his father took him to a car show and said Duesenbergs were "the best cars in the world." The passion simmered until 2003, when he began building one of the country's most significant car collections at lightning speed.

O'Quinn thought nothing of paying world-record prices for some of the world's rarest autos—if he wanted them. He had a voracious auction appetite, and he often bought multiple high-end cars in a single weekend.

At the time of his death, O'Quinn owned 850 cars, including a jaw-dropping 23 Duesenbergs. O'Quinn's Duesenbergs included the Whittle Mistress Car, the Rudolf Bauer car (the last Duesenberg), and the recently restored Father Divine

"Throne Car." He reportedly also had the world's largest collections of Rolls-Royce Silver Ghosts and electric cars. And he had stated that he was going to assemble the world's largest collection of Figoni et Falaschi.

Virtually every marque and type of car was represented in his collection: Auburn, Bugatti, Cord, Delahaye, Duesenberg, Ferrari, Packard, Maserati, Mercer, Stanley, Stutz, Talbot-Lago and more. He also owned gas cars, steam cars, electric cars, brass cars, antique cars, classic cars, special interest cars, muscle cars, and super cars.

THE GIRLFRIEND & THE ESTATE

At the time of his death, O'Quinn had been in a relationship with his constant companion, Darla Lexington, for more than ten years. Both were previously married and divorced, and even though they were not married to each other, O'Quinn frequently introduced her as his wife, and they both wore wedding rings. They were always seen at car events together, often bidding together at auctions. In fact, it was Lexington who encouraged O'Quinn to attend his first car auction.

During the last few years of O'Quinn's life, Lexington assumed management of his car collection. She controlled much of what happened with the cars, and she hired the numerous employees who cared for them.

O'Quinn repeatedly spoke of his intention to open a museum to house his car collection, but he never took any steps to create a museum or a charitable entity for that purpose.

Billionaire John O'Quinn and Darla Lexington in happier days with part of the huge car collection.

This is John O'Quinn's beautiful 1934 Duesenberg Model J Riviera Phaeton. It has a double overhead cam 265-horsepower straight eight engine, at rest here at the Louisville Concours d'Elegance at Churchill Downs in 2009. It is one of just three fitted with the Riviera Phaeton body by Brunn. *Jim Rugowski*

O'Quinn died on October 29, 2009, in what can only be described as a freak accident. He was driving his Chevrolet Suburban on wet Houston streets when he apparently lost control, veered off the road, and hit a tree. Both he and his companion, a longtime law firm employee, died in the crash. Neither was wearing a seat belt.

The disposition of O'Quinn's estate was controlled by his 2008 will. It left the bulk of his estate to the John M. O'Quinn Foundation, a charitable entity he established in 1986 that focuses on helping children, public education, and the environment. Oddly, no provision was made for Lexington, although she was named as the beneficiary of a substantial life insurance policy. Perhaps even odder, no mention was made of what should be done with his car collection. It was simply lumped in with the remainder of the estate that passed to the foundation.

The legal battles started soon enough. Lexington claimed that she owned 28 of the most significant cars and she intended to honor O'Quinn's wishes and use those as the nucleus for a world-class car museum.

"If I can show what John wanted and intended, everything will work out fine," Lexington said.

Dale Jefferson, a friend of O'Quinn's—and once Lexington's attorney—was now the attorney for the executor of the O'Quinn estate. Jefferson took exception to Lexington's statement.

"John O'Quinn was unmarried at the time of his death," Jefferson said. "It is our position that all of his property, including the cars in question, belongs to his charitable foundation."

Jimmy Williamson, Lexington's attorney, responded, "John and Darla lived together as husband and wife for many years, and his estate has a fiduciary responsibility to her beyond his death—and to carry out his wishes which he stated publically on many occasions."

The legal battle intensified when the estate executor contracted to sell five of the estate's most significant cars: at RM's Monterey auction in August 2010, a 1938 Talbot-Lago T150-C Speciale Teardrop; a 1936 Mercedes-Benz 540K Special cabriolet; and three rare Corvettes, including a pilot production vehicle. Lexington filed suit and asked for a temporary injunction to prevent the sales, arguing that the five cars were among the 28 that she owned.

In tearful testimony, Lexington lamented that the people administering the estate, "act as if I never knew John O'Quinn." She produced several witnesses who claimed that O'Quinn had, in fact, gifted the cars to her. Her legal team even showed a Discovery Channel TV segment in which O'Quinn stated that he had purchased the Talbot-Lago for her.

The estate argued that O'Quinn's statement that he purchased a multi-million-dollar car "for Darla" didn't mean that it belonged to her. To have given the car to her, he would have had to either title it in her name or made some affirmative transfer of ownership to her—neither of which occurred.

O'Quinn was a very experienced attorney, and he would have known that such a large gift to her would have required the payment of a substantial amount of gift tax. No such gift tax returns had been filed. Further, the estate said that the sale of these cars was critical to prevent a default on O'Quinn's $100 million credit line.

Lexington's legal hurdles were quite high. An executor has broad powers to sell estate assets as deemed necessary to administer the estate. Establishing that O'Quinn wanted her to have the cars—or that she deserved them—would not be enough. She had to prove that she actually owned the cars before O'Quinn died, which would be very hard to do without written documentation. And she had to establish that preventing the sale was necessary, as she could still claim entitlement to the proceeds from the sale of "her" cars.

This 1929 Rolls-Royce Springfield Phantom I Riviera Town Brougham is also from O'Quinn's collection, seen here at Louisville in 2009. The Phantom I was introduced in 1925 to replace the Silver Ghost. It has a 468-cubic-inch six-cylinder overhead valve motor. O'Quinn's car is one of just ten bodied by Brewster & Co. *Jim Rugowski*

THE DECISION AND DENOUEMENT

The case was heard by the judge on August 6, 2010. On August 9, just three days before the start of RM's Monterey auction, the judge ruled that the sales could go forward, stating that Lexington failed to establish "a probable right to recover ownership of the five automobiles at issue."

These five cars sold at the auction—the Mercedes-Benz 540K alone sold for $913,000—but that did not end the litigation. Lexington still had a common-law marriage action pending, and she still sought recovery of the funds generated at Monterey, as well as ownership of the 23 other cars.

Many who knew O'Quinn were amazed that his will left nothing to Lexington, as they were sure that he would have wanted her to be very well provided for. They were equally amazed that nothing specific was provided for the car collection. Many believe that he planned to make such changes to his will, but he just never got around to doing so.

This case points out some very important lessons for car collectors. First off, no one ever expects to die in a day or so, but it happens. Our system of law provides that one's wishes about the disposition of their property are to be found only in a valid will or a living trust.

No matter how convincing any other evidence might be about what someone "wanted" to happen, that evidence will be ignored. If you want a loved one to inherit any part of your estate, you'd better get it written into your will or trust.

More specific to car collectors, your automobiles require specific attention in your estate-planning documents. There is not much doubt that O'Quinn was serious about creating a museum for his collection, but he never did it and he didn't create any mechanism for its creation after his death.

Note that his existing foundation probably can't do that now, as its stated purposes are very different, and a car museum would probably not be an attractive investment. The foundation probably has no alternative than to sell the cars and put the proceeds to a more productive use from its perspective.

To gain assurance that your car collection is going to remain intact after your death, you not only need to establish a legal structure for it, but you also need to provide a reliable funding mechanism for it to happen.

In the end, Lexington and the John O'Quinn Foundation settled the case during a pretrial hearing in early January 2012.

The exact terms of the settlement are confidential, but Lexington received some cars from the once vast collection and a cash payment that will allow her to live comfortably for the rest of her life.

O'Quinn's giant collection of cars has been mostly sold off to new owners. As of December 2012 more than 600 of the more than 850 cars have been sold.

Proceeds from these sales have gone to the John M. O'Quinn Foundation, which has become one of the top charitable organizations in Houston, Texas.

THE BILL COSBY
SUPER SNAKE

BY LINDA CLARK

"I need a car that does one hundred eighty or better to get to work," Cosby said in his famous recording about his one drive in a monster 427 Cobra. "It's faster than anything that Steve McQueen owns."

FASTER THAN STEVE MCQUEEN

BILL COSBY'S LONG AND VARIED CAREER—as a comedian, actor, author, television producer, jazz musician, and educator—resembles his automotive pursuits.

Cosby has covered a lot of territory, from collecting antique, custom, and sports cars, to hosting numerous automobile events, to cofounding an Indy-car race team during his decades-long love affair with cars.

Through his many connections, Cosby met famed car painter Junior Conway—owner of the House of Color in Los Angeles, California, which specializes in painting Porsches, Lamborghinis, and other high-end cars. Conway got his start working for George Barris in the 1950s before opening his own shop a decade later.

In a *Sports Illustrated* interview, Conway talked about his obsession with paint and reminisced about the 1960s, when he did a lot of work for celebrities like Steve McQueen, Ann-Margret, and Bill Cosby.

I SPY A SUPER SNAKE

And that's when our story begins. By 1963 Cosby was a successful stand-up comic and subject of a *Newsweek* feature. In 1965 Cosby landed his first acting role as Pentagon secret agent Alexander Scott in the NBC adventure series *I Spy*, which was television's attempt to emulate the success of the James Bond films.

In 1966 Cosby was shopping in a department store when he bumped into his friend Carroll Shelby. Cosby, who liked fast cars, drove Ferraris at the time. Shelby, the Texas-born creator of the Shelby Cobra, thought he ought to be driving an American-made performance car and offered to build a "Cobra to end all Cobras" for the comedian. Cosby has told slightly different versions of the story through the years—from running into Shelby in a grocery store to getting a phone call from Barry Galloway, who was Shelby American's comptroller. But in any case, Cosby agreed to Shelby's offer and anticipated delivery of the car "like a kid waiting for Christmas to come."

The supercharged 427 Cobra, dubbed the Super Snake, arrived one night while Cosby was relaxing at home. He heard a knock at the door, and it turned out to be Barry Galloway (dressed all in black, as Cosby has humorously told it), who was there to hand Cosby the keys and watch him start the monster car up.

No one told the hair-raising tale of what happened next better than Cosby himself, on his 1968 comedy album, *Bill Cosby 200 M.P.H.* Suffice it to say that the 800-horsepower roadster packed more punch than any sane person needs in a street car.

One of only two built, the Cobra Super Snake, CSX3303, had a twin Paxton supercharged 427-cubic-inch V-8 engine with twin Holley four-barrel carburetors and an 11.5:1 compression ratio. Officially, the 2,280-pound roadster went from 0 to 60 miles per hour in 4.5 seconds. Shelby had signed a plate on the dashboard that read, "This car is guaranteed to do 200 mph."

Painted in Shelby's trademark Guardsman Blue, the AC Ace-based roadster had a roll bar, side pipes, and hood scoop. As a manual transmission clutch couldn't handle its outsized horsepower, the Super Snake was fitted with a three-speed automatic transmission.

The Super Snake stood out, even among the fast transatlantic hybrid Cobras that Shelby—a former Texas chicken rancher and ex-racer—built from 1962 to 1968. Cobras jammed Ford V-8 engines (289-, 260-, or the fearsome 427-cubic-inch) into the light, British-made AC Ace roadster. The combination of powerful engines and light cars created some of the wildest sports cars ever made.

Before building Cosby's car, Shelby had constructed a twin Paxton car (CSX3015) for himself in 1966. This car sold at auction in 2007 for a record $5.5 million, including a 10 percent buyer's premium. Shelby used it as his personal car and entered it in the Turismos Visitadores, a road race in Nevada—a road race, at the time, without a speed limit—where he was "waking up whole towns, blowing out windows, throwing belts and catching fire a couple times, but finishing."

Super Snakes had the 427 Cobra's aluminum body and beefed-up tubular steel frame, with coil springs in place of leaf springs (used on the smaller 289 Cobras) and fat tires and wheels residing under the flared fenders needed to accommodate them.

A 427 Competition car—made street legal with the addition of mufflers, minimal bumpers, and a windshield—formed the basis for Shelby's twin Paxton model. It retained a racing rear-end, brakes, and exhaust headers. The Super Snake built for Cosby, however, was based on a non-Competition 427 roadster.

Although Super Snake was the official name of a 427-powered 1967 GT500 car, it was also what the twin Paxton–supercharged Cobras were often called. "That came about in 1968," Colin Comer wrote in *The Complete Book of Shelby Automobiles*, "when Al Dowd of Shelby American placed an ad to sell CSX3015 and referred to it as Carroll Shelby's personal Super Snake."

THE NEED FOR SPEED

After driving his teeth-rattling Super Snake just once—and with more than a little urging from his wife, Camille—Cosby returned the car to Shelby American. In 1969 the company shipped it to one of its dealers in San Francisco, S&C Ford, on Van Ness Avenue. Later that year, S&C sold it to customer Tony Maxey. In 1970 Maxey died from injuries he suffered in a crash after he lost control of the Super Snake and it veered off a cliff.

The big-block Cobra was totaled and its wreckage hauled to a scrap yard, where it was sold. The engine and suspension were used in a Ford hot rod, and the serial number and rights to it were assigned to a new chassis and body that a shop in England used to recreate the Cosby car in the mid-1970s.

More recently, the car's current owner was reported to have removed the engine and twin Paxton superchargers from the hot rod, and reunited them with the recreated Cosby car to more closely replicate its original configuration.

Cosby's passion for high-performance cars was well known. Although he had owned a Maserati, he was especially fond of Ferraris, about which he said, "When you buy one, they automatically give you twelve speeding tickets."

The comedian also liked to tell the story about his 1949 MG TC roadster, which he had made into a V-8-powered hot rod in the late 1960s at Shelby's shop. When asked why he wanted it modified, Cosby told Shelby, "I want to mess with some people, man!"

Coincidentally, Shelby credited a 1949 MG TC roadster with changing his life, after he drove one to victory in a road race in Norman, Oklahoma, in 1952. From that point forward, Shelby said he wanted to be involved with racing and sports cars. That same historic race car sold at auction in 2008 for $313,500.

During the 1970s Cosby was a pitchman for Ford and appeared in many of the company's print and TV ads. When the Frederick Crawford Auto-Aviation Museum in Cleveland held their first Concours d'Elegance in 1978, Cosby served as master of ceremonies.

Cosby was also a close friend of the late Bill Harrah, whose shop in Reno, Nevada, continued to operate after Harrah's death and restored Cosby's Mercedes-Benz 300SL roadster in 1983. Cosby was a regular headliner at Harrah's hotels and had his 1935 Aston Martin Tourer on permanent loan to Harrah's Automobile Collection.

In 1984 Cosby produced and starred in one of that decade's defining sitcoms, *The Cosby Show*, which aired until 1992. His 1987 book, *Fatherhood*, was a bestseller.

Two years later, Cosby joined forces with Raynor Manufacturing Company of Dixon, Illinois, to sponsor race car driver Willy T. Ribbs on the Indy-car circuit for five years. Team manager Ray Neisewander III told newspapers at the time that Raynor-Cosby would spend $4.5 million in the first year. "I'll probably be in the pits, catching the fuel that spills," Cosby joked about the cost. Ribbs drove in the 1991 and 1993 Indianapolis 500 races.

Cosby has played the drums since childhood and has hosted the annual Los Angeles Playboy Jazz Festival since 1979. Also known for his charity work, he drove a Porsche 911 Turbo in the New York City leg of the 2001 Porsche Drive for Hope to raise funds for cancer research and for families of victims of America's 9/11 tragedy.

Although he was born and raised in Philadelphia, Cosby's main home is in Shelburne Falls, Massachusetts, a small, scenic town about 130 miles northwest of

Boston. It's a 171-year old farmhouse that he and his wife have lived in since 1964. It sits on 286 acres in the foothills of the Berkshire Mountains. There's ample room for his dozen or so cars, including his prewar Aston Martin, a Rolls-Royce, and several sports cars.

But when it comes to cars, Cosby is best known for his one drive in a monster 427 Shelby Cobra Super Snake.

"I need a car that does one hundred eighty or better to get to work," Cosby said in his famous recording about his one drive in a monster 427 Cobra. "It's faster than anything that Steve McQueen owns."

It turned out that 200 miles per hour was just a little too much.

JAY LENO'S DUESENBERG

BY TONY PIFF

After spending a half-century inside a leaky garage next to an open window, the paint was shot, the wood was rotten, and the sheet metal corroded beyond rescue. One fender had a hole rusted completely through. A set of disintegrating tires stored inside had ruined the interior. And, having driven 107,000 miles before being retired, the engine and mechanicals were severely worn.

LENO'S DILIGENCE PAYS OFF

JAY LENO DIDN'T KNOW what was in the small yellow garage behind Bill Johnson's house, but there were rumors of a rare treasure entombed inside, locked away for decades. Leno, a man who loves cars—especially cars with interesting stories—had a hunch about this one, and he was determined to get inside that little garage.

"I learned about Bill in the eighties," Leno says. "Quiet guy, didn't say much." The garage was conveniently located in Burbank, just a few miles from NBC Studios, where Leno hosts *The Tonight Show*, and not far from Leno's Los Angeles home. So one day Leno simply drove by in his Stanley steam car, caught Bill's attention, and made his acquaintance.

Leno asked what was in the garage, but Bill just smiled and kept mum. Little did Leno know, Bill would maintain that smiling, silent grin for 20 years. But Leno is a patient, friendly guy.

Jay Leno's collection of classic and modern cars is well documented. Many celebrities and sports stars were motorheads long before they found fame, and Leno's collection is at the top of A-list stars. Though this isn't the Deusenberg from the story, the photo provides an excellent glimpse into part of his well-cared-for warehouse. *Getty*

Perhaps you've heard the story of one of Leno's other miraculous car finds. There were rumors circulating within the old-car community of a Duesenberg Model J in storage in a Manhattan garage. Someone had reportedly seen it, maybe, but of course no one could remember where it was. Or perhaps no one was telling.

So what did Leno do? He started pounding the pavement.

"I hit every garage in New York City," he says. "I'd just ask the attendant, 'Any old cars in there?'" The approach unearthed plenty of luxo-barges from the 1970s, but no Duesenbergs were forthcoming. Then, many garages later, on the third floor of a garage on Park Avenue, Leno spied the fabled Model J, parked next to a Rolls-Royce.

The Model J was the top-of-the-line Duesenberg, a supercar in its day, built for Hollywood stars and captains of industry. You could buy a Cadillac for $5,000 or a Ford Model T for $500, or you could shell out $25,000—in 1930s dollars—or more for a Model J. But the Great Depression put such showy displays of opulence out of fashion, and Duesenberg ceased production by 1937.

The Manhattan Duesie was built as a town car, with an open-air chauffer's compartment and a formal passenger's compartment. This particularly ostentatious design only grew more dated as the years went on, which helps explain why it was parked in 1941 and never moved.

This is exactly the kind of story that motivates Leno as a collector, who is passionate not just about Duesenbergs, but about the experience of driving his cars. "You're resurrecting a lifestyle," he says, "giving people an idea of a kind of a life that won't be repeated." For Leno, "saving a piece of history" is integral to the experience. He restores cars, but he doesn't buy restored cars.

And the Manhattan Model J needed everything. After spending a half-century inside a leaky garage next to an open window, the paint was shot, the wood was rotten, and the sheet metal corroded beyond rescue. One fender had a hole rusted completely through. A set of disintegrating tires stored inside had ruined the interior. And, having driven 107,000 miles before being retired, the engine and mechanicals were severely worn.

Despite the car's decrepit condition, the owner initially refused to sell. Hoping to throw other would-be Duesenberg hunters off the trail, Leno spread a false rumor that a modern elevator installed in the garage was too small to accommodate the Model J—and that the car was now permanently entombed. Leno bided his time.

Then, in a confusing series of miscommunications, it seems that the owner's payments to the garage were misapplied, and the garage offered the car for sale to settle the debt. Leno paid a market-correct price for the car, only to find himself embroiled in a highly publicized lawsuit. Details of the settlement that followed were never released, but with all parties satisfied, the Model J made its permanent home in Leno's collection, where it underwent a full restoration.

THE BURBANK MYSTERY CAR

It was a different story when Leno got an update on the Burbank mystery car in 2005—years after he spotted that mysterious garage and first met Bill. Bill, now 92, had entered a nursing home, and he was ready to let his secret be known. And Leno, after two decades of suspense, was eager to buy whatever was inside that humble yellow garage.

Bill agreed to let Leno and his close friend Randy Ema into the locked garage. When the door was lifted, Leno and Ema peered into the dim space and were floored. A 1927 Duesenberg Model X stood proud and imposing under a heavy blanket of dust, flanked on all sides with relics of 1947—the last time the window-less structure was opened. Leno recalls, "There were oil cans, an unopened six-pack of Orange Crush Soda, old Burbank newspapers." He adds, "I was surprised to learn that Burbank had a strip club in 1947."

That humble garage that spoke to Leno for 20 years was a time capsule—and a treasure-trove. According to Ema, a Duesenberg historian and restorer, there were just 13 Model X cars built, and only four are known to survive today.

Bill's daughter, who lived in the house for much of her life, hadn't seen the car since childhood and was completely unaware of its significance. Leno advised her to have the car appraised, and he happily paid the market price. He bought not just the car, but the entire contents of the garage.

"Oh yeah, I keep everything," he says.

Unlike the weather-ravaged Manhattan Model J, the Burbank Model X was well preserved. The sealed garage and the dry California air kept rust at bay, and whoever had parked the car five decades ago had the foresight to roll up the windows. The delicate interior upholstery was completely intact with no sign of moths.

The mechanical components, however, had numerous problems. A missing tie rod meant the car could not be steered. It had to be winched out of the garage on a skid. Ema recalls, "We did brakes, gas tank radiator, a little bit of wiring." The engine was a mess.

But the mechanical issues were really a blessing in disguise.

As classic cars appreciate in value, they tend to get restored—which was Bill's plan for the Model X back in 1947. But, as collectors like Leno and Ema will often say, "It's only original once." The mechanical problems were just too complicated and expensive for Bill to handle, and the car was left unmolested in its chamber for Leno and Ema to discover.

Furthermore, while replacing mechanical components is expensive and inconvenient, it is nonetheless a straightforward process. "We manufacture all this stuff," says Ema. "We have all the original drawings, patterns, tooling, and stuff. We don't have to guess."

By contrast, it is impossible to replace the natural patina that a car acquires through years of gentle use. That patina, when it can be preserved, is what gives a car its character and, for Leno and Ema, its value. Aside from replacing the incorrect bumpers and headlights on the Model X, Leno says, "We kept it complete as it was."

While a typical restoration by Ema's shop takes a year and a half, the Burbank Model X was finished in less than eight months. The car has since been shown at the

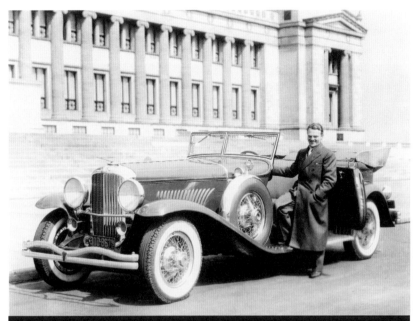

This is the vehicle rumored to be hidden away for which Leno searched for years—a Deusenberg Model J. Another star of the silver screen claims this one—James Cagney!

Pebble Beach Concours d'Elegance, where barn finds and unrestored Preservation cars have their own judging class.

And what of the car's life before that Burbank garage? According to Ema, a man named Arthur Johnson purchased the car new in 1927 in Indiana. Certain distinctive features on the chassis suggest it may have been a display car, but there are no known photographs of the car in that period, and no Duesenberg historian is aware of it being shown at an event.

By 1940 the car was languishing in disrepair in Chicago, which is where Bill purchased it. He drove it to Burbank, but burned out the valves in the process. It never left his garage again.

Ema stays busy, keeping about three projects in the pipeline at any one time, including plenty of Pebble Beach Best in Show contenders. He owns two Model A Duesenbergs and a variety of other classics. "Antiques, classics, sports cars—it's all fun," says Ema.

Leno's ever-growing car collection now has its own web series, *Jay Leno's Garage*. At last count, Leno owned 123 cars and 93 motorcycles. The assortment follows

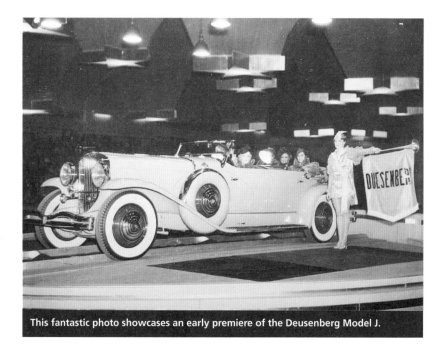

This fantastic photo showcases an early premiere of the Deusenberg Model J.

no theme except Leno's personal interest in novel driving experiences, from Brass Era electric cars, to vintage Italian exotics, to a McLaren F1, to the military tank–engined 810-horsepower Blastolene Special. His daily driver is a Model T.

Eight of the cars are Duesenbergs. Asked whether he plans to add more Duesies to the collection, Leno chuckles and says, "Sometimes they just sort of come out of the woodwork." Other times, as with the Manhattan Model J and the Burbank Model X, the lure of the barn find is irresistible.

Although Leno's two finds were some of the last unrestored Duesenbergs, Ema says that he and the small inner circle of marque historians knew that those two particular cars would eventually surface.

Of the 481 Duesenbergs ever produced, more than 40 are still completely unaccounted for, but it's been decades since a "lost" Duesenberg was discovered. "We haven't found one since 1962," says Ema, and he doubts that there are others to be found.

As with all collectibles, no matter how long a stubborn owner hangs on to a prized possession, the cars almost always come to market when the estate is settled. "We've gone through two and a half generations since then," says Ema, "so the likelihood of finding another one is next to impossible."

That doesn't mean the rumors and myths will stop. Ema says, "There's still a Model A Duesenberg sitting outside in L.A." But he won't say where.

Even if Ema is right and there are no more Duesenbergs to be found, stories like these stories still stoke the flames at the heart of the old-car hobby.

If these majestic chariots could go unnoticed by millions of passers-by in downtown New York City or a Los Angeles suburb for more than half a century, how many other untouched classics must be hiding in plain sight, just waiting for someone to look down the right alley, or befriend the right soft-spoken owner, or make the right detour from their daily commute?

THE REAL CHITTY BANG BANG

BY LINDA CLARK

Chitty Bang Bang was an aircraft-engined, chain-driven monster race car Count Louis Vorow Zborowski introduced to England's famed Brooklands racing fraternity in 1921. The car's name, which some believe came from the massive engine's noise as it idled, was actually based on the theme of a lewd World War I Royal Flying Corps ballad.

NOT ONE MAGICAL CAR,
BUT THREE

AY THE WORDS *Chitty Bang Bang* and most people think you're talking about a movie musical starring Dick Van Dyke. But there was a real Chitty Bang Bang—actually three of them.

While driving through Pennsylvania in 1982, I saw an old car parked by the side of the road with its hood open. Stopping to help a stranded motorist is a pulse-raising event, given the shaky times we live in, especially when the car turned out to be one of the rarest and most legendary automobiles in the world: the Chitty Bang Bang.

This awesome car—which has a huge, noisy airplane engine and was disabled only briefly by a clogged fuel line—was the Chitty II, but more on this later. First, the legend.

Chitty Bang Bang was an aircraft-engined, chain-driven monster race car Count Louis Vorow Zborowski introduced to England's famed Brooklands racing fraternity in 1921. The car's name, which some believe came from the massive engine's noise as it idled, was actually based on the theme of a lewd World War I Royal Flying Corps ballad.

The three Chitty Bang Bangs inspired a book. Ian Fleming, creator of the immortal James Bond, wrote a children's fantasy about a very special car. It was originally titled *Chitti-Chitti-Bang-Bang*, but was later spelled with a *y* and minus a Chitty.

Fleming was recovering from a 1963 heart attack when he wrote *Chitty-Chitty-Bang-Bang: The Magical Car* for his son, Caspar. Sadly, Fleming died after a second attack on August 12, 1964, Caspar's 12th birthday and just two months prior to the book's publication.

MGM/United Artists brought the story—and a wondrous race car—to theaters all over the world in the 1968 *Chitty-Chitty-Bang-Bang* movie starring Dick Van Dyke. The Fleming family, which retains literary rights, chose British author Frank Boyce to pen the first of three planned book sequels, *Chitty-Chitty-Bang-Bang Flies Again*, published in 2012.

The stories of the real Chitties are almost as fantastic as the book and movie.

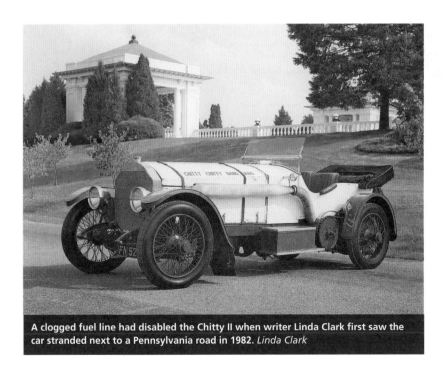

A clogged fuel line had disabled the Chitty II when writer Linda Clark first saw the car stranded next to a Pennsylvania road in 1982. *Linda Clark*

There were actually three real Chitties and a fourth on the drawing board when Zborowski was killed at 29 years old after crashing into a tree while driving a Mercedes in the 1924 Italian Grand Prix at Monza.

Amateur racers outnumbered the professionals at the Brooklands 2.75-mile circuit in Surrey during the roaring 1920s, and handicap racing was contested among a wide variety of cars. The rich and cosmopolitan playboy Zborowski was then racing several cars: the Mercedes that had won the 1914 Grand Prix; a 1919 5-liter Ballot; a fast Salmson; a 3-liter, eight-cylinder Miller imported from the United States; and a Type 30 Bugatti, which he raced at the Indianapolis 500 in 1923. He also had a financial stake in Aston Martin and owned seven acres of exclusive Manhattan real estate in New York.

Zborowski was the son of a Polish count and a wealthy American heiress who was a granddaughter of William Backhouse Astor Sr. of the prominent Astor family. Zborowski was educated briefly at Eton and resided on the 225-acre Hingham Park estate near Canterbury in Kent.

In 1903 Zborowski's father, Count Eliot, died while driving in the La Turbie Hillclimb in France while Louis was still a schoolboy. When his mother died eight years later, Louis was only 16.

Except for the 350-horsepower V-12 Sunbeam driven by Kinelm Guinness, Count Zborowski's Chitty Bang Bang in 1921 was the fastest of the amateur-built, post–World War I airplane-engined track monsters. Chitty was built in workshops

The enormous Chitty II stops traffic and draws in spectators wherever it goes. Unlike the original Chitty, the Chitty II has fenders, a soft top, and front headlights.
Roy Query

The Chitty II has a Bligh Brothers touring body, and it really doesn't resemble the Chitty Chitty Bang Bang of movie fame.

adjoining the count's country home, under the engineering guidance of Capt. Clive Gallop, who served his apprenticeship with Peugeot in France before the war. A renowned wartime pilot, Gallop also later became one of the venerable "Bentley Boys."

Chitty's mechanicals were an inline six-cylinder, 23-liter Maybach aircraft engine coaxed into a stretched pre–World War I Mercedes chassis. Draped with a high-built four-seater body by Bligh Brothers of Canterbury—a coachbuilder in which Zborowski held a stake—it was typical of the portly four-seater race cars of that Brooklands era. With its narrow Palmer Cord tires and negligible braking power (not to mention primitive radiator and crude exhaust pipe), the Chitty was dangerous at best.

But the brave Zborowski considered anything less than the Chitty's 305 horse-power and lap speed potential of 113 miles per hour boring. The oversized exhaust pipe was reportedly intended to dupe handicappers. Because the engine alone weighed as much as a complete Austin Seven Tourer, Zborowski had to put several hundred pounds of sand in the tonneau to offset the car's heavy nose.

Painted gray, the Chitty was a sensation at the Easter 1921 Brooklands race, which was its first race. After winning the Short Handicap at 100.75 miles per hour, the Chitty won the Lightning Short Handicap and placed second in the Senior Sprint race. The only car to beat the Chitty was the count's own Grand Prix Mercedes, driven by his friend Hartshorne Cooper.

The Chitty's chassis had been strengthened by plating and bracing, and the Maybach's lubrication system had been converted from wet to dry sump to reduce engine height. The Maybach had six individually cast cylinders of nearly 4 liters capacity each. The enormous engine was 2 yards long and developed 305 horsepower at a mere 1,500 rpm. Its four overhead valves per cylinder were operated by exposed pushrods and rockers. Dual camshafts ran in the crankcase, and the flat-top cylinder heads were undetachable.

To start the Maybach, Zborowski relied on his flamboyant crew to turn the 40-inch starting crank, which lacked even a handgrip. Back in the cockpit, an auxiliary magneto had to be wound manually.

Zborowski and Chitty continued to pile up successes, achieving 120 miles per hour in one race. The Chitty Bang Bang's racing career, however, came to a spectacular end in the fall of 1922 when Zborowski crashed during a practice run at Brooklands after a tire burst. The front axle was torn off the car, and the count's mechanic was thrown out, but Zborowski escaped injury.

CHITTY BANG BANGS?

Although the car was rebuilt, Zborowski never raced Chitty again. It passed to millionaire and railway founder Capt. Jack Howey and then to the Conan Doyle brothers (sons of Sir Arthur, writer of the Sherlock Holmes books), who ran it at a speed trial at Brooklands in the early 1930s. It was bought for spare parts in 1934 by John Morris, the Maybach engine being offered to Bill Boddy, editor of *Motor Sport*.

Even before the accident, Zborowski and Gallop had begun constructing an improved Chitty II. Chitty II featured a shorter wheelbase and a six-cylinder overhead valve Benz aero engine rated at 230 horsepower. It also had a narrower four-seater body on a prewar chain-driven Mercedes chassis. The engine displaced 18.8 liters, and the coachwork was once again by Bligh Brothers. Built for Continental touring rather than racing, the black Chitty II ran only once at Brooklands—unsuccessfully.

Undergeared for the track, the Chitty II was nevertheless a habitable touring car with fenders, a soft top, and lighting kit. It had a touring range, on a full tank, of around 300 miles. It also took part in several road races, including a Sahara Desert expedition in Algeria in 1922.

The Chitty's enormous engine was two yards long and developed 305 horsepower at a mere 1,500 rpm. *Roy Query*

Like the original Chitty, this car had only rear-wheel and transmission brakes and an antique scroll clutch, which required kid-glove treatment to protect the transmission. The Chitty II's gearbox weighed 310 pounds, and the driving sprockets had 38 teeth; those on the first Chitty had 40.

Between Chitties, the count acquired a 1921 six-cylinder overhead camshaft Hispano-Suiza touring car. Zborowski's great affection for this smooth-running, four-wheel braking French car inspired his most refined Chitty.

Chitty III, also known as "The White Car," was at first built with a 7.4-liter, six-cylinder Mercedes engine. Disappointed with its performance, Zborowski later replaced it with a 14.7-liter Mercedes aero engine tuned to produce over 180 horsepower. A light racing shell was placed over a Mercedes chassis enhanced with a shaft-driven transmission and four-wheel brakes, superimposed with a Westinghouse servo system based on locomotive parts.

Zborowski ran Chitty III at Brooklands in 1922 and achieved its fastest-ever Brooklands lap, 113.45 miles per hour. The Chitty III competed again in the Southsea Speed Trials, reaching 73.10 miles per hour, but the car had to be withdrawn at the last Brooklands race of 1922 after a clutch ball bearing broke during practice.

Though it was never called Chitty, the biggest and fastest car conceived by Zborowski and Gallop, in 1923–1924, was the Hingham Special, powered by

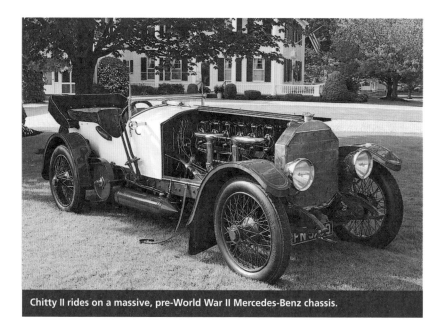

Chitty II rides on a massive, pre-World War II Mercedes-Benz chassis.

a 27-liter V-12 Liberty aircraft engine and reverting to chain drive. At the time of Zborowski's fatal accident at Lesmo corner during the 1924 Grand Prix at the wheel of a straight-eight 2-liter Mercedes, the beginnings of Chitty IV were at the Hingham workshop. It was to have been a saloon Chitty, but the count's death put an end to the project.

J. G. Parry-Thomas, the "Welsh Wizard," bought the incomplete Hingham Special from Zborowski's estate and rebuilt it with four Zenith carburetors and his own pistons. Thomas went on to break the land speed record twice with the car and was killed in a third attempt at Pendine Sands in Wales. The car passed into the beach track's hymnals as "Babs," the name Thomas has given his mechanical mastodon.

Although it's known that the Chitty I vanished forever after 1934, what became of some of the other Chitties after Zborowski's death remains the subject of speculation. After Parry-Thomas's death, Babs was buried at Pendine, only to be excavated and restored some 40 years later by Owen Wyn Owen, an engineering lecturer at Bangor University in Wales. Doing much of the work himself, Owen spent 15 years on the restoration. Babs is now housed in the Pendine Museum of Speed half the year and the Brooklands Museum the other half.

Chitty IV remains unbuilt, and Chitty III's fate remains a mystery. Zborowski not only won his fastest lap at Brooklands with Chitty III, but he also used it as his personal transport, even driving it to Stuttgart when he was negotiating to join the Mercedes racing team. History records that it was owned briefly in the late 1920s by Zborowski's friend and fellow railway investor Capt. Jack Howey, who also owned Chitty I for a short time. It's speculated that Chitty III had at least two more owners before being scrapped in the 1930s.

The sole survivor is Chitty II, which passed through three owners in England before it was bought by American industrialist Harry Resnick of New York in 1969. Subsequently the car rested for almost 30 years at the Crawford Auto-Aviation Museum in Cleveland. Loaned to the National Motor Museum in England in 1992, it sat alongside one of the 1968 Ford-powered Chitty Chitty Bang Bang movie cars that had been built by Alan Mann of Surrey. Since 2000 Chitty II has been owned by Gary Bahre of New Hampshire.

Just one of the six imitation cars created for the 1968 movie was roadworthy. Built by Alan Mann in 1967, it had a Ford V-6 engine and automatic transmission, plus a genuine UK registration. Actor Dick Van Dyke drove the car in the film.

Five other prop cars were built by Warfield Productions and MGM/United Artists, one of which was destroyed after filming. Another car was displayed at a Chicago restaurant for many years before being sold at auction in 2007 for $505,000. The other three cars were used primarily to pitch the movie in print and television ads—and at live events.

Another rendition of the car was built for the British stage musical, *Chitty Chitty Bang Bang*, which bowed at the London Palladium in 2002. Like the film, the stage version was a multimillion-dollar production with a cast and crew of over a hundred, including 10 dogs. Built for around $1.4 million, the car broke a Guinness World Record for most costly stage prop. The musical won two Olivier Awards and earned about $112 million during its nearly four-year run.

A less successful Broadway version of the show opened at the Hilton Theater in New York in 2005. Although it boasted the same director and choreographer as the London play and won five Tony Awards, it closed after just eight months. Even the producer's initial $15 million investment wasn't recouped.

The now green-and-tan Chitty II was originally painted black, but was cosmetically restored in the 1940s.

FRAUDULENT LORD BROCKET

BY LINDA CLARK

The police couldn't fathom how a truck could breach the security of Brocket Hall, load up three Ferraris, a Maserati, and four engines, and make a successful getaway without being seen or heard. Yet this is what Brocket argued had happened—he even told the media the cars and rare engines had been stolen to order, likely by foreigners.

AN ARISTOCRAT'S ARISTO-CARS

LORD BROCKET MADE HEADLINES in the 1990s when he was sent to prison after being found guilty of conspiracy to defraud an insurance company. The larger-than-life aristocrat now enjoys notoriety as an ex-convict, bestselling autobiographer, travel writer, and former United Kingdom reality TV show contestant.

More commonly known as Charlie Brocket, Lord Brocket is from an ancient Irish family that changed its name from O'Cahan to Cain when it emigrated to Liverpool in the 1800s and later made a fortune from brewing. Brocket was born in England to Ronald Nall-Cain and Elizabeth Trotter in 1952, and his father died when he was only nine years old.

Although still a boy in 1964, Brocket was eager to drive, so he had the mechanic on his stepfather's estate build a contraption from a Humber Scout Car, an old Ford, a truck radiator, and some tractor parts. Because it was neither car nor agricultural vehicle, Brocket nicknamed it The Thing. His first real car, a used MG 1100, couldn't match The Thing's oddity, but Brocket and two chums souped it up to reach 110 miles per hour.

Brocket was educated at Eton, trained briefly as an architect, and then served five years with the 14th/20th King's Hussars as a lieutenant in Northern Ireland and Germany. He bought an MGB but lack of space for his mess kit meant it had to be sold. Next came an Austin Cambridge that Brocket crashed into a telephone pole when he dozed off at the wheel after a night of heavy dining (the bill for the pole and severed cables came to nearly a third of his annual British Army pay).

Undeterred, he bought a Mercedes 190SL convertible but was disappointed with its performance. Despite its limitations, the 190 gave Brocket a taste for expensive cars, and he subsequently bought a Mercedes 280SL convertible. When he left the army in 1976 he bought a Maserati Indy with a 4.7-liter V-8, although it was well worn and rusty.

In 1979 Brocket bought his first Ferrari, a 1969 365GT 2+2 that he turned into a concours winner with a costly restoration. Although not the world's prettiest Ferrari, the Pininfarina-styled 365GT was the first 2+2 with power-steering, self-leveling rear suspension, and air-conditioning as standard. Of the 800 made, Brocket's was one of only 52 right-hand-drive examples. Brocket had the whole

Lord Brocket rests easy beneath Brocket Hall among his priceless collection of Ferraris, Maseratis, and more. *Alamy*

car stripped down to bare metal and resprayed in black by Ferrari specialist Jim Bosisto, employed Alfetta Racing for an engine and suspension rebuild, and found Moto-trim of Surrey for an interior re-trim in tan Connolly hide, replete with new black carpets.

The title of Lord Brocket passed to him in 1971 when his grandfather, Arthur Nall-Cain, died. Brocket also inherited the 46-bedroom redbrick Georgian family manor, Brocket Hall, situated on 543 acres of parkland in Hertfordshire overlooking Broadwater Lake. Brocket Hall, though, was a crumbling ruin—his grandfather left him no money to fix it.

Brocket Hall was one of England's most renowned homes, the original having been built in 1239. The Brocket Hall of today was designed by noted architect James Paine for the owner, Sir Matthew Lamb, in 1760. Two prime ministers— Lords Melbourne and Palmerston—lived at Brocket, and its rich history includes romantic liaisons and even murder. The famous poet Lord Byron slept at Brocket. And at the outbreak of World War II in 1939, City of London Maternity Hospital evacuated to Brocket Hall.

The hospital was badly damaged by enemy bombing in 1940, but 8,338 babies were born within the safety of its walls from 1939 through 1949. Known as the Brocket Babies, today they hail from countries around the world, including

Lord Brocket remains a well-known aristocrat in England. That's his first wife, Isabell Lorenzo, on his arm. *Alamy*

Australia, New Zealand, the United States, Canada, France, Scotland, Wales, and the Canary Islands.

With a loan from American Express (several British banks rebuffed him), Lord Brocket turned the family mansion into a world-class hotel and golf course. Brocket became known for inviting friends to weekend demolition parties to smash down walls, redo the electrical wiring, and rebuild the antiquated plumbing. By 1985 the revamped Brocket Hall was the leading conference venue in Britain. According to Britain's *Daily Mail*, at its height, his conference business was making 25,000 pounds a day.

In 1981 Lord Brocket met Cuban-born *Vogue* model Isabell Lorenzo, the world's fifth-highest-paid model at the time, while she was working on location at Brocket Hall. After they married in 1982 Isabell gave up modeling to assume the duties of being Lady Brocket and eventually raise their three children, William, Antalya, and Alexander. Isabell also spent time in two of Britain's top drug rehab clinics for her much-publicized cocaine addiction. After the birth of their third child, she added painkillers and sleeping pills to the mix.

Throughout his manor's transformation and his wife's bouts with addiction, Lord Brocket never lost his enthusiasm for exotic cars. By the mid-1980s he had acquired 15 Maseratis and Ferraris. After their value increased almost tenfold in just a few years, Brocket decided to buy more cars as an investment. He found a bank willing to fund his new business of buying and selling high-end sports cars and managed to buy Niki Lauda's Ferrari 312B3 Formula One car, as well as the Works Maserati 300S driven by Juan Manuel Fangio and Stirling Moss. He was also frequently seen around London being chauffeured in his Bentley Turbo R. He regularly hosted Ferrari Owners Club (U.K.) meets on the grounds of Brocket Hall.

According to people who knew him, Brocket bought and sold cars at a furious pace in the late 1980s, often paying far too much for them. Like so many active traders, he mistakenly thought the rising market would go on forever. When the 1980s wound down, Brocket owned some 50 high-priced sports and race cars, mostly Ferraris, bought with money loaned to him by England's Midland Bank (now part of global banking giant HSBC). Just as Brocket's cars were beginning to lose value, his income from Brocket Hall's hotel and golf business was falling. Many companies that spent lavishly in the mid-1980s boom were retrenching—cost-cutting was in, and golf junkets and conferences were out.

By early 1991 Brocket's sports car business was deeply in the red. He owed banks millions of pounds and yet had to borrow even more just to keep Brocket Hall running. Then the Midland Bank called in its 4.5-million-pound (around $8 million) loan and threatened to seize Brocket Hall. And that's when Brocket hatched a master plan to get out of debt and back in the limelight—he would over-insure several vehicles, stage their theft, and watch the insurance dollars roll in. It was an ego-driven insurance scam that was doomed from the start.

In May 1991 Brocket had his security guard, Mark Caswell, and his mechanic, Stephen Gwyther, dismantle four of his cars: a 1952 Ferrari 340 America, a 1955 Ferrari Europe, a Ferrari 195 Sport, and a 1960 Maserati Tipo Birdcage. They hid the cars in a friend's garage in North London.

Police were suspicious from the start. They were called to Brocket Hall the morning of May 28, where they "discovered" that the showroom where Brocket kept part of his car collection had been broken into over the Spring Bank Holiday weekend. The police couldn't fathom how a truck could breach the security of Brocket Hall, load up three Ferraris, a Maserati, and four engines, and make a successful getaway without being seen or heard. Yet this is what Brocket argued had happened—he even told the media the cars and rare engines had been stolen to order, likely by foreigners. He claimed that he had recently received purchase offers on two of his cars from nondescript "Japanese buyers."

The apparent robbery was quick to make headlines. In London's *The Independent* collector-car experts likened the theft to stealing Picassos. But Lord Brocket was not always portrayed in the best light; it was widely reported that he thought himself above the law, often telling his chauffeur, "Don't tell me about the law. I make the law."

Brocket insisted the thieves had carried out a "professional job" by removing the alarm system, and he wasted no time filing a 4.5-million-pound claim with his insurance company, General Accident. But the loss adjuster, David Cook, was dubious; valuable cars like Brocket's don't just vanish. Later, he discovered that Brocket had been lax in reporting prior losses. That gave General Accident a technical reason not to pay up.

Brocket wouldn't hear of it. He sued General Accident, hoping to force their hand. Instead, a lengthy court battle began. Brocket lied to his lawyers, insisting there had been a robbery, and forced his car dealer, 37-year-old Richard Furtado, to do the same.

Meanwhile the police vigorously investigated the alleged break-in and discovered some of the remains of the four cars in a locked garage in North London. They found other parts at the bottom of Broadwater Lake on the grounds of Brocket Hall. According to *The Economist* newsweekly, the four chassis plates belonging to the cut-up cars were found under the floorboards of the garage at Brocket Hall. It was speculated that Lord Brocket hid them in the hope that he might one day be able to rebuild the cars and sell them as originals.

Brocket was separated from his wife by that time and facing a contentious divorce. In England a divorce can be granted only after three years of separation. In 1994 Lady Brocket was arrested for forging drug prescriptions. By that time, she also had attempted suicide twice. Worried that she might be called as a witness, she told Lord Brocket's mother and uncle that his lordship was behind the theft. Brocket denied the accusation—his wife, he insisted, was a drug addict with a fertile imagination and couldn't be trusted. He assured his family that he had nothing to do with it.

At first the police bought Brocket's argument that his wife was too influenced by drugs to be reliable. But just weeks before Brocket's case against his insurer was scheduled to go to trial in 1994, Brocket dismissed his suit. This made the men at Scotland Yard suspicious again. Not long after, they discovered that behind the scenes at Brocket Hall, the baron had serious financial problems.

Ultimately it was another minor participant—Barry Flynn, who never got fully paid for his part in the scam—who gave the game away. But even then, Brocket thought police would never be able to link him to the theft.

In February 1995 Brocket was arrested. Two of his co-conspirators, Mark Caswell and Stephen Gwyther, told police the full story. But Brocket, who was charged under his full name (Charles Ronald Nall-Cain), pleaded not guilty. He never believed Scotland Yard could build a case against him.

To put pressure on him to change his plea, police gathered evidence of a second fraud. Brocket, they alleged, had commissioned two replica Ferraris and sold one of them as if it was the original car. Four days before he was to plead again in court on the first charge of conspiring to defraud an insurance company, the Crown Prosecution Service and the police arrested Brocket and charged him with a second crime of obtaining money by deception.

At his December 1995 plea hearing at Luton Crown Court, Brocket admitted to staging the robbery, just as Mark Caswell and Stephen Gwyther had admitted earlier. But two others who were charged—car salesman Richard Furtado and Michael Campbell-Bowling, a financial consultant from Fulham—denied the charges. Judge Daniel Rodwell released Brocket on 32,000 pounds bail.

Believing he was planning to escape by private aircraft to Scandinavia, the authorities put Brocket under police surveillance the weekend before he was sentenced on February 9, 1996. Sentencing the 44-year-old peer at Luton Crown Court, Judge Daniel Rodwell described Brocket's crime as "disgraceful" and rejected his claim that he had set up the fraud "in panic" over his aristocratic family seat and business debts. Brocket was sentenced to three years in prison for conspiring to defraud and another two years for obtaining money by deception. Before he could serve his sentence, he and Isabell divorced in 1995. Despite her problems, Isabell was awarded custody of their three children and took them to live with her parents in Puerto Rico.

Judge Rodwell gave Caswell and Gwyther 21-month suspended sentences, believing that they had been coerced by Brocket. Campbell-Bowling was eventually cleared of all charges, and he died in 2011. In a funny twist of fate, Furtado now runs an automotive investment business in Naples, Florida.

After all was said and done—the media hype, the purloined cars, the fraudulent insurance claim—Brocket was bankrupt. He was forced to lease Brocket Hall for *60 years* to a German-managed Asian business group, CCA (Club Corporation of Asia), based in Hong Kong. CCA spent around $40 million further developing the estate, including construction of a second 18-hole golf course. In 2056 the lease will revert to Brocket's descendants, in effect terminating his involvement for the rest of his natural life. After serving two and half years of his five-year sentence, Brocket was released from prison early for good behavior on August 7, 1998.

STEVE MCQUEEN'S SUNGLASSES

BY LINDA CLARK

McQueen's visage sold thousands of pairs of Persol folding sunglasses. And in the process, he transformed his own $300 or so Persols into a $70,000 windfall.

MCQUEEN'S SUNGLASSES
SELL FOR $70,200

STEVE MCQUEEN DIED IN 1980, but the famous Hollywood actor—known as the King of Cool—hasn't lost a bit of fame, especially among gearheads.

One of those gearheads placed an anonymous bid of $70,200 for a pair of 1960s-era Persol Ratti 714 folding sunglasses McQueen wore in the 1968 film *The Thomas Crown Affair*. A 1967 Rolls-Royce Silver Shadow from the movie fetched the same price.

Over two hundred items belonging to the Hollywood legend were sold by his widow, Barbara, at a 2006 Bonhams & Butterfields auction held at the Petersen Automotive Museum in Los Angeles.

McQueen, an expert motorcycle and race car driver, died in 1980 of a heart attack after surgery to treat a rare form of lung cancer. In both film and on television, he portrayed the ultimate outsider, yet everything McQueen touched became "cool."

One of his motorcycles, a 1937 Crocker Hemi-head V-Twin, brought in a world record price of $276,500 at the auction. His 1934 Indian Sport Scout went for $177,500.

Much of the actor's collection had been sold before, but many of the remaining items showed up in the auction. McQueen's motorcycle clothing was included, like his Belstaff jacket, which sold for $32,760, and padded motorcycle sweatshirts. A Wells Fargo MasterCard, stamped Steven T. McQueen, with the back signature section unsigned, went for $9,945.

One of McQueen's favorite vehicles, a 1958 GMC 101 Series turquoise half-ton pickup truck, sold for $128,000. McQueen had hot-rodded its 336-cubic-inch V-8 engine. He regularly used this truck in and around Beverly Hills, the star-studded city near Hollywood that is more used to Rolls-Royces, Bentleys, and Ferraris on the street.

Then there were nostalgia items like a classic Wurlitzer Model 1015 Jukebox, still containing records of the music McQueen grew up with, such as Bing Crosby, Glenn Miller, and Perry Como, which sold for $26,910. An 8 1/2-inch Buck-style folding knife, engraved with an eagle's head and "To Steve from Dutch," Von Dutch being the celebrated motorcycle and automobile pin-striper, fetched $38,025.

Bidders included private collectors from France, England, and the United States, and the Petersen Museum itself bought several items. The entire auction brought in $2.9 million.

Of all the memorabilia sold, few items raised more eyebrows, got more press coverage, or appreciated more than McQueen's folding Persol 714 sunglasses. They had custom tinted blue lenses made for him by the late optician to the stars, Dennis Roberts. A favorite of the actor's, he wore the legendary shades both off screen and on. But as with all things McQueen, the value had less to do with the sunglasses than with the provenance.

The handmade Italian sunglasses were reportedly worn by McQueen's business tycoon-turned-bank robber character in *The Thomas Crown Affair*. McQueen also wore Persol sunglasses in 1968's *Bullitt* and 1972's *The Getaway*, but not always 714s. McQueen was also filmed wearing Persol's 649 model.

Founded in 1917 by Giuseppi Ratti, Persol is among the oldest brands of sunglasses in the world. Originally a designer of sunglasses for pilots and race drivers, Persol is currently famous for its sports sunglasses. The model 714 pair McQueen owned was the folding version of the model 649 sunglasses Persol brought out in 1957. Pre-dating McQueen by seven years, they entered into legend when Marcello Mastroianni wore Persol 649 sunglasses in the 1961 film, *Divorce Italian Style*.

However, demand was so enduring for the 714 folding model, which bowed in 1962, that Persol reintroduced a limited edition run of them in 2007. Some sales outlets in the United States even advertised them as "Steve McQueen's Classic Sunglasses."

McQueen's life was filled with ironies. He played leading men in the movies, but his first starring movie role was in 1958's sci-fi horror flick, *The Blob*. He was most in his element when dressed down in jeans and cotton T-shirts, yet *GQ* named him one of the 50 Most Stylish Men.

The King of Cool excelled at taking classic American sportswear and giving it a rugged edge. Hallmarks of McQueen's style included sport coats, zip-up windbreakers, Baracuta jackets, khakis, wrinkled button-down shirts, Desert boots, V-neck sweaters, and shawl-collared cardigans. As a racing enthusiast,

McQueen never lost a step in style nor swagger as he aged—and he always looked good. *Getty*

the style icon was a fan of racing jackets, aviators, leather jackets, gloves, boots, and denim. McQueen was the first man to grace the cover of fashion magazine *Harper's Bazaar.*

McQueen did for Heuer and Rolex wristwatches what he did for Persol 714 sunglasses. Demand was so strong for Heuer's square blue-faced Monaco 1133B Caliber 11 Automatic watch, which McQueen wore throughout his 1971 *Le Mans* movie, that it was reissued twice. His own Monaco sold for $87,600 in 2009. The Rolex Submariner that he preferred off-camera also was auctioned that year for $234,000.

Interestingly, Rolex may have played a role in the real-life great escape that the 1963 film of the same name was based on. Rolex watches had acquired enough prestige by the start of World War II that Royal Air Force pilots often bought them to replace the inferior standard-issue watches. But when captured and sent to POW

McQueen's trademark visage beneath a stylish pair of custom, blue-tinted 60s-era Persol-brand sunglasses has become a much-loved and remembered trademark of the original *Thomas Crown Affair. Silver Screen Collection*

camps, their watches were confiscated. So Rolex founder Hans Wilsdorf offered to replace watches that had been seized and didn't require payment until after the war.

In 1943 while a prisoner of war, Cpl. Clive J. Nutting, one of the organizers of the great escape, ordered a stainless steel Rolex Oyster 3525 Chronograph by mail directly from Hans Wilsdorf in Geneva, intending to pay for it with money he saved working as a shoemaker at the Stalag Luft III camp. The watch was delivered to the camp with a personal note from Wilsdorf, who was reportedly impressed with Nutting because, although not an officer, he had ordered the expensive Rolex chronograph while most other prisoners had ordered cheaper models.

The chronograph is believed to have been ordered specifically for use in the great escape, because it could have timed patrols of prison guards, or timed the 76 ill-fated escapees through tunnel "Harry" on March 24, 1944.

After the war, Rolex sent Nutting an invoice for the shipping cost only. The watch and its related correspondence between Wilsdorf and Nutting were sold at auction. Nutting served as a consultant on the film, which was based on Paul Brickhill's 1950 nonfiction book about the mass escape from the Nazi's Stalag Luft III camp, in which Brickhill himself was a prisoner.

McQueen's lead role as USAAF Capt. Virgil Hilts in that film cemented his superstar status. Insurance worries prevented McQueen from performing *The Great Escape*'s famous motorcycle leap over a wire fence, which was instead done by friend and fellow cycle enthusiast Bud Ekins. But through the magic of editing, McQueen was able to ride both as the escaping POW and the German soldier chasing him.

George Orwell once said that by age 50 every man has the face he deserves. When McQueen died at 50, he had a face that everyone knew. His tilted grin, china blue eyes and hard, almost weathered features had defined a generation of action heroes, from TV bounty hunter Josh Randall to big-screen Detective Frank Bullitt.

Although not the face that launched a thousand ships, as Helen of Troy's did, McQueen's visage sold thousands of pairs of Persol folding sunglasses. And in the process, he transformed his own $300 or so Persols into a $70,000 windfall.

That was partly due to good management and partly due to McQueen's eye for quality, since Persols had an elegance and exclusivity that Ray-Bans never did. Those timeless shades were popularized in film too. They were first noticed on James Dean in 1955's *Rebel Without a Cause* and later worn by Audrey Hepburn in 1961's *Breakfast at Tiffany's*. Sean Connery also wore Ray Bans as James Bond in

1963's *From Russia With Love*, but they never garnered the cache that McQueen's Persols did.

Decades after his death, McQueen remains a magnet for big brand advertisers. *Forbes* ranked him number 10 on its 2007 list of Top-Earning Dead Celebrities, and *Marketing Week* found him as popular in 2012 as he was in the 1970s. Ironically, McQueen didn't make that many movies and was known to be combative with directors and producers. And by today's standards, he avoided the limelight as much as any celebrity can.

But he was real. When McQueen drove a race car or rode a dirt bike on screen, it was an extension of what he did in his own life. McQueen lived to ride and race motorcycles and sports cars.

Few people can identify with celebrities, because so many of them have known only wealth and privilege. By contrast, McQueen grew up at Boy's Republic in Chino Hills, California, a famous reform school for boys. Before becoming a star, McQueen was a marine who saved the lives of five of his men by pulling them from a sinking tank.

McQueen wore Clark's Desert boots, Barbour's Baracuta jackets, Persol sunglasses, Belstaff motorcycle leathers, and Rolex and Heuer wristwatches because he liked them. Although he wore them on-screen, he already wore them off-screen in his personal life. These endorsements endured because they were authentic.

That same authenticity enabled McQueen's cars to command above-average celebrity premiums. A prime example was the 1963 Ferrari 250 GT/L Lusso Berlinetta, once owned by McQueen, which sold at auction for $2.3 million in 2007.

In 2011 the 1970 Porsche 911S that McQueen drove during the opening minutes of *Le Mans*—and that became his personal car after filming—sold for a whopping $1,375,000 at RM Auction's Monterey sale. A 1970 Porsche 911S in fantastic condition is usually worth about $60,000 to $100,000. In this case McQueen's eternal cool was worth more than $1,275,000 to at least one gearhead.

Nineteen years after his death, and 27 years after the motorcycle racing documentary *On Any Sunday*, in which McQueen played himself, he was inducted into the Motorcycle Hall of Fame. Posthumously, McQueen still sells everything from cars to clothing, although his estate limits the use of his image to avoid commercial saturation.

Ford used McQueen's likeness in a 2005 TV commercial for the new Mustang. In the ad, a farmer builds a racetrack, which he circles in the 2005 Mustang. But out of the cornfield comes McQueen. The farmer then tosses his keys to the actor, who drives off in the new Mustang.

In 2009, Triumph Motorcycles Ltd., licensed by McQueen's estate, launched a line of clothing inspired by the actor's alliance with their brand. In 1964 McQueen represented the United States on a Triumph TR6 Trophy in the International Six Days of Trial, the equivalent of the off-road motorcycling Olympics. Disguised as German BMW R75 motorcycles, Triumph TR6 Trophy models were also used in *The Great Escape*'s chase scenes.

No matter how many times McQueen played an outcast, he couldn't shake free of the King of Cool tag. That's because it was McQueen—the man, not the actor—who wore those blue-lens Persols with the tortoise housing and collapsible frame and made you forget the surgeon general's warning every time he took a narrow-eyed drag from his cigarette.

LORD BROCKET STRIKES AGAIN

BY LINDA CLARK

"What a mess that Brocket incident was," Spangler recalled. "I bought the Ferrari 250 SWB for Jon Shirley for six figures. If it had been a real one, it would be worth $4 million today."

THE RETURN OF A
FISCALLY RISKY ARISTOCRAT

WHEN WE LAST LEFT LORD BROCKET, he had just been sentenced to prison in the mid-1990s for insurance fraud. But Brocket persevered and was released on good behavior on August 7, 1998, after serving half of his five-year sentence for fraudulently claiming 4.5 million pounds from his car insurance company and for selling a fake Ferrari as if it was an original.

Dressed in a black leather jacket and jeans, the dishonored aristocrat showed he had not lost his taste for flamboyant transportation; he straddled a bike, revved the engine, and gunned away on a new Harley-Davidson motorcycle.

He was jailed in 1996 after breaking up and hiding three Ferraris and a Maserati from his 20-million-pound car collection—and then claiming they had been stolen—in a bid to use insurance money pay off his debts. But according to the *BBC News*, the 47-year-old Brocket left prison to face a 600,000-pound credit card debt, along with tax bills and a personal loan of 8 million pounds.

Due to his debts, Brocket was unable to return to his ancestral home, Brocket

Hall, and now leases it to an Asian company that runs it as a golf resort (Lord Brocket gets a percentage of its income as rent).

Frequently the victim of stabbings and beatings, Brocket was moved for security reasons from prison to prison during his time behind bars. His two-and-a-half year stint in jail was spent at seven different facilities. Spring Hill men's prison, located in Buckinghamshire, was where he spent his final days as a ward of the state.

Although best-known as "the man who stole his own cars," Brocket's five-year prison term included a two-year sentence for the less-publicized crime of obtaining money by deception. After learning that he had sold a replica Ferrari as an original in 1994, police arrested him 1995, several months after his first arrest for insurance fraud. This is that story.

In 1991 while he was deeply in debt and hatching his insurance scam (see page 46, "Fradulant Lord Brocket"), Brocket simultaneously devised a scheme to build replica Ferraris and sell them as the real McCoys. According to the website www.barchetta.cc, one of the two fake Ferraris he had commissioned was offered for sale in late 1992 with an asking price of $750,000.

Well-known American car collector Jon Shirley was interested in the car, believing it was an original Ferrari 250 SWB (short wheelbase), which is what Brocket advertised and represented it as. Since leaving Microsoft Corp., where he served as president from 1983 to 1990, Shirley has amassed a collection of significant Ferraris, and cars with famous racing histories are what Shirley likes best. He regularly drives his Ferraris on the racetrack and at events all over the world, such as the Mille Miglia rally in Italy. Shirley houses his collection in a specially designed garage in Bellevue, Washington, which was featured in Phil Berg's book *Ultimate Garages III*.

Shirley had noted Ferrari collector Ron Spangler purchase the car on his behalf. Shirley had bought Ferraris from Spangler before and has bought cars from him since, including a legendary Ferrari 290MM—one of only four made—that he bought from Spangler in 1998 for several million dollars.

Often sought after for his expertise and zeal for the marque, Spangler has owned over 100 Ferraris since he began collecting them in 1962. In addition to being a senior judge for the Ferrari Club of America, Spangler has served as the Ferrari expert and private collections host for PBS television's *Motor Week* show since 1981.

"What a mess that Brocket incident was," Spangler recalled. "I bought the Ferrari 250 SWB for Jon Shirley for six figures. If it had been a real one, it would be worth $4 million today. I traveled to England first to look at it. I was greeted at the airport and later wined and dined by Lord Brocket and Richard Furtado, a Massachusetts car dealer who had moved to London and teamed up with Brocket. He was Brocket's right-hand man." (Although it's unknown whether he ever served jail time, Furtado was charged in connection with Brocket's insurance fraud in 1995. He has since moved back to the United States and is currently operating an automotive investment business in Naples, Florida.)

Spangler, who has also owned several Bentleys over the years, was chauffeured around England in the Bentley then owned by Brocket. "They knew I was there on Shirley's behalf and rolled out the red carpet," Spangler said. "Lord Brocket put me up at Brocket Hall. The setting and the grounds were beautiful.

"Brocket said Terry Hoyle was restoring the car, so I went to Hoyle's shop to look at it. I knew Terry respected Brocket, so I relied heavily on his positive presentation of the car. And it looked stunning," Spangler said.

London-based Terry Hoyle Engineering (now part of Hoyle-Fox Classics in Maldon, Essex) was well-known and revered among Ferrari collectors for its high-quality restoration work. Over the past 43 years, Hoyle has restored some of the world's finest road and race Ferraris.

"Jim Bosisto was also involved with Brocket at that time," Spangler said. "He was Brocket's chief restorer and curator of his Ferrari collection." Bosisto had pioneered the building and racing of 500cc cars in Europe in the 1940s and 1950s. Before retiring from racing, he was a member of the Bristol Aeroplane Motor Club and competed in hillclimbs and circuit races.

Shirley became the proud owner of the Hoyle-restored Ferrari in the summer of 1994. At the time it was reported that Shirley paid around $575,000 for it, believing, as Spangler did, that it was an original 1962 Ferrari 250 SWB Alloy Competizione serial number 3565.

Bosisto and Hoyle were questioned by Scotland Yard in 1994, but it was Hoyle's possible participation in the counterfeit Ferrari scheme that provided the motivation for their visit to the United States to interview Spangler. "Members of Scotland Yard visited me at Prancing Horse Farm," Spangler said. Looking back on it, he believes that Hoyle deceived him about the provenance of the car, that Furtado was likely involved in the deception, and that it would have been nearly impossible for Bosisto not to have known what was going on.

Scotland Yard was able to gather enough evidence to arrest Lord Brocket in late 1995 and charge him with the crime of obtaining money by deception, adding another crime and possible jail time to his prior arrest for conspiring to defraud his insurance company.

A prime piece of evidence was the real serial-numbered 3565 Ferrari. It was discovered after decades of slumber in the garage of a man living in Alsace, France, in 1994 and proved the Ferrari bearing the same serial number fabricated by Brocket was a fake.

"That's when Shirley and I learned that the Ferrari 250 SWB was a replica and not the real thing," Spangler said. "Brocket had had the car built on the chassis of a far less valuable 250 GTE 2+2, and to hide the fraud, the car was given the serial number of the long-missing 250 SWB."

In January 1997 Shirley sold the Brocket-built 250 SWB as a replica to a California car dealer for a fraction of what he had paid for it. In February the dealer offered it for sale in the *Ferrari Market Letter* for $195,000. His ad emphasized how well-executed the replica was and assured potential buyers that it had the competition engine and competition ribbed gearbox. Ironically, the fact that it had been sold as a real one by Lord Brocket gave it a celebrity-like provenance.

It was purchased by Swiss collector Dominik Ellenrieder, who went to great lengths to try to make the fake SWB "legitimate." The car received prototype status in 1997 in California, according to the www.barchetta.cc website. Today the bogus SWB no longer uses the 3565 serial number. By 2001 the car was back in England, having been bought by a British collector who later sold it to an anonymous bidder in Monaco through the London-based auction house Coys.

The real 1962 Ferrari 250 GT SWB Berlinetta s/n 3565 was likewise sold at a Coys auction after it was unearthed in Alsace in 1994. According to the Ferrari Owners Club of Great Britain, it was sold to a German enthusiast who had it restored by Piet Roelofs Engineering, a Dutch company that specializes in reproducing parts for vintage Ferrari race cars. The German owner later had it auctioned by Coys, who sold it to a London-based collector, who offered s/n 3565GT for sale through Coys again in 2001.

Brocket reportedly commissioned a second replica Ferrari, a rare 250 GTO. Though he never tried to sell it, some enthusiasts think they've seen the pseudo 250 GTO at events in Europe. As far as his *real* collection goes, Brocket's 42 or so Ferraris were dispersed many years ago. After paying off his massive debts and his divorce settlement in 1995, whatever remained of his car collection was liquidated after he went to prison in 1996.

Now in his early 60s, Brocket has carved out a niche for himself as a likeable but roguish minor print and television celebrity. He remarried in 2006 to photographer Harriet Warren, with whom he has a daughter. They split their time between a restored farmhouse in southern France and their London apartment.

In the world of ex-convicts, Brocket is luckier than most. He garnered some income from his bestselling 2004 autobiography, *Call Me Charlie*, and earns money from rental income from Brocket Hall and also from speaking fees and travel writing. Right after leaving prison, he was often seen tooling around London in a Volkswagen, but has since graduated to a BMW and a Mercedes, according to London's *The Telegraph*.

He might be spurned at Brocket Hall, but according to *Arnold Palmer's Kingdom*, a quarterly golf magazine, he is far from forgotten, as dozens of pictures of him posing with political and show business stars of the 1980s and 1990s can still be found on the mansion's corridor walls.

THE COBRA RISES

BY COLIN COMER

Is it possible to crash and burn the value
out of a famous Shelby Cobra race car?

ONE WILD RIDE

THE HOT AND WILD LIFE OF CSX 2136—a 289 Cobra that was built in 1963 to compete in the 1963 SCCA/US Road Racing Championship—shows that it is almost impossible to scorch and smash the history out of a storied race car . . . especially if wealthy collectors are willing to pony up big bucks to rebuild a wreck.

From the very start, CSX2136 lived fast and hard.

CSX 2136 joined the Shelby American Team for the 1963 SCCA/USRRC race at Road America in Elkhart Lake, Wisconsin. Driven by Dave MacDonald and Bob Bondurant, it finished fourth overall and first in the GT class. At Riverside on October 13, Lew Spencer drove it to third in the *L.A. Times* GT race. MacDonald drove it at the Hawaiian Grand Prix later in October to second overall. CSX 2136's last appearance as a Shelby team car was at the Nassau Speed Weeks on December 8, 1963, where Frank Gardner drove it to seventh overall and first in GT in the Nassau Trophy Race.

Ed Leslie acquired CSX 2136 from the Shelby Team in 1964 and drove it to class wins in seven of the 11 SCCA races entered in 1964, including the ARRC finale at Riverside. Leslie also drove the car during an overall and GT class win at the Laguna Seca USRRC race in 1964.

All of this history brings us to the wacky and wonderful world of vintage race cars and their complicated life stories.

This pristine 1963 Shelby 289 Le Mans Replica Cobra was crashed and burned almost to oblivion, but the restored automobile sold at auction for a startling $1 million. *Acme Photo*

OF RACERS AND REPLICAS

So let's start over—right at the beginning. First, in the nomenclature of the Cobra world, CSX 2136 is not a Le Mans Cobra. It is what both Shelby and AC Cars called a Le Mans Replica—one of the six such cars Shelby built following their success with the two actual Le Mans cars.

CSX 2136 was indeed an incredibly successful Shelby—and later privateer—team car. Like almost any winning race car, it had its fair share of bumps and bruises from 1964 to 1966. In 1967 Stan Bennett purchased it with a blown motor, fixed it up, and raced it. Somewhere along the way it was crashed to the extent it needed a new nose.

Bennett sold the repaired car to John Bachnover during September 1967. Bachnover later sold it to David Greenblatt. Greenblatt continued to race the car until significantly damaging CS X2136 during a race in the early 1970s.

To add insult to injury, the heavily damaged CS X2136 later caught on fire on Greenblatt's trailer and burned to the ground. Greenblatt was paid for the loss by his insurance carrier, who then took the remains of CSX 2136 and placed them into storage. By 1975 the insurance company lost track of the remains, the owner of the storage facility passed away, and what remained of CSX 2136 was scrapped.

CHANGING HANDS

Grab some popcorn because now the tale gets better.

In 1977 Michael Leicester met Greenblatt, and the conversation turned to CSX 2136. Greenblatt ended up selling Leicester two spare wheels and his 1969 bill of

This is not the 289 you'd find in a 1965 Ford Mustang. This car was a very successful racer in its day, but it has never looked better than it does in this photo. *Acme Photo*

The restored Cobra proved that it is almost impossible to crash and burn the history out of a winning race car. *Acme Photo*

A long legal battle erupted between two collectors, as one collector had built a replica of the car, while another collector restored the battered remains of the actual car. *Acme Photo*

sale from Bachnover for CSX 2136 for the sum of $1 and a sports racing car valued at $3,600.

In 1978 Leicester commissioned Brian Angliss—who later bought AC Cars—to build him a new Cobra body and chassis, oddly enough also wearing the identifier CSX 2136.

In 1979 the Shelby American Auto Club—the group that celebrates and guards all things Shelby—received a letter from Leicester explaining how he owns the lost Cobra CSX 2136 and how it was undergoing a "ground-up restoration."

July 1980 saw the new Angliss 2136 Le Mans Replica delivered to Leicester. In December 1980 Gilles Dubuc stumbled upon—and purchased—the earthly remains of the real CSX 2136 in a Canadian junkyard. He later sold them to Ken Eber.

Of course, a legal battle soon erupted between Eber, the rightful owner of the only bits of real CSX 2136 DNA left, and Leicester, who owned the carefully crafted "new" CSX 2136.

Eventually the Royal Canadian Mounted Police were called in to examine Leicester's ownership documents and his car, and they determined it to be a re-creation. The original paperwork for the real CSX 2136 in Leicester's possession was transferred to Eber, and Leicester was somehow allowed to renumber and call his car CSX 2136R.

The shattered, burned original CSX 2136 was completely rebuilt and restored.

Chris Cox purchased the car in 1997, and he soon sold it to Richard Scaife. Scaife later consigned it to RM Auction's 2006 Amelia Island sale, where the late John O'Quinn purchased CSX 2136 for $1,650,000.

The car went up for sale after John O'Quinn's untimely death, and it sold for $1,010,694 at RM Auctions' Monaco sale on May 1, 2010.

So, in the case of CSX 2136, we need to examine the age-old question: Is it possible to crash (and sometimes burn) the history out of a winning race car? Was it a good buy at just over $1 million, just a few years after *Sports Car Market* magazine declared it a fair deal at $1.65 million?

It all depends on your views on race history versus originality. There is no question that the car in question is all that remains of the original car that won the races and was piloted by some of the best Cobra drivers of all time.

A Le Mans Replica Cobra is among the most desirable of all Comp Cobras, and unless you are a blood relative, Cobra restorer/racer extraordinaire Bill Murray won't restore your Comp Cobra—ever. So, we know CSX 2136 is well restored and well sorted.

If you are the type that feels George Washington's axe is still the same axe he used in spite of three new handles and two new heads—and you have been looking for a Comp Cobra that will get you in the door at any vintage event on the planet, then CSX 2136 was a great buy.

If you don't care about racing, but you want to know that the aluminum on your Cobra was hammered out and installed at AC Cars in 1964, then CSX 2136 would be considered more sizzle than steak.

The sale price reflected roughly a 100 percent premium over a decent 289 street Cobra in 2010, but I suspect it also represented at least a 50 percent discount from what CSX 2136 would be worth if Ed Leslie had parked it in a garage in 1965 and it had been dragged out, dust, dents and all, and run over the same RM Monaco auction block.

I guess the answer to my above question, at least on this car's 2010 auction day in Monaco, is that you can't crash and burn the history out of a great old race car—but you can crash and burn out a significant part of its value. And I believe that 2136 was well bought for an end user who wants to race, and it was well sold if you base a car's value on how many original bits it retains.

If nothing else, the new owner of CSX 2136 has a great story to tell his buddies about his new car over a few beers.

THE $4.4 MILLION BARN FIND BUGATTI

BY LINDA CLARK

Described by his family as "generous" but "eccentric,"
Carr had a hoarding instinct that led him to collect
everything from 60 years' worth of office supply
receipts to 1,500 German beer steins.

ONE MAN'S TRASH...

MAGINE OPENING THE DOOR to your late uncle's small unassuming suburban garage and finding a rare car inside that's worth $4 million.

That's what happened to an English engineer in 2007, when he unlocked the door of the garage left to him and seven other relatives by his 89-year-old uncle, Dr. Harold Carr. The garage was in Gosforth, an affluent suburb of Newcastle, and the car was a Bugatti Type 57S Atalante coupe.

It had been sitting in Carr's cluttered, dusty garage since its last tax disc expired in December 1960. Despite its splotchy black paint job, torn and sagging seats, and rusty wire wheels, this barn find Bugatti sold for $4.4 million, including buyer's premium, at the Bonhams Rétromobile auction in Paris in 2009.

Alongside the Bugatti were two other vintage but less valuable cars—an Aston Martin and an E-Type Jaguar. The heirs sold the Aston Martin, but the Jaguar was in such bad shape that it had to be scrapped.

A childless bachelor, Carr left his estate to his nieces and nephews. They were aware of his Bugatti and other cars but had no idea what they were worth. Carr had both engineering and medical degrees, but he worked as an orthopedic surgeon and was often seen tinkering with his cars while wearing surgical gloves. In later years, Carr became a recluse.

Described by his family as "generous" but "eccentric," Carr was compared by some in the media to reclusive American millionaire Howard Hughes, due to his passion for machinery and aviation and his obsessive compulsive disorder. Carr had a hoarding instinct that led him to collect everything from 60 years' worth of office supply receipts to 1,500 German beer steins.

Friends of Dr. Carr told London's *The Daily Telegraph* that he likely knew the true value of the Bugatti and that he never answered the door when collectors called on him. Instead, they had to resort to writing offers on notes for neighbors to leave in Carr's letter box.

Of the 43 Type 57S cars built by Bugatti, only 17 were ordered with the Jean Bugatti–designed Atalante coupe coachwork. The coupe left by Dr. Carr, chassis number 57502, was even more valuable because it was originally owned by prominent British race driver Earl Howe, and because its original equipment (except for some of the interior) was intact, a restoration was possible without relying on replacement parts.

"It has all the finest attributes any connoisseur collector could ever seek, in one of the ultimate road-going sports cars from the golden era of the 1930s," said James Knight, head of the international motoring department at Bonhams when the auction house announced the car's sale. Knight and a select group of others knew of 57502 for years but didn't divulge its whereabouts.

GOLDEN PEDIGREE

The Type 57S (Surbaisse, or lowered) was built by the Molsheim, France, company from 1936 to 1938 as a high-performance variant of the firm's road car, the 3.3-liter twin overhead-cam straight eight-cylinder Type 57. Appearing in 1934 the Type 57 rivaled Alfa Romeo, Bentley, and Delage in price and performance, but when customers wanted more speed, Bugatti unveiled the 57S.

Apart from a lowered and shortened chassis, the 57S shared basic components with the Type 57. Its high-compression engine had a dry-sump oiling system derived from the T59 Grand Prix car but was otherwise similar. A Roots blower was optional, but only two supercharged 57SC (Compresseur) cars were built at the factory.

The 57S shared the 57's four-wheel cable-operated mechanical drum brakes and four-speed manual gearbox. Due to its larger diameter tires, the 57S had a slightly higher speed than the Type 57. Like the standard car, the 57S could be ordered with factory or custom coachwork. The standard chassis cost £590 ($1,629), whereas the 57S chassis was priced at £1,100 ($3,037).

Despite a variety of beautifully styled bodywork, a fine, modern engine, and uncompromising vintage chassis, occupants had to endure the 57S's sweltering cockpit. The car also had little ground clearance and no independent front suspension (although the 57S had a semi-independent front system) or synchronized gearbox, but hydraulic brakes were introduced in 1938. For twice the price of the standard 57 chassis, the Type 57S, popularly known as the Sport chassis, included special touches like a V-shaped radiator in addition to its lower center of gravity and more potent motor.

The 57S rode on a 130-inch wheelbase and weighed less than 3,000 pounds. Advertised horsepower of its high-compression engine was 175, or 200 horsepower with the Roots blower. The production run of the 57S was brief, in part due to its excessively high manufacturing cost.

It would be hard to find a Bugatti with a more impressive pedigree than this one. Its original owner, Francis Richard Henry Penn Curzon, succeeded to the peerage in 1929 on the death of his father, becoming the Fifth Earl Howe. He resigned his seat in the British House of Commons and at the same time began his long and notable involvement in motor racing.

Howe won Le Mans in 1931 driving an Alfa Romeo, co-driven by Sir Henry Birkin. He competed at Le Mans six times between 1929 and 1935. Howe was close friends with the famed Bentley Boys, and when Dudley Benjafield established the British Racing Drivers' Club, Howe was elected its first president in 1929. Under Howe's 35-year stewardship, the BRDC went from a private dining club to one of the most successful and prominent motorsport associations in the world.

In 1928 Howe, as Viscount Curzon, had driven a Type 43 Bugatti with some success in the Ulster Tourist Trophy Race, achieving fastest lap in Class D. From 1929 to 1939, Howe campaigned several more Bugattis—Types 51, 54, and even a Works Team Bugatti Type 59. So it's not surprising that he chose a Type 57S as his personal road car.

Howe took delivery of his new 57S on June 9, 1937, from Sorel of London, the UK agents for Bugatti. According to the Bonhams catalog, it was liveried in

Howe's racing colors of light blue and black, furnished with pigskin upholstery and equipped with twin spot lights and a split front bumper. Early on Howe added distinctive rear-view mirrors and a luggage rack, replaced the split front bumper with a single bumper, and added a similar rear bumper.

In the May 2009 issue of *Sports Car Market*, Simon Kidston noted that Howe also installed a removable panel in the dashboard to provide access to the troublesome magneto, extra air vents in the cowl, and ashtrays in the tops of both doors. Howe's new Bugatti was registered DYK 5 and was a familiar sight in the paddock at British motorsport venues. It shared the motor house at Howe's Amersham home in Buckinghamshire with a stable of other European and race cars. After hitting a tree with it in 1946, Howe parted with the 57S, but he retained the DYK 5 registration.

According to Bonhams, Howe sold the 57S to the London dealer Car Mart on the condition that the company not sell it in its "Howe blue," so it repainted the car maroon and reregistered it as EWS 73. Continental Cars Ltd. of Send, Surrey, bought 57502 and sold it to architect John P. Tingay of Eastcote in Middlesex in 1947 for £2,000—a considerable amount of money in those days.

Tingay upgraded the car to 57SC specifications with modified manifolds and the addition of a Marshall K200 supercharger, because Roots units were no longer available. The next owner in January 1950 was Metal Castings Ltd. of Worcester, whose director, Harry Ferguson of Stanklyn House, Stone, Kidderminster, became the owner in March 1951.

Lord Ridley of Blagdon Hall, Seaton Burn, near Newcastle, became the next owner in December 1953. Having campaigned Alfa Romeos and built his own Ridley Special to compete with Herbert Austin's diminutive supercharged racing cars, Ridley would have been a close acquaintance of Howe's in prewar racing circles. Although Ridley owned the Bugatti for only a brief time, it was likely seen regularly in Newcastle by Dr. Harold Carr, whose family owned a wholesale business, JJ Macy's, in that city.

Dr. Carr appreciated the finer things in life and no doubt knew of the motor racing exploits of Howe and Ridley. His choice of a Bugatti Type 57S was not by chance. Prior to acquiring 57502, he had corresponded with well-known sports and competition car dealer J. H. Bartlett of Notting Hill Gate, expressing interest in a Type 57 Atalante coupe. He had also contacted the Board of Trade in February 1955 regarding the possibility of importing a Type 57 from Belgium. Whether by design or coincidence, Dr. Carr bought 57502 for £895 ($2,520) from J. H. Bartlett in April 1955.

No one knows to what extent Dr. Carr used the 57S, but Bonhams believed that he had spent some time trying to enhance the performance of the de Ram shock absorbers and Scintilla Vertex magneto ignition. The car's odometer showed 26,284 when it was discovered after Dr. Carr's death. The car was not used during the war and was known to have remained partially dismantled for 47 years in preparation for a full rebuild.

Due to the doctor's reclusive nature, 57502 remained largely out of sight until his death on June 14, 2007. Being a highly coveted model for collectors, with at least four thought to be in the Musée Nationale de l'Automobile in Mulhouse, France, Bonhams made it the centerpiece of their Rétromobile sale in Paris on February 2, 2009.

The car sold for $4,408,575, including buyer's premium. This was less than exuberant presale estimates of $9 million by analysts caught up in the hype and hyperbole. But even with the deep pockets required for its restoration, some experts deemed this extraordinary barn find to have been fairly priced.

Bonhams didn't comment on who the winning bidder was or what the car's fate might be, but Simon Kidston reported in *Sports Car Market* magazine that 57502's new owner plans to do as little as possible cosmetically and retain the Marshall blower, which is part of the car's lineage.

A CAR OF A
DIFFERENT COLOR

BY LINDA CLARK

A Boston newspaper said the Moxie Horsemobile was "the joining of the horse and the automobile in a motor contraption that is ornamental, ingenious, and wonderful."

THE HORSE CAR

BEFORE TELEVISION, advertising on wheels was more popular than it is today. Products ranging from Quaker Oats to Electrolux vacuum cleaners had mobile campaigns. Companies often mounted huge custom-coachwork replicas of their product on a car or truck chassis. The giant roll of Pep-O-Mint Life Savers on a 1918 Dodge truck and the big can of V8 Cocktail Juice on a roadster were eye-catchers.

Few companies employed mobile ads more effectively than the Moxie Beverage Company, however. By 1899, the Moxie Bottle Wagon, an 8-foot-tall replica of a Moxie bottle pulled by a horse, was a familiar sight throughout New England.

Moxie was also quick to capitalize on the newly created horseless carriage. By 1908 the Massachusetts company's Rambler- and Buick-based Moxie cars had become a common sight in 17 states. It was often said the first car ever seen in many towns had "Moxie" painted on its side.

As cars gained popularity, Moxie soda, which had been derived from a patent medicine in 1884, was marketed as the ideal beverage for "safe driving" or "one for the road." Since tipsy patrons no longer had a trusted horse to get them home, why not drink Moxie? Moxie had been touted as a whiskey substitute since its founding, but the company needed a new mobile campaign that would stand out in traffic.

Frank Archer, a Maine native and son of a doctor, had joined Moxie in 1896. Archer was Moxie's advertising genius. He also had a flair for showmanship. Following Moxie's unsuccessful attempt to motorize its Bottle Wagon, Archer came up with the idea of a horse car. However, he was unable to build one that wasn't top heavy and dangerous to drive, so Archer asked his friend Fred Wright, a Dort dealer in New York City, for help. Wright asked Hal Carpenter, who had worked for Pierce-Arrow in Buffalo, New York, to see what he could do.

The 28-year-old Carpenter happened to be a Moxie drinker and enthusiastically went about mounting a harness maker's dummy horse on a 1917 Dort Speedster chassis. The combination of superior mechanical skills and a lighter horse did the trick—it was driven from the horse's saddle and attracted attention wherever it went. A Boston newspaper said the Moxie Horsemobile was "the joining of the horse and the automobile in a motor contraption that is ornamental, ingenious, and wonderful."

Carpenter had to rearrange the clutch and brake pedals, extend the gear shift lever, and put the steering shaft down through the horse's neck and chest. To

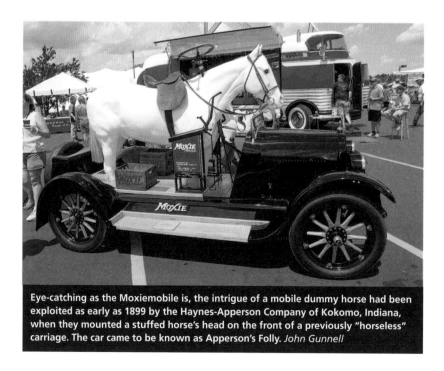

Eye-catching as the Moxiemobile is, the intrigue of a mobile dummy horse had been exploited as early as 1899 by the Haynes-Apperson Company of Kokomo, Indiana, when they mounted a stuffed horse's head on the front of a previously "horseless" carriage. The car came to be known as Apperson's Folly. *John Gunnell*

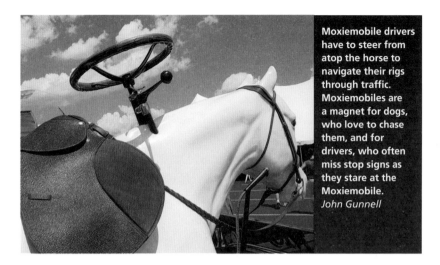

Moxiemobile drivers have to steer from atop the horse to navigate their rigs through traffic. Moxiemobiles are a magnet for dogs, who love to chase them, and for drivers, who often miss stop signs as they stare at the Moxiemobile.
John Gunnell

accelerate, the driver had to put his foot on the right-hand stirrup platform and slide it forward to move a curved-bar pedal that opened the throttle. That way, Carpenter told Frank Potter in the book *The Moxie Mystique*, the driver could stand up on the stirrups and ride over rough roads without the danger of being thrown off.

The dummy horse used for the Carpenter horsemobile was made of papier-mâché, as was the one used for Archer's earlier rig. The Carpenter Moxiemobile, as it came to be known, was the only one to have a black horse. Later Moxiemobiles were built using white aluminum horses formed in custom-made molds.

While the Dort-Moxie was the protoype, Moxie wanted to use prestige platforms for its official advertising vehicles. Except for one built on an Essex chassis in 1922, Moxiemobiles were built on Buick, LaSalle, and Rolls-Royce chassis. Their horses used both western and English-style saddles.

The men who drove the Moxiemobile in its late 1920s to early 1930s heyday, noted Marc Stern in *Special-Interest Autos*, wore English riding habits. These included a white ascot, riding coat, breeches, boots, and hat. The hat was especially useful as the Moxiemobile had little clearance under low-hanging branches, so drivers got their share of bumps and bruises.

Driving the Moxiemobile was a risky job in itself. The driver had only manual steering to navigate the 18-foot-long cars through traffic, all while seated 12 feet in the air. The rigs were a magnet for dogs, who loved to chase them, and for other drivers, who often missed traffic signals as they stared at the Moxiemobile.

Although the cars retained the full range of dashboard gauges, the driver was too far away from the gauges to read them.

Until the early 1920s, Moxie outsold Coca-Cola and had bottlers in 38 states. It was an impressive feat for Moxie founder Dr. Augustin Thompson, who was born in 1835 in Union, Maine. He grew up on the family farm, and when the Civil War began, he enlisted in the Union Army. He enlisted as a private and retired as a lieutenant colonel.

After the war Thompson went to medical school. After graduating he established a practice in Lowell, Massachusetts. To supplement his medical practice income, he developed patent medicines, which were popular at the time. In 1884 Thompson entered the growing soft drink trade by modifying one of his medicines into a "nerve food beverage" named Moxie. It's speculated that the name was inspired by Thompson's boyhood home, where there was a Moxie Falls, Moxie Cave, and Moxie Pond.

But it was Frank Archer, whom history has dubbed the "Father of Moxie," who took Thompson's famous "nerve food," carbonated it, and sold it cold around 1906.

John Wissink, of Spring Lake, Michigan, owns this handsome Moxiemobile that was recreated by Howard Mark of Deland, Florida, on a 1923 Buick truck chassis. *John Gunnell*

While it was still in service in the 1940s, the 1929 LaSalle Moxiemobile attracted a lot of attention at this Massachusetts parade. The men who drove Moxiemobiles wore English riding habits that included a white ascot, riding coat, breeches, boots, and hat. *Evan Kempton Collection*

It's delightful "never sticky or syrupy" formula, an extract of the gentian flower, gave Moxie its distinct bitter taste.

LONG SHELF LIFE

The only surviving original Moxiemobile, built on a 1929 LaSalle chassis, was restored in 1971 by the Monarch Company, owner of Moxie at that time. In 1984, it was sold to Q. David Bowers and Eddie Clark, both of New Hampshire. Today it's co-owned by Bowers and Eddie's son, Ben Clark. Their beautifully restored example is on display at Clark's Trading Post in Lincoln, New Hampshire.

A few authentic replicas exist, thanks in large part to the efforts of Moxiemobile expert Wil Markey of Dallastown, Pennsylvania. Markey has been restoring and collecting antique cars and trucks for over 60 years. But he got into the business of building Moxiemobile replicas by accident.

"Around 1989 I had a chance to see the Moxiemobile co-owned by Q. David Bowers," Markey said. "I liked it so much that I wanted to buy it. But it wasn't for sale and I really couldn't afford it. So after doing some research, I decided to make my own," Markey said.

"I bought a 1929 LaSalle, and after studying some original Moxie photos, converted it to a Horsemobile. It took a few years to complete. When it was done, I took it to the Antique Automobile Club of America's big Hershey meet and someone there wanted to buy it. It was amazing. I sold it at Hershey. That's what got me going," Markey recalls.

"Moxiemobiles tended to not survive because the early ones had wooden horses that deteriorated. They were also accident-prone since they tipped over easily. And they were dangerous to drive because the saddles tended to slide off, especially when taking corners. That's why I bolt down the saddles and straps on my replicas," Markey said.

"As for the horses," Markey noted, "the aluminum ones that Moxie used weren't very authentic looking because they lacked the muscles you normally see on a horse. They were too smooth. So I found a place in Michigan that makes realistic-looking fiberglass horses with muscles showing on them."

The world's only surviving Moxiemobile, a modified 1929 LaSalle, at the 2009 Moxie Festival in Maine. Co-owned by Q. David Bowers and Ben Clark, this beautifully restored original resides at Clark's Trading Post in Lincoln, New Hampshire.
Dave Sacerdote

"The fiberglass horse I use is life-size. First I cut a few inches off the legs, then stuff them with rags and pour fiberglass into them and put a bolt in the middle. I place a steel plate between the horse's hooves and the car, covered with some green indoor-outdoor carpet. After first putting the horse on the carpet so its hooves make an impression, I bore down through the steel plate and put nuts and bolts where needed to fasten the horse to the car," Markey recounted.

"People always think I'm going to fall off when they see me driving down the street in my Moxiemobile, not realizing I bolted down the saddle and straps. You're sitting so high you can see over the traffic, and when you go around corners, there's nothing to hold onto except the wheel," Markey said.

"I've built four Moxiemobiles—three LaSalles and one Rolls-Royce. I sold three of them. One of the LaSalles went to Holland and in 2007 the Rolls-Royce went to Florida. Over the past twenty-three years, I've driven all of them to the annual Moxie Festival in Lisbon Falls, Maine. It's a three-day affair with a big parade, swap meet, and car show sponsored by the New England Moxie Congress," Markey said.

The Moxie Festival was launched in 1982 by Frank Anicetti, a lifelong Moxie drinker and third-generation owner of the Kennebec Fruit Company in downtown Lisbon Falls. Known locally as the Moxie Store, since Anicetti sells Moxie memorabilia, during the festival there's a line outside the door of people waiting to buy Moxie ice cream cones.

"A loosely-knit band of Moxie zealots and fellow travelers" is how the New England Moxie Congress describes itself on its website. Members are dedicated to preserving all things Moxie. It is the only known club for Moxie collectors, so members come from near and far.

In addition to the Moxie Horsemobiles, some members own the Moxie cars that were used for advertising, which ranged from Stanley Steamers and Locomobiles to Ford Model A "Tudor" Sedans.

STRAIGHT FROM THE HORSE'S MOUTH

Eye-catching as the Moxiemobile was, the intrigue of a mobile dummy horse had been exploited years before by the Haynes-Apperson Company of Kokomo, Indiana. The company built a car around 1899 that was startling to see, although the idea had been to make a car that wouldn't startle horses.

Apperson's Folly, as the car came to be known, was the brainchild of Uriah Smith of Battle Creek, Michigan. A stuffed horse's head was mounted on the front of a previously "horseless" carriage. This was meant to create the illusion of a horse and buggy and thus fool approaching horses so they wouldn't panic, as they often did, when confronted with the strange new, noisy machines. But the car was judged a failure. Smith returned to Michigan, and Elmer Apperson consigned the hapless horse's head to whatever pastures such absurdities go.

Horses never lost their appeal, though, and even Moxie sold toy versions of its famous Moxiemobile. Manufactured by toy and tricycle maker American National Company of Toledo, Ohio, these 8 1/2-inch-long replicas of the real-life Moxiemobile are sought-after collectibles.

The lithographed tin toys were made from 1917 to 1925 and came with red or blue cars with a rider and horse. The rider wore a Moxiecloth jacket and the cars resemble Archer's own 1916 prototype. The toys bear the Moxie trademark and say "patented February 27, 1917" underneath. A blue one sold at a Bertoia Auction in Vineland, New Jersey, in 2012 for $5,750.

American National also built an orange Moxie Horsemobile pedal car in the early 1920s with bottle cap hubcaps. It's unknown how many were built, but Moxie aficionados believe only one or two still exist. Their value is estimated to be around $15,000.

The company itself was split into two after the Great Depression. Frank Thompson, son of founder Augustin Thompson, became president of the Moxie Company, which retained bottling rights to New England. The other company was Moxie Company of America, headed by Frank Archer, which had bottling rights to the entire nation except New England.

In 1967 Moxie bought National Nugrape Company, and the two soda companies formed the Moxie-Monarch-Nugrape Company of Doraville, Georgia. Moxie largely faded into memory as Monarch went on to become a huge success with NuGrape, Suncrest, and other soda brands.

Moxie can still be purchased in New England, where it lives on in the hearts, souls, and taste buds of stalwart devotees who consider it "wicked good stuff."

THE JEFFRIES
PORSCHE

BY TOM COTTER

As he investigated his new purchase, he began
to notice some unusual features; the Porsche had two
switches next to the steering wheel for the coils. It also
appeared that the car once housed a dry-sump oiling
engine, as was typical in racing Porsches.

I N 2009, I WROTE A BIOGRAPHY about California customizer Dean Jeffries (*Dean Jeffries: 50 Fabulous Years in Hot Rods, Racing & Film*). One of Jeffries' most significant custom creations was a Porsche Carrera that he customized as a young man when he rented space behind George Barris' shop.

The rare sports car was molded into an appealing shape and featured non-traditional headlights, taillights, and scoops, and it was painted pearl silver. Jeffries speaks proudly that even though it was frowned on to customize sports cars—especially Porsches in the 1950s and 1960s—his Carrera was universally appreciated by enthusiasts and even got a "thumbs-up" from a Porsche factory representative. The car was featured on the cover of the October 1959 issue of *Rod & Custom* magazine.

One day a man walked into Jeffries' Hollywood, California, shop and said he wanted to buy the Porsche that was sitting outside. "That's fine and dandy," Jeffries told him. "But I want all cash."

The man said, "Fine, because that's all I deal with."

When Jack Walter bought this intriguing Porsche in the 1970s, he just liked the look. He didn't know that it left the factory with a four-cam Carerra engine, that famous California customizer Dean Jeffries had customized it, or that it had been featured on the cover of magazines decades earlier. *Jack Walter*

Jeffries didn't know that the man was wanted for murder and bank robbery. He paid cash for the car and, as Jeffries said, "Drove down the road." To this day Jeffries regrets selling the Porsche, and has said for many years that he would love to buy it back to add to his small collection.

The man, Albert Nussbaum, apparently drove the car from Southern California to his sister's house near Fort Lauderdale, Florida, trying to avoid the police. Ultimately he was arrested, and the car remained in his sister's driveway for two to three years.

The Porsche disappeared until 1964, when it reappeared briefly repainted in white. The rare and temperamental four-cam Carrera engine had been removed, and a standard pushrod Porsche motor had been installed in its place.

Amelia Island Concours d'Elegance founder and co-chairman Bill Warner followed up rumors that the car still existed somewhere on the East Coast. He found the owner and made arrangements to bring it to the 2009 Concours for Jeffries to see for the first time in nearly 50 years.

As Jeffries walked around the car, which was halfway through a restoration, he had tears in his eyes. He had thought of this day for almost half a century.

How had such a famous car gone undiscovered for so many decades? Jack Walter knows.

Walter was your average car-crazy teen in 1971. He had just graduated from high school and was eager to own a Porsche.

"I had been a Porsche nut from an early age," said Walter, 58, of Atlanta. "When I was fourteen years old I read a 1966 *Car & Driver* story about a black Porsche Speedster called *Ode to a Bathtub*. It left a huge impression on me."

Upon graduation, Walter went searching for a Speedster of his own. He saw an advertisement for one being sold by Atlanta-based race driver Jim Downing, who at the time had a little shop.

"It was painted with primer and he was asking six hundred dollars for it," said Walter. "I only had four hundred dollars, so I brought my dad along hoping I could borrow the extra two hundred dollars. But he just saw this old Speedster and wouldn't loan me the money."

Walter's father hoped to satisfy his son's desire for a sporty convertible by buying him a Corvair Corsa Turbo convertible for $275. The car had a dropped

When Jeffries' pinstriping, painting, and customizing career was just starting out in the 1950s, he used this car as his calling card at car shows. He originally painted the car pearl silver, then painted it pearl gold (as shown), then painted it silver again before selling it to a "killer and a bank robber." *Jack Walter*

Dean Jeffries was reunited with the partially restored Porsche after nearly 50 years at the 2009 Amelia Island Concours d'Elegance in Florida. Jeffries will come to Amelia again to see the finished product when it is completed. *Jack Walter*

valve, so his dad wanted him to invest some "sweat equity" into the car before it could become roadworthy.

"I rebuilt the engine and had it balanced," he said. "I had it up to two hundred forty horsepower." Still, as cool as it was, the hot little Corvair failed to satisfy the young Walter's desire for a Porsche.

Walter used to hang out at a friend's house whose older sister, Peggy Dale, was a sports car enthusiast; she owned a Fiat Spyder. Her mechanic, Sandy, found a strange-looking Porsche coupe while on a Florida trip in 1969, so he bought it and towed it home.

As soon as she saw it, Peggy wanted to own the Porsche, but Sandy wasn't interested in selling it. But her mechanic friend had a gambling problem and called Peggy to borrow some money to pay off the "leg-breakers" who were on their way over to his house.

"No, I won't loan you money, but I will buy your Porsche," said Peggy, who at the time was 24 years old. Even though he had wanted more money for the car, Sandy accepted $1,100 because he had recently crashed the car into the back of a truck and it sustained some body damage.

Peggy bought the car and Walter remembers the first time he saw it while he was over visiting Peggy's brother. "I saw it at her parent's home and I made three laps around the car before I walked into the house," he said. "Sell me the car," he told Peggy.

She ignored him, proud of her new set of wheels.

Walter said that Peggy used the Porsche every day. She lived near a downtown Atlanta bar, so unfortunately she parked the unique car in the streets. Every time Walter saw her he would ask, "When are you going to sell me the car?"

In 1971, Peggy told Walter she was trying to raise money so she could travel to Katmandu. "I'll sell you the car for what I paid: one thousand one hundred dollars," she said.

"I said, 'OK!'" said Walter.

He drove the car home. Immediately his father asked why he bought the beat-up Porsche.

Walter said the registration slip identified the car as a Sebring coupe, but he really thought the car was just a local Florida custom. He began saving to get the damaged nose repaired.

As he investigated his new purchase, he began to notice some unusual features; the Porsche had two switches next to the steering wheel for the coils. It also appeared that the car once housed a dry-sump oiling engine, as was typical in racing Porsches.

About this same time—1971 or 1972—Walter said that he saw an ad in *AutoWeek* magazine asking for photos and information on a custom Porsche that was built by Dean Jeffries in the late 1950s.

"I still didn't know I owned Dean Jeffries' Porsche, but I certainly knew who Dean Jeffries was," said Walter. "He built the Monkeemobile and the Kyote Dune Buggies. I always wanted one of those dune buggies."

Eventually he got the Porsche's nose repaired "with lots of Bondo," and started to drive the Porsche quite a bit, even though he still owned his Turbo Corvair.

"So I sent photos of my car to the guy who advertised in *AutoWeek*," he said. "I wrote, 'Is this what you're looking for?'"

"I got back a six-page letter with copies of magazine articles and a letter from the man. He said he had seen it at a car show in the 1950s."

Finally he knew what he owned.

Walter joined the Atlanta Region of the Porsche Club of America, but when he wrote on his application that he had a customized Porsche, they gave him a bad time. That is, until he told them it was the Dean Jeffries' Porsche; then members started telling him that Jeffries actually enhanced the car's original lines.

"I couldn't believe I own this car," he said. "I actually built Dean Jeffries model cars when I was a kid. I was so excited."

In 1973, a friend of Walter's who owned a Porsche 550 Spyder suggested that he consider purchasing a proper four-cam engine for the Jeffries Porsche.

"He knew a guy in Jacksonville who had three Carrera engines, so I said, 'OK, let's get one,'" said Walter. "We drove down in his friend's new Honda Civic hatchback and picked up the engine. I paid nine hundred dollars."

TRADING UP

Walter tells a funny tale of driving back to Atlanta in the Honda with the four-cam engine in clear view through the large hatchback window.

"A Porsche comes blasting past us in the fast lane, then slams on its brakes when the driver saw the engine we were hauling," said Walter. "It turns out it was [Porsche race driver] Hurley Haywood, who just wanted to see it."

In 1974, Walter painted the Porsche white with a dark blue GT40-type stripe that ran from front to rear. (It was in this configuration that *Rod & Custom* ran a photo of the car in 1990.)

Then the car went into a 20-year hibernation.

Walter was in a funk. He had too many cars and not enough time.

"A friend of mine said he walked into his garage when he turned fifty years old and realized that he'd have to live to one hundred in order to finish all his car projects," said Walter. "He sold off a bunch of projects and used the money to fix up his favorites.

"It took me a couple of years to come to the same conclusion. I had a Porsche sunroof coupe—six hundred forty serial numbers after the Carrera—that I sold. I sold a BMW 2002tii as well." His new goal was to restore the Porsche he had owned since 1971.

"I want to bring the Porsche to display at Amelia Island restored to the exact way it looked when it rolled out of Dean Jeffries' shop in 1957," he said.

He has located a restoration shop that is doing an exquisite job on the body, and he will have the interior duplicated.

But the restoration is expensive, certainly more than his job at Lockheed can comfortably afford. Luckily Bill Warner from Amelia Island talked paint sponsor

BASF into donating the paint for the project. And Dean Jeffries himself sat down with a company rep to ensure the color and the metallic flake would be just right.

"Dean Jeffries said he'd like to buy it back, and I said I'd trade it for his GT40," said Walter.

"I'm just an engineer and can't really afford to own a car that valuable. When the car is done, I might just let it go to a Porsche collector with deep pockets.

"A standard Carrera coupe is worth three hundred thousand to five hundred thousand dollars these days. Certainly this one is more valuable. At least it might allow me to retire a little bit early."

"There was a main house with an outbuilding, and next to the house was the GTO. The Ferrari was sitting on an open trailer that appeared abandoned rather than parked. No effort was made to preserve the car—it was left uncovered and completely exposed to the elements. It appeared it was being punished, purposely left near the salvation of indoor storage, but denied access for some unknown sin. The tires on the car and the tires on the rusty trailer were flat, but it didn't matter; this was a car that wasn't going anywhere.

Instead of hiding the car, it was exposed to be seen by anyone driving by. Occasionally, someone would stop to look at the car, and like the old ladies who peer from behind windows waiting to yell at kids retrieving balls from their yards, the owner took perverse pleasure taunting people with the sight of the car—and then denying them access to it."

№ 2

WRECKS
& RUINS

THE BURIED BELVEDERE

BY DALE NOVAK

A sealed time capsule that was stored with the car
didn't leak, and its contents—newspapers, rolls of movie film,
vinyl records, plates, and other documents—were in perfect
condition. But the Belvedere, the star of the show,
was in sad shape.

VALUING MISS BELVEDERE

O N JUNE 15, 1957, a 1957 Plymouth Belvedere was buried in Tulsa, Oklahoma, to commemorate Oklahoma's 50th birthday. It was intended to be a time capsule for a future generation to unveil 50 years down the road. The Plymouth was brand-spanking new, with only four miles on the clock. Fifty years later, when the car was scheduled to be exhumed from its crypt, it would be given to the Tulsa resident who could guess the current population of the city 50 years in the future.

In 1957 Raymond Humbertson guessed 384,743; the actual Tulsa population in 2007 was 382,457. Humbertson's guess was the closest, so he won the car. He had died, however, in 1979, so the car was passed on to his two sisters, one of whom still owns it today.

Virgil Exner's Forward Look design was considered ultra-modern and stylish, so the Belvedere was chosen as a fine representative to send to the world of 2007. A case of Schlitz beer and a large can of gasoline—to be used to start the car if the world of 2007 no longer used gas to power their vehicles—were stored in the trunk.

The car was sealed in an underground concrete vault that was billed as strong enough to withstand a nuclear war. Nuclear war, maybe, but not a good rain shower—the vault was not watertight.

It's a great story, and it could have had a great ending. But in 1973 work crews doing some excavating around the Tulsa Courthouse (in the vicinity of where the car was buried) ruptured a water main. The area flooded terribly, and water made its way to the concrete encasement, completely submerging the sleeping Mopar.

When it was unearthed in 2007, it was hoped that the car would come out of its dark resting place in an overall preserved, good condition. But that simply wasn't to be. The car was shrouded in a cover, but a rusty rear fin poking out showed the crowd that the car hadn't spent the past 50 years high and dry. The car had sat in water for decades, and it was a rusty mess. The seats were mostly rust springs.

A sealed time capsule that was stored with the car didn't leak, and its contents—newspapers, rolls of movie film, vinyl records, plates, and other documents—were in perfect condition. But the Belvedere, the star of the show, was in sad shape.

With a collective sigh, the crowd went home, and the story quietly, over time, simply dissipated. Humberton's family didn't want to give up, so they shipped the car to Dwight Foster in New Jersey.

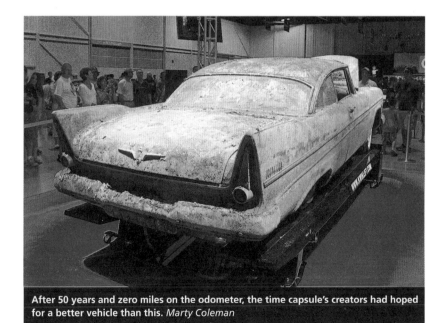

After 50 years and zero miles on the odometer, the time capsule's creators had hoped for a better vehicle than this. *Marty Coleman*

Dwight Foster's company, Ultra One Corporation of Hackettstown, New Jersey, sells a rust removal chemical called Safest Rust Remover, designed to remove rust safely without compromising metal. Dwight was tasked with trying to save the car from further deterioration and resurrect it, as best he could, with an eye on preservation.

The interior of the buried Belvedere before any restoration work had started. *Ultra One*

The 1957 Belvedere as it looked right after it emerged from decades of soaking in water in an underground vault.

The buried Belvedere rests easy on a trailer in Tulsa, Oklahoma. In hindsight, this may have been a better place for it than the vault!

When he received the car, it didn't roll, the leaf springs had all but disintegrated, and the chassis was about as fragile as papier-mâché. The water, which became something like an acid bath, had compromised everything—a toxic soup the car had remained submerged in since 1973.

Dwight still has the car, and he's still carefully peeling off decades of crusty rust and molten debris. The car now sits on a stabilized chassis. It rolls, and the 1957 tires have been fitted with inner tubes to hold air. His plan is to continue to preserve the car so it can be put on display or eventually sold, if the family decides to take that route.

"I'd like to see it end up in the Smithsonian," Dwight says. "The family turned down a few offers in the past with hopes that the car would end up in a museum

The original paint is finally visible on the buried Belvedere after months of painstaking work to remove the rust.

The interior of the buried Belvedere. Though the restoration had begun, the rust and decay were still everywhere.

or be part of a tour that can display the car so the public can enjoy the history and the story. I think that's a fine idea, as the car is too special to just let it sit in a warehouse somewhere."

A pristine original Belvedere with minimal mileage is worth about $40,000 to $50,000. Obviously, that's not this car, because it's not even truly an automobile any longer—it's an artifact.

What about other cars that have been found? Ones that will never work again but instead are appreciated as works of automotive art?

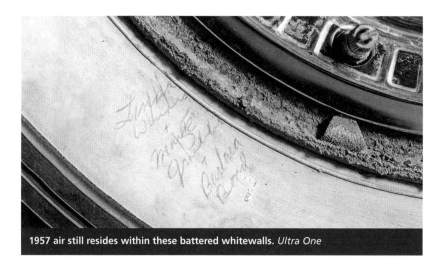

1957 air still resides within these battered whitewalls. *Ultra One*

In 2009 a 1925 Bugatti Brescia Type 22 Roadster was pulled from the bottom of Lake Maggiore in Switzerland. It had been sitting on the bottom of the lake for about 70 years. When it was recovered, it was in similar condition as our subject car. It had to sit on a dolly just to be moved because most of the car had succumbed to the lake water in a similar fashion as the Belvedere.

That car sold at the Bonhams Automobiles d'Exception Auction at Rétromobile in Paris on January 23, 2010, for $364,700. At the time, a fully sorted, well-prepared #2 condition Bugatti had a valuation range of $150,000 to $400,000.

The difference for this sale, or at least at the time of this sale in 2010, is that the Bugatti was offered as a newly discovered treasure. In other words the sizzle was sold while the steak was hot off the oak-fired grill. Sell 'em while they're hot, so to speak.

NOT A RARE CAR, BUT A RARE STORY

A 1957 Belvedere hardtop is not hard to come by. A total 67,268 were built. Sure, this one is rare due to its history—no argument there. But you and your spouse aren't going to drive it down to the ice cream shop now or ever. It will never be functional as an automobile again. So on this scale, the car has virtually no value.

But as an automotive oddity, it has some merit. A unique collector, or let's say at least two of them, could presumably bid this car to a distinctive level given the proper amount of marketing and a large television audience. On that scale, and with the stars aligning, I would guesstimate that the car would fetch a figure larger than $25,000—but I don't think it would exceed $100,000.

At first glance, the cleaned-up Belvedere looks almost drivable, but it is too delicate to ever take the road again.

Some have questioned if the work by Dwight's shop has aided or diminished the value. This is debatable, and I'm sure if we asked several collectors we'd get several answers. The car was certainly more haunting and historical in its as-discovered condition. The clay and rust preserved the car in an eerie state of decay. In that form, it had a unique look. By cleaning it up, perhaps some of the history has been washed away.

But on the other hand, Dwight's work has preserved the car and stabilized the sheet metal. It is ready, according to Mr. Foster, to be on display, provided that it is properly transported and cared for. One could look at this somewhat like a five-hundred-year-old painting that is no longer visible because of fading and oxidation. Conservators carefully remove the surface oxidation, waxes, and dulling varnishes. These preservations increase the value of the work of art when properly executed. Isn't that what was done here? Shouldn't the car be considered an object of art?

Looking at the history, the current state of the car and unique one-of-one provenance coupled with a market that seems to be yearning for the odd and unusual, I'd suggest a value range of $40,000 to $60,000 at a widely publicized auction. I think the car might have pulled a considerably stronger number in 2007, while the sizzle was still following the steak. But auctions can and do surprise us, so the true number is anyone's guess.

That said, I'm with Dwight—I'd rather it find its way to the Smithsonian. It would be a more fitting end to this story.

FIERY HISTORY OF THE JAGUAR XKSS

BY LINDA CLARK

Jaguar was able to resume 50 percent of production within just five days of the fire, but nearly three hundred cars had been turned to scrap. The 16 remaining XKSS cars were delivered and remain treasured keepsakes among Jaguar aficionados.

JAGUAR IN THE GOLDEN AGE OF RACING

L IKE THE C-TYPE BEFORE IT, the Jaguar D-type was one of the landmark race cars of the 1950s. Not only did it have Malcolm Sayer's beautiful, iconic design, but it also fulfilled Jaguar founder William Lyons's desire to win France's 24 Hours of Le Mans.

Frank "Lofty" England was the mastermind behind much of Jaguar's track success. He served his engineering apprenticeship with Daimler before joining Jaguar in 1946. Owing to his 6-foot-5-inch height, England acquired the nickname Lofty in the 1920s, and it stuck with him for life.

Jaguar had no motorsport plans after the end of World War II, but Jaguar and England quickly realized the potential of Bill Heynes and Walter Hassan's XK engine. The company's newly formed Racing Department provided six top prewar drivers with lightweight, preproduction, aluminum-bodied XK 120s in 1949, and the results were encouraging.

Although small victories piled up with the XK 120 model, Jaguar boss William Lyons and England realized it was too heavy and aerodynamically compromised ever to win at Le Mans. Their solution was to install the XK 120 drivetrain in a new lightweight chassis and streamlined body. The Malcolm Sayer–designed XK 120C (for competition), later known as the C-type, raced for the last time at the 1951 Le Mans race.

England's new racing team outsmarted 19 cars with engines bigger than the C-type's, and Sayer had shaped Jaguar's first Le Mans winner. He went on to design the iconic D-type. After working for the Bristol Aeroplane Company, Sayer was steeped in the laws of aerodynamics by the time he went to work for Jaguar in 1950. Sayer's working methods involved plotting the coordinates of curves with slide rules and logarithmic tables. He also pioneered the use of wind tunnels to test a car's aerodynamic properties.

After another Le Mans victory in 1953, Lofty England decided that Jaguar had taken the C-type as far as it could, and he developed a new car around the winning XK engine. The resulting D-type was unveiled at the 1954 24 Hours of Le Mans race, where drivers Duncan Hamilton and Tony Rolt were beaten into second place by only one lap by the Ferrari 375 of Formula One stars Jose Gonzalez and Maurice Trintignant.

Le Mans in 1955 was expected to be a contest between Jaguar and the Mercedes-Benz team of Alfred Neubauer. But an accident triggered by driver Mike Hawthorn's D-type caused the deaths of Mercedes driver Pierre Levegh and 83 spectators, as pieces of the crashed Mercedes-Benz 300 SLR sliced through the crowd. Mercedes-Benz withdrew from the race and urged Jaguar to do the same, but England refused.

After the race, which Jaguar's D-Type won, Lofty England drew criticism for his decision, but maintained for the rest of his life that he didn't think Hawthorn was responsible for the tragedy and thus saw no reason to withdraw. According to people who knew him, this was typical of England's hard-nosed manner in which he ran the team.

The 1956 24 Hours of Le Mans was the last outing for the works Jaguar team. But there was no swan song for Lofty England's crew. A new, long nose D-type variant managed sixth place, and, fortunately for Jaguar, England encouraged private teams and ensured that they got as much help as Jaguar could offer. It was one of those teams, Ecurie Ecosse, which scored the D-type's win that year. The Scottish team also won the race with an England-supplied, ex-works long-nose car in 1957.

In America the Briggs Cunningham team raced several D-types. A 1954 works car on loan to Cunningham won the 1955 12 Hours of Sebring in the hands of Mike Hawthorn and Phil Walters, and in May 1956 entries for Maryland's Cumberland National Championship Sports Car Race included four D-types in Cunningham's white and blue racing colors.

An unsung hero of Jaguar's track victories was engineer Norman Dewis. Dewis set up a testing department when he joined Jaguar in 1952 and created over six hundred tests. He set a speed record with the D-type in 1953 and drove in both the Mille Miglia rally in Italy and at Le Mans. But what Dewis was proudest of, according to Jaguar, was his development of the disc brake with Dunlop.

OUT OF THE FRYING PAN, INTO THE FIRE

Following Jaguar's withdrawal from racing, Lofty England returned to his role as head of Jaguar's service department. He turned down an offer to buy the Vanwall Formula One team and then began climbing the corporate ladder within Jaguar. When Sir William (who was knighted in 1956) retired from Jaguar in late 1967, Lofty England and Bill Haynes succeeded him as co-directors of the company.

McQueen sold the XKSS to casino owner and car collector Bill Harrah in the 1970s, but bought the car back in 1978 and owned it until he died in 1980. *Time & Life Pictures*

There were still 25 D-types in inventory when Jaguar ceased racing in late 1956, and, according to *Road & Track*, Briggs Cunningham encouraged Jaguar to add another 25 D-types, the total of 50 meeting the Sports Car Club of America's rules to qualify for production sports car racing in the United States.

At the same time, race driver Duncan Hamilton urged Jaguar to build a road-going D-type, having given his own 1954 works car a veneer of civility in the form of a windshield and weather protection for use as an occasional road car.

Jaguar changed the model number of the cars from XKD to XKSS, the initials standing for Super Sport. Externally, the factory added minimal bumpers to protect the aluminum bodywork, a luggage rack for touring, turn signals, larger taillights, and a full-width windshield. Specially designed body-colored alloy panels anchored into the bodywork held the side pillars of the curved windshield in place.

For the XKSS, the distinctive D-type headrest and fin were removed. For creature comfort, side windows and a rudimentary folding fabric top were added. Also, the center divider between driver and passenger was removed and the rider got a door.

Little changed mechanically. XKSS buyers got the same 250-horsepower, dry-sump 3.4-liter DOHC straight-six engine that moved the Jaguar to 60 miles per hour in just 5.2 seconds on the way to its 149 miles per hour top speed, according to *Road & Track*. The XKSS cars also had the same rack-and-pinion steering and disc brakes as the Competition D-type.

The cars weighed around 1,950 pounds and rode on a 90.6-inch wheelbase. D-types had a complex multi-tubular front frame, with separate monocoque center and tail sections. They also featured an all-synchromesh four-speed transmission. Suspension was conventional upper/lower wishbones and torsion bars in front, with a live axle and trailing links in the back.

The steering wheel and seats were nonadjustable. While developing the roadster, according to noted British sports car expert Hartmut Lehbrink, Jaguar invited four people of different stature to try out the seats, and a universal seating position was established. Instruments consisted of a large speedometer and tachometer to the left of the steering column and small oil pressure and water temperature gauges to the right.

Jaguar unveiled the road-going XKSS at the December 1956 New York Auto Show, where Jaguar took orders from buyers anxious to get their street-legal D-types. Work on converting the 25 remaining D-Types to XKSS specifications was underway when disaster struck.

A fire at the Browns Lane factory in Coventry on February 12, 1957, destroyed not only nine of the cars, but all the special tooling, jigs, and wooden bucks needed to form the XKSS's body. The fire ended the production run of the XKSS cars just as they were peaking in popularity.

The fire was etched in the memory of a worker who rescued cars as the factory burned around him. Brian Martin, a father of two from Solihull, was working on an assembly line and was putting in overtime on a saloon car that had come off the production tracks.

Martin told Britain's *Coventry Evening Telegraph* that he had finished the job and was preparing to head home when he heard the fire alarm. "I looked back and saw the roof on fire, right next to the tire bay, which is where I had moved from. The lining of the roof was melting and sending burning material on to the floor and starting fires everywhere," he told the newspaper.

Help! was Martin's first thought, but he and all the office staff bravely tried to save as many of the drivable Jaguars as they could. The blaze gutted half the factory, which employed four thousand people.

Martin told the newspaper the fire started around 5:45 p.m. and had high praise for the Coventry Fire Brigade, whose 19 engines arrived at Browns Lane within 20 minutes, and their crews were able to save at least half the plant from ruin.

In Britain's House of Commons on February 28, the Minister of Labour assured House members that all the regulations of Britain's Factories Act were properly observed and that Jaguar had an excellent record "not only in its products but in its relationship with its workers and the care it takes of them."

Jaguar was able to resume 50 percent of production within just five days of the fire, but nearly three hundred cars had been turned to scrap. The 16 remaining XKSS cars were delivered and remain treasured keepsakes among Jaguar aficionados. Twelve of the cars were reportedly shipped to America, two to Canada, one to Hong Kong, and one remained in Britain.

CHANGING HANDS

At least two of the XKSS cars went to California. One went to American movie and television actor Hugh O'Brien, best known for his starring role in the ABC western *The Life and Legend of Wyatt Earp*. The other was sold to building contractor James Patterson of Altadena, a suburb of Los Angeles. Patterson later

Between takes of the CBS television series *Wanted: Dead or Alive*, Steve McQueen often tinkered with his beloved Jaguar XKSS. *Time & Life Pictures*

sold the car to radio and television personality Bill Leyden, famous for announcing *The Liberace Program* on radio and hosting six TV game shows on NBC.

While the car still belonged to Leyden in 1958, actor Steve McQueen, then just beginning his role as bounty hunter Josh Randall in the CBS television series *Wanted: Dead or Alive*, saw the XKSS parked on a studio lot in Los Angeles. He subsequently bought the car from Leyden for a reported $5,000 and twice almost lost his license speeding in it.

In his book *Jaguar Sports Racing Cars*, Phillip Porter notes that McQueen's car was originally painted white with red interior, but he had it repainted British Racing Green, had the interior redone in black leather, and added a locking glove box. In the 1970s McQueen sold the car to casino owner Bill Harrah to add to his

1,450-plus car collection in Reno, Nevada. Around 1978 McQueen bought the car back and owned it until he died in 1980.

In 1984 McQueen's XKSS was sold at auction to his friend Richard Freshman for $148,000. Freshman then had the car refurbished by Jaguar experts, Lynx Motors Ltd., in Britain. Freshman later sold the car to Margie and Robert Petersen of *Hot Rod* magazine and Petersen Automotive Museum fame.

A Jaguar reunion at the 2010 Pebble Beach Concours hosted 12 of the surviving 16 XKSS cars, including the one once owned by McQueen. There are actually 18 XKSS cars, because two of the original D-Types were returned to Jaguar in 1958 to be converted to XKSS specifications. One of those two belonged to American fashion designer Ralph Lauren.

When new, the XKSS sold for $5,600, about twice the price of an XK 120. But in 2003, an XKSS sold for over $1 million. Its original owner was James Grove of St. Louis, Missouri, but it had passed through many more owners and undergone several restorations by 2003.

Some Jaguar fans think the XKSS's appeal was diluted by the replicas built in both America and Britain. Cars with genuine pedigrees are more likely to fetch top dollar, such as the C-type once owned and raced by Phil Hill that sold at auction in 2009 for $2,530,000. But because none are on the market, on that rare occasion when an XKSS is offered for sale, it will no doubt be significant.

Its jaw-dropping appeal remains. A review in the May 3, 1957, issue of British magazine *The Autocar* ran out of superlatives for the XKSS. Short legs were recommended for a ride of any duration in the cramped passenger cabin, the reviewer wrote, but the lower limbs of the many people wanting to accompany him on the test drive suddenly seemed miraculously to shrink.

Tragedy—in the form of the 1955 Le Mans crash and the 1957 factory fire— seemed to haunt the C- and D-type Jaguars. That said, there are far fewer authentic XKSS cars now, and that rarity has made an already iconic car into a coveted jewel of the automotive world.

A PRINCELY
COLLECTION ROTS

MICHAEL SHEEHAN

The Rolls had become so hot with the windows up
that the steering wheel's foam padding had melted into
a puddle on the driver's seat and the leather wrap hung from
the barren steel rim like a used condom. The entire interior
was fuzzy with mold from the heat and humidity,
rendering the interior a gray, furry blanket.

DAYS OF THUNDER
(AND RAIN, WIND, AND MORE)

IMAGINE SEEING HUNDREDS of deluxe Ferraris, Lamborghinis, and McLarens—many with hardly any miles on the odometer—rotting away in tropical heat and humidity.

Although much has been written of the Sultan of Brunei's car collection—and there is no lack of spy photos of his collection on the Internet—the estimated 2,500 cars are actually *not* the Sultan's—they were the property of Prince Jefri, the Sultan's third brother. As the minister of finance for Brunei (until 1997), Prince Jefri controlled the revenue from oil and gas through the BIA, or Brunei Investment Authority, and a network of companies under the name Amadeo.

The 1997 Asian financial crisis depressed oil prices and triggered a financial crisis in Brunei. The sultan ordered Arthur Andersen to audit the BIA books, which revealed that between 1983 and mid-1998, some $40 billion in "special transfers" were made by the BIA and that Prince Jefri had personally squandered

$14.8 billion. In July 1998 Prince Jefri's Amadeo investment group collapsed under $10 billion in debt.

In 2000 Prince Jefri settled with the government of Brunei and began returning assets. Those assets included more than five hundred properties in Brunei and abroad, more than two thousand cars, a hundred paintings, five yachts, and nine world-class aircraft. According to court documents, the prince spent $78 million at Pininfarina Spa for coachbuilt right-hand-drive Ferraris, $475 million at Rolls-Royce, and $900 million at British jeweler Asprey.

WILL FLY TO BUY

In early 2002 I was offered a package of 13 very special Ferraris and McLaren F1s from the collection of a Brunei importer. After the usual negotiations, I agreed to buy two McLarens (a Ferraro F40 LM and a 288 GTO Evoluzione for clients), with an option to buy another 16 McLarens and Ferraris.

In May 2002 I flew to Brunei and stayed at the Empire Hotel. Commissioned by Prince Jefri and built at a cost of $1.1 billion, the Empire Hotel is beyond opulent. The Empire was built to accommodate over a thousand guests, but I never saw more than a dozen people anywhere in the hotel at any time. I also visited Jerudong Park, the largest and most expensive amusement park in Southeast Asia, which was also commissioned by Prince Jefri for a modest $1 billion. Like the Empire hotel, it was

Prince Jefri's 1988 Ferrari Testa Rossa F90 Speciale was just one of hundreds of unused Ferraris, Lamborghinis, and McLarens rotting away in the tropical heat and humidity of Brunei.

empty. A strict Muslim country, Brunei has no alcohol, virtually no nightlife, and thus no tourists.

I was picked up by an ex–New Zealand Special Forces (SAS) officer working as a bodyguard for the Brunei royal family. The car collection was a few kilometers down the coast and housed in a large compound surrounded by a high wall topped with razor wire, further protected by a bombproof front gate. Once inside, we had to turn in our cameras and passports and stay with our guide, as armed Gurkhas with very serious German shepherds patrolled the compound.

We first went through eight two-story buildings—each about 250 feet long by 60 feet wide—with each level holding about 120 cars. Each level had a semblance of a theme, with the first building filled with Porsches from 959s up to the late 1990s. Another floor held mainly black-on-black 1996–1997 Mercedes-Benz 500 sedans. Yet another building held coachbuilt Rolls-Royces, Bentleys, and Aston Martins, while the next one housed mainly 1990s-model Ferraris, including a few dozen 456s and 550s. Several 550s were fitted with experimental XTRAC automatic gearboxes. About a half a dozen were coated in radar-reflective matte black coatings and fitted with infrared cameras for night driving—high-tech stuff for the late 1990s.

A lower floor revealed rows of right-hand-drive Testarossas, 512 TRs, and 512 Ms. Another building contained mainly coachbuilt Ferraris, with four 456 four-doors, four 456 Venice Cabriolets, more 456 Venice station wagons, five FXs, a pair of Mythoi, and an incredibly ugly one-off called an F90. The token Enzo-era Ferrari was a right-hand-drive 275 GTS, serial number 7795.

Between the eight large buildings was a glass-walled showroom with three McLaren F1s, a 288 GTO Evo, an F50, and an F40 LM. The F40 LM was black with a black leather interior, red piping, air conditioning, and power windows. As in the other buildings, the air conditioning was off, rendering the showroom a very efficient greenhouse. Inside, the cars were cooking away. A windowless theater sat beneath the building, filled with rows of right-hand-drive F40s, 288 GTOs, and other exotics.

At the back of the compound were two long two-story buildings about 50 feet apart. A corrugated tin roof between them offered some protection from the blistering sun—but not from the rain. Under the shade were another three hundred or so 1995–1997 500 SELs and SLs, all black/black, many with the windows down, all rotting into oblivion. Millions of dollars of beautiful and rare collector vehicles were virtually open to anything the Southeast Asian weather decided to throw

Prince Jefri—the Sultan of Brunei's third brother—took this Ferrari 550 Spider to Monaco.

at them—from humid, tropical heat to the whirling winds and rain of monsoon season. Many of the vehicles were AMG specials with wood- or carbon-fiber-trimmed interiors, big motors, etc. We called this group "the reef," as turning them into an artificial ocean reef was probably their best use.

A late-1090s Rolls-Royce convertible was near the Mercedes-Benz fleet, but it was under a real roof and better protected. The Rolls had become so hot with the windows up that the steering wheel's foam padding had melted into a puddle on the driver's seat and the leather wrap hung from the barren steel rim like a used condom. The entire interior was fuzzy with mold from the heat and humidity, rendering the interior a gray, furry blanket.

A single-story building held 60 or so truly unique cars, most in a very bright yellow—including a row of four-wheel-drive Bentley station wagons and a dozen late-model Lamborghinis. A few non-yellow cars, such as a black 456 Venice wagon with mirrored side windows, were also in this building. A side room was filled with high-end motorcycles, whereas another room was filled with hundreds of empty Rolex, Cartier, and Patek Philippe watch presentation boxes.

Behind one of the buildings was a row of "lesser" cars, including the collection's token Corvette—all destroyed by the sun and rain. The mechanics deserted the collection in 1998, and nothing was in drivable condition. What had once been the planet's largest collection of coachbuilt and high-end exotics was now a vast automotive tomb, patrolled only by a few Gurkhas with dogs.

POSTER CHILDREN FOR
A STUDY IN DEFERRED MAINTENANCE

There were fewer than a hundred Ferraris, and only a few hundred cars in total were commercially viable. All had minimal mileage—but all were also poster children for deferred maintenance.

The lesser cars were beyond saving. None had been started in five years. Our offer was cheerfully accepted by the importer who offered the cars, but none of them came with any service records. Even worse, none had titles, and attaining a bill of sale or export documents was almost impossible, as the mid-level bureaucrats were paralyzed by indecision of the fear of making a political mistake and issuing export paperwork.

Although my trip to Brunei was an amazing cultural and automotive experience, we were never able to get a car out of the collection. Eight more years in a steamy tropical rain forest has certainly not helped any of those former beauties.

The local officials have no plans to save or to sell the collection, and the cost to turn it into a tourist attraction would be staggering. Over the last eight years, fewer than a dozen significant cars have been removed as gifts to well-connected expats. Another few hundred pedestrian Mercedes-Benzes have been given to Brunei locals, but the bulk of the collection is still there, where it will die and then rot into oblivion.

THE FORGOTTEN FERRARI GTO

BY STEVE AHLGRIM

The actual location of the GTO was never really a secret. The network of Ferrari spotters knew where it was. They kept the location to themselves, but it didn't take much prodding to get them to spill the beans.

THE WORLD'S MOST VALUABLE CAR
DECAYS ON A TRAILER

THE FERRARI 250 GTO in the field had already been there for nine years when I first heard the story.

Ferrari folklore held that a rare and valuable Ferrari 250 GTO was sitting in a field next to a house crumbling away to dust. The house was on the outskirts of a small town somewhere in Ohio. It was real American gothic: narrow, white, two stories on the way out of town, sitting where the small in-town lots widen into rural property.

There was a main house with an outbuilding, and next to the house was the GTO. The Ferrari was sitting on an open trailer that appeared abandoned rather than parked. No effort was made to preserve the car—it was left uncovered and completely exposed to the elements. It appeared it was being punished, purposely left near the salvation of indoor storage, but denied access for some unknown sin. The tires on the car and the tires on the rusty trailer were flat, but it didn't matter; this was a car that wasn't going anywhere.

The car was supposedly integral to some tragedy in the owner's life. The episode had turned him into a bitter recluse, and the GTO was the focal point of his reticence.

The car was a monument to his disappointment, and he would watch it decay as it had ruined his life. Instead of hiding the car, it was exposed to be seen by anyone driving by. Occasionally, someone would stop to look at the car, and like the old ladies who peer from behind windows waiting to yell at kids retrieving balls from their yards, the owner took perverse pleasure taunting people with the sight of the car—and then denying them access to it.

The exact location was never divulged, as the storyteller was always trying to buy, sell, or at least liberate it from the field. The story explaining why it was there and why it was abandoned was equally sketchy. There was some indication that the owner was buying a small fleet of exotic cars to use in an exotic car rental business. Some tragedy followed, and the GTO as well as a couple other cars were abandoned where they sat. The description was right out of a scene from a science fiction movie where a nuclear holocaust has frozen everything in time.

One narrative had the owner's son killed in a car accident; the owner then grounded the cars so no one would ever be hurt in one of them. Another version had the owner distraught after the rental business failed and never wanting anything to do with the cars again. Whatever the scenario, the GTO was real. Pictures of the car sitting on the trailer were circulated, and it was a topic of many Ferrari gatherings.

WORTH MORE THAN ITS WEIGHT IN GOLD

The Ferrari 250 GTO is the most valuable car on the planet. One reportedly sold for $35 million in mid-2012. That sale eclipsed the next highest known sale of any car by millions of dollars.

The number is particularly staggering because the GTO isn't some elusive, one-of-a-kind car that may not come to market again in this generation; GTOs aren't even all that rare by Ferrari standards. There were 39 GTOs built between 1962 and 1964, and all of them are still around today. Most are in the hands of serious Ferrari enthusiasts who take them to rallies, display them at shows, and even race them at vintage collector events. If you go to vintage sports car events, there's a good chance you've seen more than one.

The value in a 250 GTO is that it is the ultimate expression of a Ferrari. It's a car that could be driven to the racetrack, soundly thrash the competition, and then be driven back home that night.

It is incredibly attractive, with the fastback silhouette that's become an icon for Ferrari design. They are all in the hands of wealthy Ferrari enthusiasts who don't need to sell them to buy another car or anything else. From a low of around $5,000 several decades ago, it will take over $30 million to buy one today.

Whatever offer an owner is presented, the next offer is sure to be higher, so few GTOs change hands.

A WILD LIFE

The late Innes Ireland jumped out of planes in the military before becoming a successful engineer. He then gave up his engineering career to become a race car driver and, later, an exemplary automotive raconteur.

In 1962 Innes accompanied Col. Ronnie Hoare, the United Kingdom's Ferrari distributor, on a trip to the Ferrari factory in Italy. They were there to pick up two brand-new Ferrari 250 GTOs, chassis numbers 3589GT and 3505GT. The two had a playful trip back to the UK, stopping at many of Ronnie's favorite restaurants. The two also swapped the GTOs back and forth to add to the fun.

Innes would be racing 3505GT upon their return, with the car later passing to Sir Stirling Moss. It eventually became the very car that sold for the $35 million record price in 2012. The other GTO, 3589GT, passed to someone else, but it would not be the last time Innes encountered the car.

Tom O'Connor Jr. came from a very wealthy Texas family. One of his ancestors had turned a small dowry of land and cattle into a half million acres of fenced cattle ranch. Keeping 100,000 head of cattle nourished is a huge job, which was often disrupted when a pesky brown substance oozed from newly drilled water wells. The O'Connor ranching fortune was soon dwarfed by a new fortune in oil.

Tom and his son-in-law went to an SCCA race in Galveston in 1961 and got bitten by the racing bug.

In true Texas style, just a few months later, Rosebud Racing—a name derived from the Victoria, Texas, chamber of commerce's slogan "City of Rosebuds"—was a flourishing operation with a small stable of race cars. The 1962 season brought more cars, more races, and the hiring of professional drivers; Pete Lovely, Richie Ginther, and Innes Ireland drove for the team.

Rosebud's first race cars were Lotus models, but in late 1962, the effort was enhanced with the acquisition of a serious Ferrari race car, 250 GTO, 3589GT. In 1963 O'Connor added a Ferrari 250 Testa Rossa to his stable, but rather than campaign the TR, the engine was oddly removed and mated to a Lotus 19 chassis.

The first outing with the GTO was the Bahamas Speed Week in December 1962. Innes was reunited with his old friend and finished third in the Tourist Trophy race. Other 250 GTOs filled the first and second places. The teams competed in more races, but come 1964, the thrill was gone. Rosebud Racing was swiftly disbanded and the cars dispersed.

Victoria, Texas, was the O'Connors' family home, and they were the town's major patrons. The GTO was given to the Victoria High School auto shop. Innes Ireland ended up with the 250 Testa Rossa (less its engine), which went with the Lotus.

The auto shop had about as much use for a Ferrari 250 GTO as it did for a piano—in a community where tractors were nearly as common as cars, an exotic Ferrari race car wasn't a relevant teaching tool. The car was a regular at homecoming parades and graced some special occasions, but it mostly took up space. In 1972 GTO 3589GT, now also known as the Victoria High School Ferrari, became the subject of a *New York Times* classified ad.

MAROONED IN OHIO

James Korton of Cleveland, Ohio, was browsing the *New York Times* when he came across the ad for the Victoria High School Ferrari GTO. He and his son were assembling cars for a muscle car rental business, and the GTO seemed a good fit. A

It's mind boggling to imagine a Ferrari 250 GTO—the most valuable car on the planet, with examples selling in the $30 million range—decaying on a trailer, but that was the case for more than nine years in Ohio. *Alamy*

deal was arranged for a reported $6,500. Korton picked up the car in Victoria and brought it home to North Royalton, Ohio, a small town just south of Cleveland. Korton also acquired a Mercedes-Benz 300SL Gullwing, a Ferrari 275 GTB, a Lamborghini Miura, and a few other cars for the business.

Korton's son tragically died, and the rental car business was stillborn. Korton felt that if he hadn't bought the cars, his son would still be alive. He lost interest in them, yet he couldn't bring himself to part with them.

The actual location of the GTO was never really a secret. The network of Ferrari spotters knew where it was. They kept the location to themselves, but it didn't take much prodding to get them to spill the beans. Attempts to buy the GTO were unequivocally met with disinterest and sometimes outright hostility. Descriptions of being greeted with a shotgun were probably exaggerations, but a steady stream of amateur and professional buyers were unceremoniously turned away.

The car's problems weren't over. The GTO loaded on an open car trailer was doomed to spend 15 years next to Korton's house. The Miura was left at a Sunoco station on Route 82, where a mechanic blew the engine and earned the station a lawsuit. That car eventually was sold, perhaps to settle the suit. And in late 1972 the GTO was entered in a classic car auction in Hershey, Pennsylvania, where it was a no-show.

HEAVEN SENT?

Frank Gallogly was a successful financier with a fancy for Ferraris. He had used some of his earnings to buy Grand Prix SSR, a Ferrari dealership on Long Island.

Frank set his sights on the GTO, and rather than pounding on Korton's door unannounced, he started corresponding with him by letter. They had developed a cordial relationship, so the seeds of a purchase were planted. Korton was a CPA by profession and not as crazy as assumed.

He recognized that the GTO had become a valuable asset. He also acknowledged there was a huge tax implication with the sale of such a large asset. Additionally, he understood that he could optimize the sale if he completed it before new capital gains laws went into effect at the beginning of the next year.

Korton was a graduate of Notre Dame. As a grateful alumnus, he wanted to do something special for the school. A good 250 GTO was worth over a million dollars at the time, and although the 3589GT needed extensive restoration, he knew the proceeds of the sale would be substantial.

Korton decided to gift the earnings to the school. Korten might have been eccentric, but he wasn't dumb; his proposal to Notre Dame went something like this:

He would donate the car to the school, which it would in turn sell to Mr. Gallogly. The profit from the sale would be used to purchase an annuity that would pay income to Kroton during his life and revert to Notre Dame upon his death. Once again it seemed 3589GT would be donated to an educational institution.

Notre Dame was no stranger to large endowments, but it didn't like the deal. At the last minute, the school pulled out, putting the GTO sale in jeopardy. The Glenmary Home Missioners, however, were not so picky. Glenmary missioners proclaimed and witnessed the Good News of Jesus Christ, the power of God's love, mercy, and justice through evangelical and social services in rural America. The group found Korton's offer very appealing, and a deal was made. Funds were transferred, and the Ferrari GTO, along with Mercedes-Benz 300SL Gullwing and Ferrari 275 GTB, were freed from purgatory.

RISING FROM THE DEAD

Up to this point, Gallogly had not seen the car. He had seen pictures, and he had established that he was getting the real 3589GT, but he had not seen the car in the flesh.

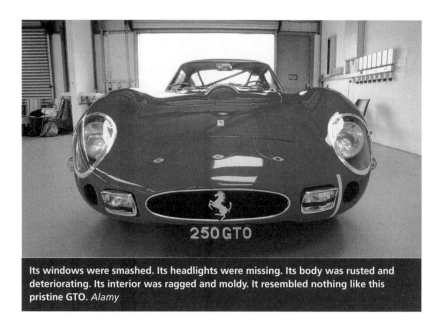

Its windows were smashed. Its headlights were missing. Its body was rusted and deteriorating. Its interior was ragged and moldy. It resembled nothing like this pristine GTO. *Alamy*

What he found was frightening.

The deterioration from racing and years in the elements was substantial. The paint and interior were shot. The Plexiglas windows were heavily crazed; nearly everything cosmetic needed to be restored or replaced.

Mechanically the car was equally depleted. It hadn't been started or moved in over a decade. It had to be winched onto the transporter because the brakes had frozen solid. It would be a long, long journey to bring 3589GT back to its glory, but at least the process was started. The Victoria High School 250 GTO/GTO in the field at last would be resurrected . . . or would it?

The restoration of 3589GT was a huge project. It proved overwhelming for the first owner, so a new shop was contacted. Unfortunately the new garage was booked solid, and it could not start on the car for months. Enter Englebert Stieger, a Swiss national who amassed a fortune from a textile manufacturing business. Stieger was putting together the Turning Wheel Collection, a world-class assemblage of automobiles and, in particular, Ferraris. No Ferrari collection is complete without a 250 GTO, so the hunt was on, and 3589GT was the target.

Selling the project of your life before you've seen it completed is not an easy decision, but the prospect of another year or more of restoration and repair bills makes you think twice. Add a pile of money that multiplies your original investment, and the scale can be tipped.

It took some grueling negotiations, but a deal was reached—3589GT and 51 boxes of parts were packed in a container destined for a new home in Switzerland.

The story of 3589GT closes much as it starts. In 1990 Innes Ireland received a call from a friend who had a friend who had just finished restoring a 250 GTO. The GTO was 3589GT, and the owner wanted to know if Innes would be interested in doing some shakedown laps at Sears Point racetrack before the car debuted at the Pebble Beach Concours d'Elegance a week later.

It was an emotional reunion. Today 3589GT is still in the Turning Wheel Collection. It makes an occasional appearance at vintage events and GTO reunions.

THE LOST NORSEMAN

BY LINDA CLARK

That same day, Chrysler Corporation issued
a press release out of Detroit: "Idea Car Lost on
Andrea Doria." "A revolutionary new Chrysler Corporation
'idea' car, being shipped from Italy to the United States for
its public debut, was lost today in the sinking of
the Italian liner *Andrea Doria*."

CHRYSLER NORSEMAN LOST
ON THE *ANDREA DORIA*

O N THE MORNING OF JULY 17, 1956, the *Andrea Doria* ocean liner left Genoa for its voyage from Italy to New York. After stops in Cannes, Naples, and Gibraltar, the ship cruised out of the Mediterranean and westward into the Atlantic Ocean. On board were 1,706 passengers and crew, 401 tons of cargo (including 500 Necchi sewing machines and 1,000 Olivetti typewriters), 522 luggage bags, and 1,754 mail bags. There were also nine cars on board, including a Rolls-Royce and the Norseman dream car, a joint Chrysler-Ghia prototype valued at about $150,000.

As the ship neared New York on July 25, Capt. Piero Calamai, his crew and the passengers were preparing for their scheduled 9:00 a.m. arrival on Thursday, July 26. But after seeing fog near Nantucket Island, Massachusetts, Captain Calamai slowed the *Doria* down, activated the fog horn, and sent a sailor to watch for any approaching ships.

Meanwhile, the Swedish liner *Stockholm* had left New York that morning and was steaming east toward Scandinavia. Third Officer Johan Johannsen had relieved

Capt. Harry Nordenson at the helm. Like the *Doria*, the *Stockholm*, which was carrying 749 passengers and crew, used radar to navigate past approaching vessels. But no one expected a ship like the *Doria* to be hidden until the last few minutes by dense fog.

Around 10:45 p.m. the *Stockholm* showed up on the *Doria*'s radar screen, at a distance of about 17 nautical miles. Soon after, the Italian ship showed up on *Stockholm*'s radar, about 12 miles away. History is uncertain of what happened next, but it wasn't until they were within just 2miles of each other that each noticed the other ship's lights. Third Officer Johannsen turned the *Stockholm* in an emergency effort to avoid the *Doria*.

Just a mile away, Captain Calamai realized he was on a collision course with the *Stockholm*. He veered left, expecting to race past the bow of the Swedish ship. But at 11:10 p.m. the *Stockholm*'s sharply angled bow—designed for breaking ice—smashed 30 feet into the starboard side of the *Andrea Doria*. Five of the *Stockholm*'s crewmen died.

The situation on the *Andrea Doria* was much more dire. The bow of the Swedish ship crashed through passenger cabins, killing 46 passengers. With seven of its ten decks open to the Atlantic waters, the *Doria* listed to port in minutes, its watertight compartments pierced. Because the ship was listing very sharply, only half of the lifeboats could be used. Passengers in lower cabins struggled through darkened hallways flooded with water and leaking oil.

Not having suffered a fatal blow, the *Stockholm* lent its lifeboats to the evacuation effort. Several ships heard the *Doria*'s mayday and came to help. At 2:00 a.m. on July 26, the *Ile de France*, another big ocean liner, arrived and led the rescue effort. It was history's greatest civilian sea rescue, and 1,660 lives were saved. The *Stockholm* hobbled back to New York. The *Doria* stayed afloat for another 11 hours before sinking at 10:09 a.m., all its lights gleaming as it sunk below the surface of the sea on July 26.

That same day, Chrysler Corporation issued a press release out of Detroit: "Idea Car Lost on *Andrea Doria*." "A revolutionary new Chrysler Corporation 'idea' car, being shipped from Italy to the United States for its public debut, was lost today in the sinking of the Italian liner *Andrea Doria*." Chrysler was advised by its New York shipping agent that because the ship sunk over 200 feet, the car must be considered a complete loss. According to the press release, the car was covered by insurance.

Also lost in the *Andrea Doria*'s collision was the Rolls-Royce belonging to Edward L. Parker of Miami, Florida. Parker and his bride, Virginia Inez, had boarded in Cannes. They were returning from a Paris honeymoon.

NORSEMAN NO MORE

The experimental Norseman was to be a featured attraction of Chrysler's auto show exhibit for 1957. Although it was designed by Chrysler in Michigan, it had been built by Ghia in Turin, Italy, and was en route to the United States when the ship sank. Unlike the other eight cars in the *Andrea Doria*'s 50-stall garage, the Norseman was packed in a wooden crate before being loaded by crane onto the Italian luxury liner. It was placed in the ship's cargo hold instead of the garage with the passenger cars.

In many ways, the Norseman had its roots in 1949, when Chrysler President K. T. Keller hired designer Virgil Exner to create a series of concept cars to influence new production vehicles. Exner had previously worked at Studebaker and General Motors. When Exner joined Chrysler, the company's cars were designed by engineers instead of designers, leading to what many thought were stodgy designs on late 1940s and early 1950s Chryslers.

Exner was in charge of the design process, including clay prototypes and the die models used to create production tooling. He combined Chrysler's six separate styling studios into one. Although it was Keller who formed an alliance with Italian car design firm Carrozzeria Ghia, Exner forged a strong bond with designer and engineer Luigi Segre. The alliance produced at least a dozen Chrysler Ghia designs for both concept and limited-production cars, including the Chrysler K-310, Dodge Firearrow, and DeSoto Adventurer.

"Forward Look" was the name New York ad agency McCann-Erickson gave Virgil Exner's lower, sleeker, more aggressive looking 1950s designs. Exner also wanted to create cars with optimal all-around visibility. A bold step in this direction was the 1956 Norseman dream car, named for Exner's ancestry.

Its most striking features were its pillar-less wraparound windshield and cantilevered roof. It also lacked door vent window —often called butterfly windows—but had an electrically operated sunroof. Its power-operated, glass rear window retracted into the roof; a similar feature bowed on Ford's 1959 Lincoln Continental Mark IV.

William Brownlie, assistant manager of Chrysler's Advanced Styling Studio, came up with the cantilevered roof idea in early 1954. Although it was initially viewed as impractical, styling director Virgil Exner, chief stylist Cliff Voss, and designer Maury Baldwin eventually became supporters. Quarter-inch steel rods were placed where the A-pillars would have been to hold the roof in tension. In the event of a rollover, the rods would snap and allow the roof to spring upward. Chrysler ad men capriciously claimed that the cantilevered roof could support eight times the Norseman's weight. The car's fastback roof was made of a special glass by PPG Industries for strength in a rollover. PPG also supplied the shatter-proof windshield.

The fastback hardtop coupe's body panels were hand-formed aluminum shaped over wooden bucks. The aluminum panels resulted from Chrysler's research to reduce structural weight. It had a sloping hood, tail fins, and a full-length belly pan under the body for aerodynamic efficiency. The Norseman's resemblance to the 1965 Rambler Marlin fastback coupe, or vice versa, was uncanny. Was Marlin designer Dick Teague (who worked briefly as a stylist for Chrysler in the mid-1950s) inspired by the Norseman?

Riding on a 129-inch wheelbase, the Norseman was powered by a 235- horse-power 331-cubic-inch overhead-valve Hemi V-8 engine. It drove through the rear

The *Andrea Doria* was named after a 16th-century Genoese admiral of the same name. The ship's gross tonnage weighed over 29,100 tons, with a capacity of roughly 1,200 passengers and 500 crew. The ship was an icon of Italian national pride after the devastation of World War II—it was the largest, fastest, and supposedly safest of the Italian cruise ships. *Everett Collection Historical Photos*

The *Andrea Doria* slowly sinks into the North Atlantic, with the beautiful Chrysler Norseman inside. The Norseman forever rests over 200 feet deep, lost to history and what might have been. *Time Life Pictures*

wheels through a two-speed push-button Powerflite automatic transmission. The Norseman was 227.5 inches long, 57 inches tall, and 80 inches wide.

Overall smoothness of the Norseman was enhanced by its concealed automatic headlights, door handles, and trunk lid opening device. The car was painted two-tone metallic green with a touch of red inside the flared wheel openings, according to Chrysler's press release. Although Exner had ordered the car in silver with red interior, Chrysler ordered it in dark green with a green and gray interior.

Its matching green and gray metallic leather interior had four bucket seats separated by a full-length console. Pods containing gauges and controls were suspended from the upper crash pad. Reel-type seat belts were mounted in the doors and came across the occupants' laps to fasten at the center console. Unique air intakes for the cockpit were built into the front edge of the roof panel. Continuing its futuristic theme, the cabin was illuminated with special lighting.

The Norseman had spent a year on the drawing board in Chrysler's Advanced Styling Studio before being built in Italy.

Exner and his right-hand man, Cliff Voss, traveled to Ghia in 1954 with plans for the car. Engineers later fashioned a 3/8-scale clay model in Detroit. Working only from Chrysler drawings, Ghia began crafting the full-scale car in April 1955. Ghia's prototype workshop, headed by Sergio Coggiola, spent 50,000 working hours and around $150,000 to build the Norseman before crating it for shipment back to the United States.

Only a handful of photos were taken of the Norseman in Italy, and almost no one at Chrysler who designed it ever got to see the actual car. Exner was in the hospital recovering from emergency open-heart surgery on the day the *Andrea Doria* sank. It wasn't until five days later that Tex Colbert—who had succeeded Keller as president of Chrysler in late 1950—broke the news to him of the Norseman's sinking. Some of its styling innovations were resurrected on later Chrysler cars, but not the cantilevered roof.

Underwater photographer Peter Gimbel was the first diver to see the wreckage of the *Andrea Doria*, and his photos were published in the August 1956 issue of *Life* magazine. He produced two documentaries about the ship, and in 1981, he salvaged the *Doria*'s first-class bank safe. Its contents—Italian lire and U.S. silver certificates—were later restored and sold as collector items.

In 1991 dream car collector extraordinaire Joe Bortz of Highland Park, Illinois, agreed to pay a diver to locate the Norseman. It was only when a chemist convinced him that nothing but the engine block would likely have survived the salt water that he abandoned his quest.

But the chemist was wrong. Three years later shipwreck historian and diver David Bright became the first person to see the Norseman since it sank. He described it as a rusted hulk and said the only identifiable remains were the rubber tires. After another dive to the *Andrea Doria* on July 8, 2006, Bright died of heart failure from decompression sickness.

Joel Silverstein of Tech Diving Limited in Arizona has made 56 dives to the *Andrea Doria* wreck. In a 2010 interview with the website Examiner.com, he said, "It's one of the toughest, hardest dives you can do. It takes about 14 hours to reach the Doria's location 55 miles off the coast of Nantucket Island and the fierce currents make it difficult to reach the ship. And now the wreck is very much deteriorated. The tip of the bow is only 20 feet from the sand, whereas 10 years ago it was 50 feet up."

How might automotive history and design have changed if the Norseman had made it ashore? In a cruel twist of fate, British author and historian Peter Grist discovered that Ghia was a few weeks over schedule completing the car, so the Norseman missed its intended sailing and was booked on the next available ship to America: the *Andrea Doria*. In his biography of Exner, Grist notes that after it finished touring in 1957, the Norseman was scheduled to be crashed at Chrysler's Chelsea Proving Grounds to determine whether the cantilevered roof worked.

Given that inglorious fate, Grist said, Exner thought it far better that the Norseman was lost at sea, forever becoming a part of automotive folklore and legend.

THE BUGATTI IN THE LAKE

BY MILES COLLIER

The local dive club had known about the sunken Bugatti for years, but it took a tragic murder in February 2008 to start the process of bringing it back from the depths.

A 1925 BUGATTI BRESCIA TYPE 22
SPENDS 70 YEARS UNDERWATER,
THEN SELLS FOR $364,000

WHO COULD IMAGINE that a car submerged beneath the waters of Lake Maggiore in Switzerland for more than 70 years would become one of the most famous Bugattis of all time, despite its rusty (albeit gorgeous) patina?

To answer that question just begs another—how did the Bugatti end up in Lake Maggiore in the first place?

The answer makes perfect sense: to avoid paying taxes, of course.

Research has told us this much: on April 11, 1925, Bugatti Brescia Type 22, chassis number 2461, was registered in Nancy, France in the name of Georges Paiva, with the number 8843 N5. A small brass plate found on the car after its removal bears the name Georges Nielly, 48 Rue Nollet, Paris, but the registration plate is only partly legible: the last digits are RE 1. This registration was issued in Paris between May and June 1930, so perhaps Georges Nielly bought the car earlier in Nancy and had it registered in Paris. The French plates have remained on the car ever since.

The rear end of the car emerges into the sunlight after decades on the bottom of the lake. *Bonhams*

The Bugatti chassis plate is missing, as is the enamel radiator badge, but the relevant chassis number is on the round boss on the right front engine bearer. The engine number 879 is on top of the cam box, the gearbox bears the number 964, the radiator is by Chausson, and the carburetor is a Zenith, which is correct. The SEV magnetos are in the middle of the dashboard. There are indications the body was modified, with fenders added, probably at the end of the 1920s.

So far, the likely candidate for ownership in Ascona is Marco Schmuklerski, a Zurich-born architect who lived there from 1935 to1936. If he studied in Paris, it's possible he brought the car back from there, but without paying any import duties. When he left Ascona, Schmuklerski stored the car in a builder's yard. But the Swiss authorities wanted their tax money, so the car was hidden in the lake at the end of a chain. However, the chain corroded, and the car fell 150 feet to the bottom of the lake. It was discovered in 1967 by a local diver, and finally, on July 2009, the car was finally rescued from its grave.

LOCAL LEGEND

The local dive club had known about the sunken Bugatti for years, but it took a tragic murder in February 2008 to start the process of bringing it back from the depths. A club member was mugged, beaten, and died. The club raised the car to sell and use the money in a campaign against juvenile violence.

The plan worked. The Bugatti sold for $364,700 including buyer's commission at Bonhams's Automobiles d'Exception auction in Paris on January 23, 2010.

Rarely does a paradigm-changing event occur in the automobile world. Yet the sale of this artifact represents such a moment. Car collectors who read the catalog entry before the sale no doubt marveled at the $100,000-to-$125,000 pre-auction estimate for what is arguably a marine archaeology find.

That the hulk made over $350,000 on the day is simply breathtaking. That price is, after all, the value of a decently running collector-grade Brescia Bugatti. Furthermore, the result could only have been achieved with at least two bidders; and, as it turns out, both bidders were connoisseurs with world-wide recognition.

When two great and experienced collectors struggle this fiercely, I don't see the sale as aberrant. Something is going on here. Let's look beyond a facile explanation involving "two nutters with battling checkbooks."

This car represents the first instance of a buyer acting with a postmodernist sensibility that deconstructs the automobile as a rare archeological artifact. As

A local dive club pulled the Bugatti Brescia Type 22 from Switzerland's Lake Maggiore, where it had been for 70 years. *Bonhams*

many surmised before the sale, this automobile would go, not to an experiential or use-oriented buyer with a desire to restore and drive, but rather to a contemplative buyer who would want the object as-is, freshly raised from the depths of Lake Maggiore like an artifact from a Spanish treasure galleon.

Unless the car was intended to be given away, no restoration scenario imaginable makes any sense. Even if not to be restored, there is still another cost factor that may yet play a part: conservation.

While fortunately submerged in fresh water rather than salt water for 70 years, I can't help thinking that this car will require the same hugely expensive museum conservation regimen demanded by other recovered submerged relics, wherein technicians in white lab coats, latex gloves, and magnifying spectacles must meticulously inject the exhibit with hypodermic syringes of acrylic consolidant to prevent it from crumbling to dust.

Therefore, only a museum, the archetypal contemplative buyer, could possibly want this car as-is. Not surprisingly, after spirited bidding, the car was acquired by a developing museum in the Los Angeles area devoted to a fabulous collection of French coachbuilt cars.

Here's the main point: this car was bought not as another impeccable object for the museum, but as an archeological relic. In fact, its identity, beyond that of being a relatively elitist French automobile from the 1930s, had precious little relevance to the auction price. That is why, as an archeological object, its realized value exceeded the value of an intact, running Brescia Bugatti.

Second, the zeitgeist played its part here: a decayed industrial relic of past glory resonates in these turbulent times. Thus, I see emerging a reversion to the real: a reaction to the artificially enhanced, primped, detailed, and hence epistemologically confusing collector car of accepted practice.

With this purchase, the buyer/curator wanted to show an irreproachably real object, an object connected to a distant past, hoary with age and decay. To that end, this artifact is a kind of *memento mori* for the collectible automobile from an age of excess.

From the standpoint of the museum and its exhibits, I suggest that this lot was bought to contrast with the rest of the collection in the most poignant and striking way possible. It stands as an eloquent reminder of the fate that awaits almost all examples of the automobile, the single most important technological object of the twentieth century, absent the intercession of connoisseurs, collectors, and museums.

The car was in amazingly good condition after 70 years underwater. It helped that the car was not submerged in salt water. *Bonhams*

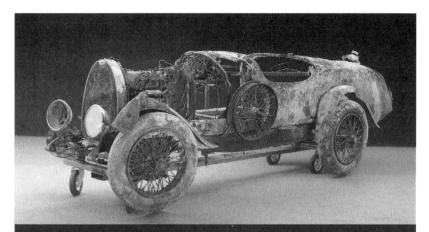

The Bugatti on display as it came from the Lake Maggiore. Notice that the car is on a wheeled cart, as the metal is very brittle. Specialists were brought in to stabilize the metal. *Bonhams*

It is impossible to restore this car, but many Bugatti lovers believe that it would lose much of its historical value if it were restored. The car is now on display in the Mullin Automotive Museum in Oxnard, California, which is the home of many important and valuable French cars from the 1920s and 1930s. *Bonhams*

There is little doubt that the Brescia will make a startling impact on the museum's visitors. They will spend substantially more time contemplating this object and will engage with it more than any other single automobile in the collection. This relic assumes a degree of historic gravitas, relevance, and, yes, romance that makes a "silicone-enhanced and airbrushed" Best in Show at Pebble Beach winner historically weightless.

So, is it a good financial move to make an artificial reef out of our collector cars with the intent of dredging them up and selling them as priceless relics decades in the future? Probably not. Yet the romantic mystique of newly discovered treasure played an important factor in this transaction. Could our subject resell in five years for a similar price? I would say not.

Shattering the longstanding valuation paradigm of automobiles as having to be useable history, this car has achieved apotheosis by becoming an archeological artifact from the modern industrial age. Consequently, it commanded a price typical of an archeological rarity. As a financial transaction: very well sold. As a cultural artifact: brilliantly bought.

THE VEYRON
IN THE LAKE

BY JOHN DRANEAS

Upon looking up, House claimed he saw a low-flying pelican coming at him and swerved to avoid it, sending him into some boulders and then into the lagoon. He claimed he was being bitten by mosquitoes and had to exit quickly. He forgot to shut off the engine, and it ran for about 15 minutes before dying an unglamorous (and arguably unnecessary) death from drowning.

BUGATTI VEYRON DROWNS
IN LITIGATION LAGOON

 STUNNING 4 MILLION PEOPLE and counting have now watched the YouTube video of a 2006 Bugatti Veyron driven straight into a lagoon in Galveston, Texas. Now it looks like it's going to be viewed at least another dozen times by a U.S. District Court jury.

According to the complaint filed by the Philadelphia Indemnity Insurance Company—which underwrites policies for Grundy Worldwide, a company that insures valuable and collector cars—the video is evidence that the car-sinkers don't have to pay the claim because the damage was intentionally caused and the policy was procured by fraud.

The complaint states (we have not received any information from the other parties) that the 456-mile Veyron was purchased by Andy House for $1,050,000. He paid for it with a zero-interest loan from his friend and business associate, Lloyd

A handsome—and very valuable—Bugatti Veyron at rest before a summer drive during a Bugatti event. *Dave Tomaro*

Gillespie. House purchased a collector car insurance policy from Grundy and listed Gillespie as a Loss Payee based upon his having financed the purchase. The policy included an agreed value of $2,200,000 for the Veyron.

For a month or so after the purchase, House put about 1,200 miles on the Veyron. He drove the car to and from work, on errands, to a biker rally, on business trips and to business functions. He also let several of his friends drive it, including Gillespie.

On the day of the crash, House drove from Lufkin, Texas, to a friend's place outside Houston. He then drove to a Taco Cabana for breakfast and then to a Sprint store to buy a battery. He then drove to Galveston to view some commercial properties for business. After stopping for lunch, he set off for a marina to look at a boat he was thinking of buying. The crash occurred en route to the marina.

CANDID CAMERA

Bugatti Veyrons attract much-deserved car spotter attention. Joe Garza was riding in his friend's car on the freeway when he spotted the Veyron traveling on the parallel feeder road. He thought he knew exactly what it was, so he grabbed his camera and starting filming the car.

Just as Garza told his friend he was going to own a Bugatti of his own someday, he was stunned to see the Veyron veer to the right and drive straight into the lagoon, coming to rest in three feet of salt water.

Garza's YouTube video captures the shock—and a bit of swearing—of seeing a $2.2 million car barrel into a shallow, muddy lagoon. Garza also calls the car "a Lambo," which is a mistake.

House safely escaped from the drowned Veyron, but not before onlookers snapped photos. He explained that he was trying to use his cell phone's GPS feature to find the marina when he dropped it on the floor.

A row of coddled, cherished Bugatti Veyrons at The Quail, which is one of the most exclusive events during the Monterey Car Week each August. *Dave Tomaro*

Bugatti Veyrons are the world's fastest production cars, with top speeds exceeding 265 miles per hour. Here some rest during The Quail in Carmel Valley, California. The car's engine has 16 cylinders and four turbochargers. *Dave Tomaro*

Two Bugatti Veyrons at rest during a Bugatti-sponsered drive from Monterey, California, to Los Angeles in 2010. These cars automatically lower themselves closer to the pavement when they approach a speed of 220 miles per hour. *Dave Tomaro*

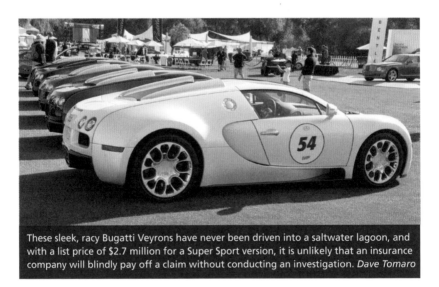

These sleek, racy Bugatti Veyrons have never been driven into a saltwater lagoon, and with a list price of $2.7 million for a Super Sport version, it is unlikely that an insurance company will blindly pay off a claim without conducting an investigation. *Dave Tomaro*

Upon looking up, House claimed he saw a low-flying pelican coming at him and swerved to avoid it, sending him into some boulders and then into the lagoon. He claimed he was being bitten by mosquitoes and had to exit quickly. He forgot to shut off the engine, and it ran for about 15 minutes before dying an unglamorous (and arguably unnecessary) death from drowning.

Garza's video was a too-good-to-be-true situation for the insurance company. The company couldn't see a pelican in it, nor could it see any effort on House's part to steer away from the lagoon or that he hit the brakes, which was confirmed by a lack of skid marks on the pavement. Additionally, Garza testified that he didn't see a pelican, didn't see House drop the cell phone, and didn't think House appeared to be distracted in any way.

ICING ON THE CAKE

Obviously hoping to drive the last nail into House's coffin, Philadelphia advised the court that a confidential informant had come forward and was prepared to testify that House had offered to pay him to steal the car and burn it so he could collect the insurance proceeds. Further, the informant claimed to have confronted House after the car was driven into the lagoon, and he claimed that House offered to pay him part of the insurance proceeds in exchange for his silence.

Philadelphia refunded all of House's premiums and denied coverage for three reasons:

- The damage was not an "accidental loss," but the result of House's intentional actions.
- The Bugatti was not used as a "collector vehicle" as defined by the policy.
- House was a dealer and the Bugatti was inventory, both of which House misrepresented when he purchased the policy. That allows Philadelphia to rescind (cancel) the policy retroactive to the date of issuance.

Of course, there are going to be two sides to the accident versus intentional act issue in this case. Who wins that battle is going to depend entirely upon whom the jury chooses to believe. There is no way to predict that outcome, and we will have to wait and see what happens.

An interesting point here is Gillespie's situation. He will undoubtedly insist that he was an innocent lender listed as a loss payee with respect to the policy and that Philadelphia must pay him the money he loaned to House.

This is a good legal point, as the insurer's obligations to the lender are separate from those to the owner. That is, if House intentionally destroyed the Bugatti, he may not get coverage, but the lender may still get paid off. That is why Philadelphia alleges that Gillespie knew all about this and assisted House in destroying the car. If that can be proven, it might well prevent Gillespie from getting his money back. If not, Philadelphia might have to pay the $1,050,000 paid for the car, but not the $2,200,000 agreed value.

Collector car insurance policies are affordable because collector cars are driven so infrequently, and owners keep their cars secured and in great condition. The risk of loss is quite small.

The big bugaboo is that the carriers don't want to insure daily drivers, which are subjected to far higher risk of loss due to the character and magnitude of the use. Consequently, collector car policies all contain provisions that limit the use of the cars.

This one is rather typical. It defines a "collector car" as "maintained solely for use in exhibitions, parades, club activities, or other functions of public interest," and "is not used for regular driving to work, school, errands, shopping, general transportation, secondary or commercial purposes, except for limited pleasure use." Philadelphia has alleged a number of facts that would seem to contradict much of that definition.

There are some problems with this argument. First off, it's just a definition and may not automatically mean that there is no coverage. It also has a lot of wiggle

It's hard to believe something as harmless as a seagull could send a modern marvel of engineering (and beauty) such as this into a lake. *Dave Tomaro*

A Bugatti Veyron on display at a classic car auction. Bugatti Veyrons built between 2006 and 2010 rarely show up at top-level collector car auctions, and they sell in the $1 million to $1.7 million range—not too shabby for a used car. *Dave Tomaro*

room with the use of the words "regular" and "limited pleasure use." And House can be expected to argue that this was just a new toy, which he only owned for a month. With time, his use would have lessened and averaged out to more limited use.

Should we take this case as a warning that collector cars shouldn't be driven? I am unaware of any other case where a collector car insurance carrier denied a claim based upon excessive use. This is probably just an extreme case that triggers a "you know it when you see it" reaction. Nonetheless, it is important to remember that these policies are premised upon limited use and to be careful that our actual use of our collector cars is consistent with the policy definition.

DEALER STATUS CAN BACKFIRE

The dealer argument rings another warning bell for collectors. Was House really a car dealer trying to buy cheap insurance—or was he just another collector who thought he could avoid sales tax by getting a dealer license? We will have to wait for the trial to learn the answer. But it does seem logical that if it is proven that House was actually a dealer trying to insure his inventory cheaply, the policy would have been procured by fraud and the insurance company can cancel it retroactively.

Using dealer status to avoid sales taxes can backfire on you. This case is another example of how becoming a car dealer may not be the best overall strategy. It can cause you income tax problems, liability problems with buyers when you sell your cars, and, as we see in this case, possible insurance coverage problems.

Again, this is probably just an extreme case and may not indicate problems for the "technical dealer collector." However, the result may just be a matter of degree.

In this case Philadelphia is using the Bugatti and an Enzo that House also insured with them to establish dealer status, and those two cars may not be enough by themselves.

However, if you have a dealer license and you regularly sell a more substantial number of cars, this may be something you should be thinking about. If you think you can be a dealer when that suits you and a collector when that suits you, you might end up getting hoisted by your own petard.

Finally, if you're ever lucky enough to own a Veyron, keep your eyes on the road at all times.

PIKEVILLE
PURGATORY

BY TOM COTTER

"We bought that car on the West Coast right after it won at Pebble Beach," he said. I was dumbstruck. This rusted hulk—which if restored would require a truckload of money and years of time—had been a gleaming, polished, and perfect example once displayed at the most revered Concours d'Elegance in the world.

THE FINEST DEALERSHIP
ON THE EASTERN SEABOARD

WHAT WOULD HAPPEN if a car dealership closed—just closed—and sat untouched for three decades?

In the showroom, brochure racks would still be filled with colorful materials showing the latest models, body styles, and colors for cars that were new when Jimmy Carter was in the White House. The parts department would still be stocked with water pumps, distributor caps, and brake shoes. And, of course, there would be rows upon rows of used cars out on the lot.

Welcome to Collier Motors, located in the tiny, rural town of Pikeville, North Carolina. Robert Collier is the third-generation owner of a dealership that was begun by his grandfather more than 100 years ago. His grandfather opened the dealership early in the 20th century as an outlet for Whippet, Studebaker, and Willys Overland vehicles. Collier's father converted the dealership to sell and service Nash and Rambler automobiles, which Robert Collier took over and owns to this day.

Hundreds of vehicles pass by the former dealership every day, the occupants never knowing what relics reside behind the metal fence and dense vegetation. Yet a walk of less than 50 feet through those trees reveals a strange combination of a time-capsule car dealership and something like Jurassic Park.

"I was a Rambler and American Motors dealership since the 1950s," said Robert Collier, 80, who along with his son Rob, still operates the former dealership. "But when American Motors was purchased by the French, I just closed down. I wasn't going to sell none of them Renaults." (American Motors Corporation was partially purchased by the French-owned Renault company in 1979.)

BORN A RAMBLIN' MAN

Collier installed an eight-foot-tall cyclone fence around the property and locked the gate, but continues to fiddle with his Ramblers to this day. Initially his old customers brought their Ramblers for him to repair, but as those cars got older and were taken off the road, his business declined.

He continued to work on his Matadors, Rebels, Marlins, and Javelins, but father and son also started to collect significant American Motors automobiles. They began to search out and purchase the rare two-seater AMX muscle cars. Today, the Colliers probably own a dozen examples, including two very low-mileage examples in excellent condition that are still sitting in the one-time showroom. Others, however, are rusting and rotting into the ground.

Probably the most interesting AMX in the Collier collection once belonged to the late Arizona senator Barry Goldwater. According to Collier, Goldwater bought the bright red coupe new for about $5,000, "But he invested at least another hundred thousand dollars in accessories and special equipment," he said.

Goldwater had a number of hobbies—ham radio, American Indian kachina dolls, photography, and UFO studies—but he also was a car buff and enjoyed modifying his AMX.

Likely through his government and armed services connections, Goldwater had several aircraft gauges installed in the dashboard, including an altimeter. He also installed Recaro driving seats and a custom steering wheel.

Displayed across the trunk deck are decals signifying all the states he had driven his AMX through during his ownership. He apparently also drove the car throughout Europe, which was documented in a three-page summary in his autobiography. Also displayed on the car's rear license tag was his ham radio frequency number.

A once-thriving AMC dealership in North Carolina was suddenly closed down in the 1970s. It remains a time capsule today, although overgrown with trees and weeds, which have taken over the parking area and used car lot. *Tom Cotter*

When Goldwater died in 1998, Collier contacted the family about purchasing the senator's car. After a short negotiation, a deal was finalized with Goldwater's son.

That's the good news.

The bad news is that since the desirable AMX has been transported from the arid Arizona climate to the humidity of North Carolina, it has been sitting outside in a back lot at Collier's facility, just rusting away.

Parked randomly throughout Collier's property are a number of Javelins, including several Mark Donohue editions that commemorated his winning of the 1971 SCCA Trans-Am Championship.

Collier said he has at least 250 used cars still parked on his property. Although they were once probably parked on gravel or grass, after 30+ years of not cutting the lawn, those cars are now parked in a mature forest. All sorts of AMC sedans, station wagons, and convertibles (some with trees actually growing through the fabric roof) are littered in rows throughout the several- acre lot. The lot, though, is not only comprised of AMC products—it also houses random brands such as Chevrolets, Fords, Chryslers, Cadillacs, and even Mercedes-Benzes.

"I think I have about two hundred fifty cars in the lot, but I'd have to count the titles to be sure," said Collier. With all the trees and plant growth around the cars, it more resembles a metallic jungle than a proper car lot.

Probably the most valuable single cars on the property are the collection of Nash-Healeys that the Colliers have assembled. Nash-Healey sports cars were manufactured between 1951 and 1954 and created out of a partnership between the Nash Motor Company (the American company, which supplied the special multi-carb high-performance engine and drivetrain), and Donald Healey (the British sports

Robert Collier inside the once stylish showroom of Collier Motors in Pikeville, North Carolina, which now sits forlorn and neglected. It contains two rare AMX two-seaters, a Packard sedan, an Ambassador convertible, and a few motorcycles. Roof leaks have caused the ceiling tiles to fall down on the cars. *Tom Cotter*

car builder who supplied the chassis, suspension, and technical expertise). The two-seater bodies were manufactured in Italy.

The cars were an odd combination of components that seemed to work better than anyone imagined. The cars performed well on the racetrack and finished as high as third place at the 24 Hours of Le Mans in 1952. But because components for the car came from three places—Nash in Kenosha, Wisconsin, Healey in Warwick, England, and the bodies from Turin, Italy—the cars were expensive for the day. The cars cost nearly $6,500, which in the early 1950s made it one of the most expensive sports cars available.

Only 507 cars were built over its three-year production life. But the car has a loyal following among collectors today. The renowned Walnut Creek, California, car collector, the late Jacques "Frenchy" Harguindeguy, who owned a fleet of classics including the Best in Show Pebble Beach 1936 Delehaye roadster, considered his Nash-Healey one of the best cars ever built and chose to drive it over all his other priceless cars.

The Colliers have four Nash-Healeys scattered around the former dealership. The good news is that two of the rare cars are parked in what was formerly the

One of the few celebrity-owned cars is this 1969 AMX, which was purchased new by Arizona senator Barry Goldwater. The Colliers purchased the car from the senator's estate, but unfortunately have kept it outdoors ever since, so it has rapidly deteriorated. *Tom Cotter*

service department. The bad news is that the other two are parked outside in the elements.

One particularly disturbing example is a Nash-Healey Le Mans Coupe, a stylish hardtop that was built to commemorate the brand's racing successes.

When I walked up to Collier's coupe, the door was ajar and the outside was indeed inside. Moss, mold, and other organic materials were equally spread on both the outside and inside of this once magnificent car. The car's once red and black body was totally covered in rust, and cancer had become firmly entrenched within the car's extremities.

What I couldn't believe was what Collier said next.

"We bought that car on the West Coast right after it won at Pebble Beach," he said. I was dumbstruck. This rusted hulk—which if restored would require a truckload of money and years of time—had been a gleaming, polished, and perfect example once displayed at the most revered Concours d'Elegance in the world.

Out of respect for the car's history, I walked back to the Nash-Healey and pushed the door shut. But it sprung back open.

What was once a used car lot is now overgrown and nearly impassable. More than 250 cars are still parked in rows on the property, but many—especially the convertibles—have trees growing right through the body! *Tom Cotter*

The Colliers have several Nash-Healey sports cars: two coupes and two convertibles. This one, believe it or not, is said to have won its class at the Pebble Beach Concours decades ago. Now it sits rotting into the earth. When asked if he would consider selling one, Mr. Collier said yes, but these days "they sell for at least two hundred thousand dollars." *Tom Cotter*

Robert Collier is an interesting fellow. He was obviously a competent businessman who ran the family dealership in the 1950s when he was in his 20s; he is mechanically astute, and he knows the value of vintage cars and parts. But he seems to have no sense of preservation. He owns significant cars, but instead of protecting the cars (and therefore his investments), they are put out to pasture where their conditions rapidly deteriorate. Hoping to save some of the cars, I asked if any were for sale.

"Sure, everything is for sale," he said.

I asked about the Nash-Healey Le Mans Coupe, which had been rusting terribly outside for decades.

"Yup, I'll sell it."

"How much are you asking?"

"Well," he said, "I'd have to think about that. But that car won at Pebble Beach, and they sell for at least two hundred thousand dollars."

There was nothing left for me to say. I shook his hand and thanked him for allowing me to see his facility. I've been haunted about the dilemma of his cars ever since.

And at this very moment, all of them are still sitting there, rusting into the ground.

THE JUNKYARD FERRARI

BY ROB COTTER

There was the 4WD Morris Minor pickup truck with the Porsche 356 motor mounted to a dual-range eight-speed gearbox, and the Bultaco motorcycle with the Honda engine and the strange sidecar that doubled as a canoe and hot air balloon gondola.

IT WAS 1979. I was 23 years old, and my sweetheart, Maureen, and I were taking time off to do the proverbial cross-country adventure that was so popular when a gallon of gas was one-quarter the price of a gallon milk.

I had recently restored an old Volvo 122 wagon for the trip. The car had a few mishaps during the 10,000-mile journey, but it came through when it mattered most. When Maureen rolled it several times down the steep passes of Yellowstone Park, both of us were unscathed from the accident. After several weeks of bending and welding, the Volvo was back on the road again, even if it didn't look quite the same.

Although the old Volvo had flipped several times, it also bounced, so the passenger side looked like it was hit by a southbound train. Amazingly, the driver's side was perfect. We were roughly only halfway through our journey, and the car's condition led to numerous conversations along the way. (I was tempted to write "His" and "Hers" on each side of the car, but that would've made for a long, cold trip.)

In Arcata, California, the heart of redwood country, we had one of our weekly breakdowns. It was the usual routine. We'd visit friends and locate the appropriate auto parts store, and then I'd spend the remainder of our visit on my back on our friend's driveway.

This time, I was pulling into downtown Arcata when I noticed quite a unique vehicle; a mid-1960s Comber camper van. At the time it was probably the only one I'd ever seen, sort of a British version of a VW Camper. I looked it over and was amazed it was still on the road and running. I went into the parts store, but when I came back outside, a fellow was staring at my Volvo just as intently. It was the guy who owned the Comber. He wanted to know if I needed any Volvo parts and instructed me to follow him and the Comber back to his place.

I remember many twisting roads meandering up steep hills. That Comber was the slowest vehicle imaginable, desperately sputtering and straining to go even five miles per hour. It made my old, demolished 122 wagon seem like a Turbo Carrera as I crawled behind him. After about 20 minutes of torturous mountain driving, we arrived at his house/junkyard/laboratory, only two miles away from where we started.

My first impression was that it appeared to be a typical foreign car junkyard from the mid-1960s. The lot contained Peugeots, Morris Minors, Humbers, Alfa Romeos—the list went on. But there were some distinctly unique aspects to the atmosphere of this salvage yard. One was the music (don't all junkyards have piped-in music as the customers rummage through rusted Citroëns?). The classical music was performed by a group called the "Harmonicats," which is an all-harmonica band, and during my time in Arcata, the music was always on and the Harmonicats were the only thing playing.

My other impression was of his office, which was housed inside a 1930s stream-lined bus. The office was decorated with rows of purple velvet drapes with gold cherubs hung from the walls every six feet or so. As strange as this all was, the office and music was pretty mundane compared with the automotive oddities that rested on these hallowed grounds.

STRANGE BREW

The scruffy-looking junkyard owner introduced himself as Lou Brero Jr. He seemed nice enough, as well as exceedingly eccentric. He mentioned he was going through a rough divorce.

We became car friends, and he shared some of his life experiences with me and showed me some of his inventions. There was the 4WD Morris Minor pickup truck with the Porsche 356 motor mounted to a dual-range eight-speed gearbox, and the Bultaco motorcycle with the Honda engine and the strange sidecar that doubled as a canoe and hot air balloon gondola.

The streamlined bus/office with purple curtains and gold cherubs was being restored and highly modified to maintain 100-mile-per-hour speeds. The back of the bus was being fitted with a drop-down tailgate that would serve as a garage for the Porsche-powered Morris. This was all in preparation for an around-the-world trip of a lifetime, and I got the impression he was waiting for some sort of financial settlement to begin his trip.

As we extracted parts from the old collection of Volvos (I needed a lot!), I learned a bit about his peculiar personality. At one point I had gotten some rusted car crud in my eyes, and Lou saw I had to stop and deal with the irritation. "Oh, let me show you how to deal with this," he said, at which point he grabbed a handful of dirt and tossed it into his open eyes. Then he grabbed a file and aggressively started grinding away at his knuckles until they bled. "Then you wipe dirt and grease into the cuts, and NOW you are ready to work on a car!"

The beat-up remains of a once great racer. This rare 340/375 MM Ferrari, which had been raced by famous drivers such as Phil Hill, Carroll Shelby, Richie Ginther, and Alberto Ascari, as well as Lou Brero Sr., sat in a storage container in a California junkyard for 40 years. *Mark Savory*

Fully restored and now owned by collector Bruce McCaw, the "Junkyard Ferrari" won Best of Show, Concours de Sport, at the 2007 Amelia Island Concours d'Elegance. *Neil Rashba*

I began to get seriously concerned about spending time with this man. But the thought of driving the 122 with a rear shock bouncing though the floorboard was worth the risk of dealing with this, um, frustrated artist.

Sometimes I went to the yard and he would be dealing with other issues, and I would mill about through the glorious rubble. This time, as I'm kicking about between the cut-in-half English taxicabs and the bombed-out Sunbeam Rapiers, I spy a unique engine block. It was a V-12!

My mind started racing. "How many brands of V-12s are there even out there?" The heads were stripped off and the cylinders looked smallish. But wait—there were more—two more V-12 blocks outside under old vinyl tablecloths! Now my goal was not only to get the Volvo parts for my ailing wagon, but to purchase from this crazy man these V-12 blocks and the magnificent piece of iron that hopefully went with them.

Lou returned his attention to me. It turns out he was chasing cats on the property with a tire iron. "Filthy, murderous bastards! They kill for pleasure. I hate them and won't have them around me," he said. I hoped he didn't feel the same about me.

As he was hauling out a cutting torch to dismember a donor Volvo, I timidly mentioned, "Hey Lou, I noticed a V-12 block over there under the tarp?" I only mentioned one in hopes that he was too distracted even to remember about the other two. "Yeah, that's to my '53 Ferrari," he mentions matter-of-factly.

I stammer, "F-F-Fifty-three F-F-Ferrari?"

"Yeah, it's a 1953, the one my father raced at the Nassau races."

I'm sure he could hear my jaw drop when it hit the ground. This led to a whole other unique chapter in this man's life. Yes, his father was a Ferrari racer and had one of the earliest Ferraris in the United States. But Lou himself raced for Alfa Romeo in Italy. He went into great detail as to being the outcast of the team, the "Young American Rebel." Alfa management had little patience for his radical style. I seemed to remember him telling me that one of their gripes was that he would spin his wheels too much on the turns; he thought it would orient his car better, but they just thought he was a showboat. And I think there was also alcohol involved.

Eventually, he said, Alfa management worked with the Italian police to have him removed from the country, thus ending his international racing career.

Closer to home, he once raced an outdated Kurtis sports car that famously beat the Corvette factory team.

I was still gobsmacked by the notion of leaving with a 1953 Ferrari. "Hey Lou, how much do you want for the old Ferrari anyway?"

His answer stunned me. "I want one million dollars."

My heart sank—I guess he wasn't that crazy. But I needed to see it before I left.

He pointed to where it was. A dozen yards away was a series of old storage containers where cars and other items were stored. *Overstuffed* doesn't begin to describe how tightly these containers were packed. Collectively the units held about 12 cars in them, and the cars were literally stacked on top of each other. Inside was a Hudson, a Packard, picnic tables standing on end, swing sets, an aluminum rowboat (powered by an inboard 305 Honda Dream motorcycle engine, with some sort of jet-drive installed, of course). And way in the back of one unit, peeking out from all that shit, was the edge of a left front fender, headlight, and the corner of a grille of a 1953 Ferrari. Underneath mounds of dust and gunk, it almost looked red. It was like getting a glimpse of a starlet from afar that you could never embrace— nor would anyone else—for a couple of decades.

This was the same car—340 MM serial number 286 AM—that won the Nürburgring 1000 in 1953, and the next year Phil Hill and Richie Ginther used the car to finish second in the Carrera Panamerican.

I occasionally think of that strange junkyard with the numerous contraptions, but only one vehicle of note popped back on the radar. In the 1990s, a group of wealthy investors and Ferrari collectors rescued the Ferrari and paid the required ransom, overpriced but a worthy cause.

For my part, I felt grateful to get out of there in one piece and with enough Volvo parts to continue our journey. I wonder if anyone knows about an all-wheel-drive Porsche-powered Morris out there?

And I wonder if Lou ever took that around-the-world extravaganza in his streamliner?

I hope so.

THE FERRARI SPINS ITS TIRES AGAIN

It has been 50 years since Lou Brero's famous 1953 Ferrari 340 MM Vignale Spyder RHD with the oversized 375 engine was last seen in public. In its early days, it came in first at Nürburgring, piloted by Alberto Ascari and Giuseppe Farina. Later it ran in the Carrera Panamerican with Luigi Chinetti and accumulated numerous first and seconds with Phil Hill, Caroll Shelby, and Lou Brero Sr. It was later sold by Lou Brero Jr. for $1.5 million, complete with an interior filled with cedar chips and a partially installed Jaguar drivetrain. But the car was complete and intact, though well-rusted and in pieces.

Just weeks later it sold again to Bruce McCaw of Bellevue, Washington, for $1.8 million and was immediately sent for restoration to Pete Lovely Racing. In 1997, it debuted at the Monterey Historic Automobile Races. With Phil Hill at the wheel, it won by lapping the entire field. It has since won the Pebble Beach Cup at the 1997 Pebble Beach Concours d'Elegance and the Concours d'Competicione at Amelia Island in 2007.

"Pontiac's drivable Plexiglas 1940 show car wasn't like anything else on the road. The first full-sized transparent car ever made in America, it bowed at General Motor's Highways and Horizons exhibit at the 1939–1940 New York World's Fair.

Pontiac's see-through body was originally styled as a 1939 Deluxe Six Four-Door Touring Sedan, but later updated with a 1940 clear Plexiglas nose clip. According to the July 1940 *Automobile Digest,* a second plastic car, a 1940 Torpedo Eight Four-Door Sedan, was built for the 1939–1940 Golden Gate International Exposition in San Francisco."

№ 3

STRANGER
THAN FICTION

THE BHAGWAN'S 93 ROLLS-ROYCES

BY LINDA CLARK

As cult leaders go, Rajneesh was straight out of central casting. His preferred garb was a satin-trimmed velvet robe and shoes, usually adorned with expensive jewelry. His waist-long beard distracted attention from his bald head, which was always hidden under a matching cap. Followers often spoke of his "delicate brown hands with perfectly manicured fingernails."

WHAT THE BHAGWAN?

UNTIL NEWS STORIES began to surface about his Rolls-Royce collection, Bhagwan Shree Rajneesh was unknown to most Americans. He possessed a variety of treasures, but his 93 Rolls-Royces—many with psychedelic paint jobs—were the most visible.

As cult leaders go, Rajneesh was straight out of central casting. His preferred garb was a satin-trimmed velvet robe and shoes, usually adorned with expensive jewelry. His waist-long beard distracted attention from his bald head, which was always hidden under a matching cap. Followers often spoke of his "delicate brown hands with perfectly manicured fingernails."

Born in India in 1931, he earned a masters degree in philosophy and taught at India's Jabalpur University in the late 1950s and early 1960s. It was while teaching that he began honing his skills as a self-described spiritual leader. By the time

Rajneesh founded his first commune in Poona, India, in 1974 he already had a small but loyal following.

A disciple of Gurdjieff, a Russian spiritual teacher who claimed that most humans live in a "waking sleep," Rajneesh couldn't resist the finer things his followers enabled him to acquire—French brandy, chocolates, Chinese jade. His mania was pens, although not fountain pens—he complained of the mess they made. If a particular brand caught his fancy, he would amass a collection, always ordering the most expensive diamond-encrusted ones from the top of the range.

Rajneesh seldom left home without a bodyguard and a driver. In Poona he owned a succession of Mercedes-Benz and large American cars. As his profile rose, so did his following. His blend of Eastern religion and pop psychology was irresistible to some Westerners. By 1976 he was attracting nearly 50,000 visitors a year to his Poona compound, mostly well-heeled Americans and Europeans drawn to his encounter therapies and free-love reputation.

In addition to the admission charges levied at Poona, the Rajneesh's books, lectures, therapy sessions, and even photographs of himself became lucrative sources of income for his company, Rajneesh Foundation International.

During daily "drive-by blessings," disciples threw flowers on the hood of Rajneesh's car.

Part of the guru's Rolls-Royce motor pool at Rancho Rajneesh.

BEHIND THE GILDED IMAGE

But all was not as it seemed. Reports of violence, prostitution, and drug dealing at the Poona retreat infuriated its Hindu neighbors. India revoked the commune's tax-exempt status in 1976 and hit Rajneesh with a $4 million bill for back levies. In 1979 three Rajneesh followers were arrested for drug smuggling in Paris, just as three other disciples were being jailed in Yugoslavia for drug trafficking. Richard Price, a founding therapist at California's famed Esalen Institute and onetime Rajneesh follower, renounced the movement soon after.

None of these legal and public relations problems put a crimp in Rajneesh's goal of establishing a city of his followers. Leaving many of his disciples to beg in India's streets, he departed for America in 1980 on a 12-month tourist visa and briefly settled in New Jersey before eyeing Oregon. In 1980 he also bought his first Rolls-Royce, a white Corniche, and had it plated with armor. It was a luxury unheard of in still poverty-laden India. But with "the unique suspension on the Rolls-Royce," Rajneesh assured his clan in the sect's newspaper, "he rides in a tranquility that compares with the endless peace discovered by the Buddha."

Rasjneesh arrived in Oregon in the summer of 1981 with 10 devotees and $1.5 million, according to *Newsweek*. He bought the 64,000-acre Big Muddy Ranch in eastern Oregon's Wasco County for a reported $5.75 million (it had formerly served as a barren backdrop in several John Wayne westerns). Rajneesh began a period of public silence, entrusting his decrees to his acid-tongued, pistol-packing aide, Ma Anand Sheela. But once secluded on the remote ranch, Rajneesh discovered it was lacking the essential water, sewer, and phone services he needed to run either Eden or the foundation's huge book-publishing business.

While waiting for his ranch to be rezoned as a city under Oregon's strict land use laws, Rajneesh began buying up property in Antelope, the nearest chartered town. It wasn't long before his disciples took political control of Antelope, changing its name to Rajneesh. They converted the general store into a restaurant called Zorba the Buddha and legalized nudity in the public park.

As the population of the Rancho Rajneesh commune and the dollars in its bank account grew—to five thousand disciples and $100 million, respectively—so did Rajneesh's obsessions. He spent most of his time watching movies, according to several accounts, and the disciples whose job it was to keep his video library stocked were flying to Portland or San Francisco almost daily to buy new films. Most of the books penned by alumni of the cult allege Rajneesh was sniffing nitrous oxide (i.e., laughing gas) on a regular basis. On one occasion, reclining in his own $12,000 dentist chair, he reportedly babbled, "I am so relieved that I do not have to pretend to be enlightened anymore."

Orange-clad followers lined Nirvana Drive every day for a glimpse of their master in his Rolls-Royce.

At the height of the controversy, the Bhagwan's disciples (all who lived in Spartan housing) still lined up along the road each day to shower flowers on the hood of Rajneesh's many Rolls-Royce cars. *Bill Miller*

Rajneesh had been buying a couple Rolls-Royces a month since 1980 and owned around 36 when he began his "drive-by blessings." Every afternoon at two o'clock, his most loyal disciples would set down their tools in the ranch's fields, leave their cash registers in Rajneesh's shopping mall, and emerge from their jobs in the commune's casino. Dressed in the "reds and oranges of the sunrise," they lined Nirvana Drive for a glimpse of their bearded, doe-eyed master slowly cruising the boulevard in one of his Rolls-Royces.

The disciples would sing, chant, and throw flowers on the hood. Helicopters hovered overhead, and a security force armed with semiautomatic weapons lurked nearby.

Once the Rolls passed, the devoted returned to their seven-days-a-week jobs in service to Rajneesh. Privileged visitors to the commune elsewhere enjoyed horseback and aircraft rides, boating, swimming, and river rafting. To complete the Club Med appeal, there were also discos, bar lounges, and gaming tables.

There were 41 commune businesses, all staffed by some of the 1,500 followers who "worshipped" at their jobs in exchange for $10 a month, free vegetarian meals, and mattress space in A-frame houses. Another couple thousand commune residents paid $250 a month to explore life with Rajneesh. Still others worked on the 70-acre truck farm that grew enough food for the entire commune. Others worked at shops like the Rajneesh deli, Rajneesh beauty salon, or Rajneesh bookstore, whose stock consisted entirely of the Rajneesh's 650 titles.

Business patronage came mostly from mail orders and the 15,000 visitors who spent an average $500 apiece during Rancho Rajneesh's annual week-long summer open house. Rajneesh also successfully courted a handful of wealthy and sympathetic patrons who were eager to make six-figure donations.

TROUBLE AT THE RANCH

Almost from the moment Rajneesh bought the ranch, Oregon and the commune were embroiled in nonstop legal battles. Rajneesh's power grabs involved everything from arson and attempted murder to racketeering and a planned mass biological attack. In 1984 cult members poisoned the food in several local restaurants in hopes of suppressing voter turnout in an upcoming election. Around the same time Rajneesh brought in thousands of homeless people from outside Oregon in an attempt to commit voter fraud.

Rolls-Royce Motor Cars officials at the carmaker's then U.S. headquarters in Lyndhurst, New Jersey, had a profitable and somewhat odd relationship with Rajneesh. The commune had its own service center, and a Rolls engineer periodically traveled there to troubleshoot cars. A company spokesman told a Trenton newspaper, "Even though it's a rather bizarre place, anybody who's got 93 cars is a good customer."

As for buying two cars a month, Rolls-Royce thought it was "a splendid marketing opportunity." At that time the company only made 2,500 cars a year and sold about 1,100 in America. In 1985 dollars a new Rolls cost from $109,000 to $173,000, and the company earned about $1.4 million from sales to Rajneesh.

The commune also had its own body shop, according to *Automotive News*, where Swami artists commissioned by Rajneesh decorated 36 of the cars with outlandish paint schemes. Psychedelic purples, gold metal flakes, and even cars adorned with jewelry, lace curtains, and cotton balls were reported by dealers who saw them. A 1984 Silver-Spur, dubbed "the Peacock Car," had sky-blue panels with clouds and iridescent red and white peacocks painted on them.

Rajneesh bought 17 of his 93 cars from the Rolls franchise in Portland, some 145 miles from the commune. Then owner Monte Shelton told *Automotive News* that he had a good relationship with the remote desert commune. The rest of the cars were

The last car to sell was a green and gold-lace Rolls-Royce with teargas guns secreted behind the fenders.

bought from dealers throughout the country, depending on who had a particular color or equipment.

The cult's attempt to steal a Wasco County election in 1984 was the tipping point that led to the commune's downfall. In 1985 Rajneesh's right-hand woman, Ma Anand Sheela, fled to Germany with several other sect leaders. She was extradited to the United States in 1986. Ultimately, she got a 20-year prison sentence and was fined half a million dollars, according to *Offbeat Oregon History*, for her role in immigration fraud, burglary, racketeering, arson, and attempted murder. In 1988 Sheela was released from prison early for good behavior and immediately flew to Switzerland.

Rajneesh tried to flee America in October 1985 but was arrested when his jet refueled in Charlotte, North Carolina. After his November 4 trial in Portland on charges of immigration fraud for using sham marriages to get his top lieutenants into the United States, Rajneesh left for India and changed his name to Osho. He spent the rest of his life in several countries, including Greece and Uruguay. He died in 1990 of heart disease in Poona, India, where his followers still run a commune.

After the cult fell, a stash of jet planes, Rolex watches, cash, weapons, armored Jeeps, wiretapping devices, and suspected bioterror labs were found on the sprawling ranch. But what drew the most publicity was the Rolls-Royce collection and vast speculation about how it would affect the used-luxury-car market if it were sold. Rajneesh himself bought eight of the cars before they were sold—many years earlier he had put them into a special car trust.

In an unusual move, and out of concern for the company's image, Rolls-Royce officials and two top dealers traveled to the now-defunct Rancho Rajneesh to inspect the fleet. "We were anxious to ensure that when they went on the market they were cosmetically and mechanically authentic Rolls-Royces," a company spokesman told a New Jersey newspaper. The president of the U.S. unit examined the cars and followed with an undisclosed offer to buy the fleet, but it fell short of the commune's $5 million asking price.

Also looking into the fleet was Consolidated International (now known as the Big Lots chain of stores) of Columbus, Ohio, whose prior major automotive acquisition was the DeLorean in 1983, when it bought the unsold cars and unused parts left in the factory after the bankruptcy. Concerned that the psychedelic paint jobs would hurt resale values, Consolidated's Eli Goldach felt the $5 million asking price was too high.

Both parties were outbid by Bob Roethlisberger, co-owner of European Auto Group in Dallas. Roethlisberger arrived at the commune three days before Thanksgiving in 1985 in a private jet armed with a $6 million line of credit from his bank and a $2 million cash down payment. According to the *Orlando Sentinel*, he paid nearly $7 million for 85 cars. A dozen transport trucks struggled through

A dozen transport trucks struggled through heavy snow in Oregon on their journey to Texas. The cost to transport the Bhagwan's favorite vehicles was upwards of $200,000.

heavy snow to pick up the cars in Oregon for their journey to Texas; the haul cost Roethlisberger over $200,000.

Roethlisberger at first planned to sell the cars at an auction in February, but later changed plans due to what he termed heavy demand for individual sales. According to the *Los Angeles Times*, when he died in April 1986 of cancer at age 40, 43 of the cars had been sold at prices ranging from $65,000 to $100,000.

The remaining 42 cars were sold at auction, including 30 to an unidentified buyer from the Middle East. Many of the cars were repainted. But to the surprise of some, filmmakers, athletes, and business owners were eager to buy the purple cars, the Autumn Car, the Rainbow Car, and the Kimono cars, for which Rajneesh had matching kimonos he used to wear for photo shoots.

In 1987 the last car to sell was a green and gold lace Rolls-Royce. It featured teargas guns secreted under the fenders!

THE ONE-PIECE-AT-A-TIME CADILLAC

BY LINDA CLARK

He'll sneak a Cadillac out, one piece at a time, in his lunchbox.

JOHNNY CASH'S PROPHETIC SONG

IT WAS THE YEAR that a peanut farmer from Georgia became President of the United States. Gas was 59 cents a gallon, and a Polaroid camera cost around $28.

In 1976 Steve Jobs founded Apple Computer, and the sleeper hit *Rocky* was the year's highest-grossing film. Barry Manilow had the longest-running number-one song, but Johnny Cash's "One Piece at a Time" was number one on *Billboard*'s Hot Country Singles chart. It was Cash's last song to reach number one.

Dubbed a "rockabilly novelty song," "One Piece at a Time" was written by Wayne Kemp. In his book *Johnny Cash*, biographer Michael Streissguth says that Kemp came up with the idea for the song after hearing about an Oklahoma airman who stole enough parts from his base to make a helicopter.

The song tells of a man who, in 1949, leaves his home in Kentucky to go work at a General Motors assembly plant in Detroit. The singer puts wheels on Cadillacs, watching them roll by every day. Sometime he cries, because he knows he will never be able to afford one.

But then he devises a plan "that should be the envy of any man." He'll sneak a Cadillac out, one piece at a time, in his lunchbox. Getting caught would mean getting fired, but he figures he'd have it all by the time he retired. So in his large lunchbox, he manages to smuggle out a fuel pump, gears, shocks, nuts and bolts. For the bigger stuff, he uses his buddy's motor home.

That plan worked fine over many years until it came time to assemble the pilfered Cadillac. The transmission was a '53, and the motor turned out to be a '73. And when he and his buddy tried to put in the bolts, the holes were gone. So they drilled it out so that they would fit and "with a little bit of help from an A-daptor kit, they got that engine running just like a song."

The headlight was another sight. They had two on the left and one on the right. But when they pulled out the switch, all three of them went on. According to the song, "the back end looked kind of funny too." But they continued to assemble the Cadillac, and when they got through, they noticed that they had only one tail fin.

It was about that time that the singer's wife came out to look the car over. "She had her doubts," says the song, "but she opened the door and said, 'Honey, take me for a spin.'"

So they drove to town to get tags for the Cadillac, and as they headed down the main drag, they could "hear everybody laughing for blocks around." But at the courthouse they didn't laugh because to type it up, it took the whole staff. "And when they got through, the title weighed 60 pounds."

Then the chorus describes putting the vehicle together one piece at a time. The songs ends with a truck driver inquiring about the "Psychobilly Cadillac," to which Cash replies, "negatory on the cost of this mow-chine. You might say I went right to the factory and picked it up. It's cheaper that way."

When an actual Cadillac was needed to promote the song, Johnny Cash's producer contacted Bruce Fitzpatrick, owner of Abernathy Auto Parts and Hilltop Auto Salvage in Nashville, Tennessee.

"Johnny's producer phoned me in April of 1976 and said he thought 'One Piece at a Time' was going to be a hit and could we come up with a car to use in publicity shots," Fitzpatrick recalled. "He knew I had a lot of Cadillacs.

"So using parts from 1949 to the early seventies, I had my guys build it. It took them about eight to ten days," Fitzpatrick said. "And when it was done, we drove the car to the House of Cash [Johnny Cash's now-defunct museum] in Hendersonville, Tennessee, to deliver it to Johnny. A photographer was there and he took a few photos."

House of Cash, the once public museum on nearly three acres of land complete with a train depot, closed because of financial difficulties in 1985. "After it closed,"

Fitzpatrick recalls, "we retrieved the '49–'70 Cadillac with our wrecker and brought it back here and crushed it. Today it's probably a Nissan or something.

"People from all over the world call me about the patchwork Cadillac," Fitzpatrick says, "but it wasn't that big of a deal when we built it. Nashville wasn't even that big then. We built the car for fun. I never got paid for it."

THE OTHER PATCHWORK CADILLAC

Although the patchwork 1949–1970 convertible was the only Cadillac officially built to promote the song, a second and equally famous 1949–1973 Cadillac was built by Bill Patch of Oklahoma. It had its beginnings in the tiny rural farming and coal mining town of Welch, about 80 miles northeast of Tulsa.

It all started when the Lions Club of Welch began construction of a new civic auditorium in 1977 to provide a meeting place for both kids and adults in the

Johnny Cash at the wheel of the official promotional "One Piece at a Time Cadillac" built in 1976 by Bruce Fitzpatrick (standing) of Abernathy Auto Parts and Hilltop Auto Salvage in Nashville, Tennessee. Fitzpatrick used parts from 1949 to early '70s models.

area. Forced to take on financial debt, the Lions Club staged musical and variety acts, garage sales, raffles, and bake sales to raise funds. Yet the debt remained overwhelming.

As Welch Lions Club member Bill Patch sat in his office one day listening to "One Piece at a Time," he was inspired to build a Cadillac just like the one described in the song. Already a collector of antique cars, Patch and his mechanics scavenged the local salvage yards for Cadillac parts and started building their One-Piece-at-a-Time car.

The result of Patch's effort was a combined Coupe and Sedan DeVille three-door 1949–1973 Cadillac. Built around a 1968 Cadillac, it had a left front fender from a 1963 model and a right front fender from a 1953 model. The left rear fender was from a 1958 model, and the V emblem on the hood and crest on the right fender were from a 1949 model. The car's right rear tail fin was a 1961, and the left tail fin a 1956. The rear bumper was from a 1960 model. The front grille and bumper were from a 1957 model.

Bill Patch of Welch, Oklahoma, built a second patchwork Cadillac for Johnny Cash. This 1949-1973 model appeared in a film often shown at Cash's tour performances of *One Piece at a Time*. Today, the car resides in Wayne Lensing's Historic Auto Attractions museum in Roscoe, Illinois.

More polished looking than the Bruce Fitzpatrick multicolored convertible, it was harder to spot the mismatched pieces on Bill Patch's black Cadillac. But upon closer inspection, you could see the abnormalities. The 1949–1973 Cadillac had two doors on the driver's side but only one on the passenger side. The same went for the headlights; two appeared on the driver's side and just one on the passenger side. The most glaring mismatch could be seen on the back of the Cadillac, where the taillights and tail fins went in opposite directions.

Ironically, building the hodgepodge Cadillac was the easy part. Patch's friends convinced him to give his automotive creation to Johnny Cash, but Cash was understandably dubious of this "out of nowhere" offer. Patch was persistent, however, and drove the car some 545 miles to the House of Cash museum.

To Patch's delight, Cash fell in love with the Cadillac and after several hours of conversation between the two men, Cash graciously accepted the gift. When Cash heard about the Welch Lion's efforts to raise funds for their auditorium, Cash even planned a way to reciprocate Patch's kindness. Cash and his wife, June Carter Cash—a very successful singer in her own right—traveled to Welch for a benefit performance.

Advertising for the benefit was minimal to enable the residents of Welch and other nearby towns first chance at the two shows of one thousand seats each. The two sold-out shows yielded enough money to send the building fund right past its goal.

Moreover, the lasting friendship that grew between Bill Patch and Johnny Cash led a few years later to a Johnny Cash and June Carter Cash encore performance in the then completed Welch Civic Auditorium to benefit the Boy Scouts and the Oklahoma Eye Bank for the blind.

Cash drove both the Fitzpatrick and Patch promotional cars in parades and they were both on display at the House of Cash, but a film of the Patch-built Cadillac was frequently shown at Cash's tour performances of "One Piece at a Time." Bill Patch also appeared with Johnny in publicity photos of the car. After it resided in the House of Cash for several years, the 1949–1973 Cadillac Coupe Sedan DeVille was purchased by collector Wayne Lensing for his Auto Attractions Museum in Roscoe, Illinois.

CRY, CRY, CRY

In 2003 both Johnny Cash and June Carter Cash died, within just four months of each other. In May June died at age 73 from complications following heart valve replacement surgery. And in September Johnny died at age 71 of complications from diabetes.

Even after its 1976 release, "One Piece at a Time" continued to cement its place in music and automotive history. In the 1980s an attempt to build a vehicle "one piece at a time" was successfully completed over a five-year period by a Chinese motorcycle assembly line worker in Chongqing. His achievement was discovered after his arrest by Chinese authorities for driving the motorcycle without the proper paperwork.

In 2001 the song was covered by Chicago rock band Tub Ring for the Johnny Cash tribute album, *Cash from Chaos: A Tribute to the Man in Black.*

THE ANYTHING CARS

BY LINDA CLARK

The main body was that of a Volkswagen Beetle,
but the front fenders were from an AMC Javelin. The tail
fins were from a Chrysler 300 letter car, and the front grille
was from a Lincoln Mark III. The doors were from a Mercury
Comet, and there were Chevrolet Super Sport
emblems below the front bumper.

A CAR OF MANY COLORS

I F YOU'VE EVER borrowed money to buy a vehicle, you know that it involves some research and doing a few calculations before making an informed decision. However, you're probably not likely to wonder where car loans came from in the first place.

But now that we've mentioned it, aren't you just a little curious? Nearly everyone's heard of Henry Ford's idea in 1914 to pay his workers $5 a day so they could afford to buy the cars they were assembling. Although Ford's main objective was to reduce worker attrition—labor turnover from monotonous assembly line work was high—$5 a day did increase car sales. However, financing new cars was something Ford strongly opposed, predicting "it would be the end of America."

General Motors founder William C. "Billy" Durant had no such qualms. He was eager to find a way for car dealers to buy vehicles in large quantities so they could keep the factories running at full tilt. Durant thought the only way to do this was to allow consumers to finance their vehicles so that dealers could, in turn, finance the vehicles they bought from the manufacturer.

Durant's vision led to the formation of General Motors Acceptance Corporation (GMAC) in 1919, the first large non-bank source for car and truck loans. By 2001 GMAC had financed $1 trillion for 150 million cars and trucks in over 40 countries. After General Motors emerged from a government-backed Chapter 11 reorganization in 2009, GMAC was renamed Ally Bank.

GMAC was the first and biggest of the so-called captive finance companies—meaning it was a lending firm wholly owned by the car manufacturer—but there were other pioneers in the field. One of the earliest and most notable was John D. Hertz, who later founded the famous Hertz rental car company.

Hertz started out in the taxi business in Chicago, building Yellow Cabs and operating the taxi service. Between 1915 and 1922 he sold thousands of Yellow Cabs. His deals were often made on credit or in exchange for shares of taxi companies. He began offering creditor payments stretched over time to his taxicab buyers as a means to get rid of his excess inventory. He was so successful that in 1925, when General Motors wanted to expand its commercial line, GM bought Yellow Cab Manufacturing Company from Hertz and his associates for $16 million.

Few commercial banks can compete with the below-market rates offered by the automakers' financing units, but banks nevertheless control about 43 percent of the car loan market, according to a 2008 report by the U.S. Federal Reserve Board.

Manufacturers Hanover Trust (now part of JP Morgan Chase) was New York City's third-largest bank, with 250 branches in the New York metropolitan area alone, when it launched its novel "AnyCar Loan" campaign in 1971. To emphasize that their loan was for "any car you have in mind," they commissioned noted customizer Gene Winfield to build an AnyCar for use in multimedia ads.

WINFIELD'S AMBITIOUS VEHICLE

Winfield masterfully combined 22 different car models into one luxury/economy/intermediate car. It was christened the *ForChevAmChrysVagen* because it was made up of parts from major American and foreign cars.

The main body was that of a Volkswagen Beetle, but the front fenders were from an AMC Javelin. The tail fins were from a Chrysler 300 letter car, and the front grille was from a Lincoln Mark III. The doors were from a Mercury Comet, and there were Chevrolet Super Sport emblems below the front bumper.

The AnyCar I was completed in just 16 weeks—from presentation of the original concept on March 30, 1971, to the finished product on July 18, 1971. For a work team of fewer than a dozen in Winfield's North Hollywood custom shop, it was a remarkable achievement.

Inside, the AnyCar's seats, door panels, and dashboard were upholstered in a bright floral print. The exterior was painted in a combination of warm colors, beginning with yellow on the front fenders and Volkswagen roof, moving to pastel orange on the doors, and finally dark orange on the rear quarter panels.

In addition to being on display at the bank's modernistic 510 Fifth Avenue branch in midtown Manhattan—which has since been designated a New York City landmark— the AnyCar I was seen in print and television ads, as well at car events on the East Coast.

Winfield's prior work had included creating TV cars for such shows as *The Man From U.N.C.L.E.*, *Batman*, *Bewitched*, and *Get Smart.* He also crafted some of the bullet-ridden cars for the movie *Bonnie and Clyde*, as well as the Klingon spaceship for the *Star Trek* TV series.

AnyCar I still exists; it was recently spotted in Europe, where it has been painted turquoise and white, and sports Wes Bank decals. Wes Bank, a division of FirstRand Bank Limited, is South Africa's leading provider of dealer financing and consumer car loans and a major sponsor of motorsports.

Manufacturers Hanover Trust called the AnyCar II "as classic as a Rolls-Royce and as modern as a Lincoln Continental." That was stretching it a bit. However, the AnyCar II does have a hubcap from a Bentley and a Lincoln Continental trunk. Gene Winfield also gave it a distinctive print top.

ANYCAR II

In 1973 Manufacturers Hanover Trust commissioned legendary car builder George Barris to create an AnyCar II. Less modern-looking than the original AnyCar, the Barris creation was what the bank called a "neo-classic car" in its loan brochure. It was essentially a 1929 Hudson body adorned with parts from 50 different automobiles dating from pre–World War II to modern.

Again featuring "something for everyone" styling, the AnyCar II had running boards and side-mounted spare tires like many prewar cars, plus lots of postwar parts from cars such as the Cadillac Eldorado, Plymouth Valiant, and various models of Lincoln, Pontiac, Oldsmobile, and Plymouth. The paint job was a mix of red, green, tan, maroon, and gray.

In addition to starring in print and TV ads, the AnyCar II appeared in two of the *Pink Panther* comedy films starring Peter Sellers as the bumbling French police detective, Inspector Jacques Clouseau.

AnyCar II has passed through several owners since 1973 and is often seen at car shows on the East Coast. When it was photographed in 2008 at a New Hampshire show, it appeared to be in excellent condition.

By 1974 Manufacturers Hanover Trust—or "Manny Hanny" as the bank was familiarly known—was one of the most recognizable bank names in America. It

Gene Winfield designed the AnyCar II with parts from 50 different car models dating from the late 1920s to the 1970s. Built around a 1929 Hudson (which Winfield found in an open field propped up on blocks), the AnyCar II was powered by a Ford V-8 engine, modern for its time.

reached its commercial heyday in the 1970s, when it ran a series of commercials with the tagline, "It's banking the way you want it to be." *Twilight Zone* writer Rod Serling and comedian Paul Lynde served as celebrity spokesmen. At the same time, a Manufacturers Hanover Trust billboard advertising "Super Checking" was a prominent feature of Yankee Stadium. The bank's heavily promoted AnyCar Loan was another huge success.

ANYCAR III AND THE MINI ANYCAR

AnyCar III made its debut in 1974 and was again the focal point of Manny Hanny's auto loan promotion. Continuing the design concept of its predecessors, it was an amalgamation of parts from at least 40 different makes and models. Again, this was the bank's way of conveying the broad range of models and body styles available to car buyers.

However, a new distinction was added to the AnyCar. This third version carried a "Mini AnyCar" under its hood that was equally as functional as the mother car. A four-speed, battery-powered vehicle, it was designed for short-range travel. It was also touted in the bank's 1974 car loan brochure as a possible "long-range solution to the urban problems of traffic congestion and air and noise pollution."

Compact in size, the Mini AnyCar was less than 27 inches wide. To release it from the forward compartment beneath the hood of the AnyCar III, the driver needed only to pull a lever and push a button inside the AnyCar. The Mini AnyCar then came down and out of its "garage."

In that no particular components of AnyCar III were dominant and no two parts were identical, the car, according to designer George Barris, was a "true asymmetrical AnyCar."

Created by Barris in his North Hollywood headquarters, AnyCar III was made up of parts from over 40 different car models mated to the body of a 1974 Volkswagen station wagon. The rear-engine vehicle was chosen to take advantage of the storage space under the front hood compartment where the Mini AnyCar was transported.

A distinctive feature of the AnyCar III was its paint scheme. Just as each of the parts were dissimilar, so too were their paint schemes. The color, identified with the particular car model from which the part was taken, was retained, thus lending authenticity to the individual parts and visual impact to the whole car. The interior was also multicolored. Each seat (left front, right front and rear) was from a different model, again with its original color retained. Brown, orange, tan, imitation wood-grain, white, and black were just some of the colors on the AnyCar III.

With the exception of a 1973 Buick Riviera trunk lid and a couple of other components, all AnyCar III parts were from 1974 models. They included parts from an Alfa-Romeo, Peugeot, Toyota, Datsun, Oldsmobile, Ford Pinto, Chrysler New Yorker, Lincoln Continental, Mercury Cougar, and Cadillac Eldorado. The current whereabouts of the AnyCar III is unknown.

By all accounts Manny Hanny's four-year AnyCar Loan multimedia ad blitz, done in coordination with marketing agency Young & Rubicam, was successful. It was somewhat of a last hurrah, as Manufacturers Hanover Trust was bought by Chemical Bank in 1992, which bought Chase Manhattan Bank in 1996, and four years later merged with J. P. Morgan to form JP Morgan Chase.

Manufacturers Hanover Trust traced its lineage to the 1800s and the likes of American financier J. Pierpont Morgan, Britain's King George I of Hanover, and fur merchant John Jacob Astor.

It took the lead on funding reconstruction after the Civil War and nearly single-handedly financed construction of the Brooklyn Bridge. It survived dozens of mergers and acquisitions over 180 years, several banking debacles—including the panic of 1837 and the Great Depression—but couldn't outlast the banking upheaval of the 1990s.

Color brochures of each of the AnyCars were issued in 1971, 1973, and 1974. Not surprisingly, each also contained a Manufacturers Hanover Trust car loan application. Today these brochures, along with newspaper and magazine ads of the AnyCars, are popular with literature collectors. Thanks to YouTube, one of the original television ads for the AnyCar Loan can also be viewed.

KNEE-STEERING BESASIE CARS

BY LINDA CLARK

The rear-engined, aluminum-bodied X-2 featured a 365-cubic-inch Cadillac engine that, with a race cam and Besasie-made turbocharger, delivered 400 horsepower. Two radiators dispelled heat with dual fans that drew in air from scoops on each side of the body. The air was then expelled out of the large grille at the rear of the X-2, whose frame was made out of chrome moly tube.

CAR-CRAZY BESASIE AND
THE EXPERIMENTAL X-CARS

THE SINGULAR—some would say weird—Besasie X-cars were born when post–World War II prosperity and the new Interstate Highway System in America created unbounded optimism between 1955 and 1969.

Nowhere was that optimism more evident than in Detroit, where by the late 1950s, flamboyant car styling had turned into dazzling entertainment. That optimism also fueled the dreams of backyard car builders, many of whom lacked sufficient talent, imagination, or money to create anything memorable.

But only one man designed and built high-performance cars that could be steered with the driver's *knees*.

Raymond Besasie was different. He had talent and imagination to spare. And although Besasie was not rich, he always managed to scare up enough money to finance his next dream car, and his X Series of custom cars were out on the cutting edge of car design and steering systems.

According to Ray's grandson, Anthony Besasie, Ray was born in 1904 in Milwaukee, Wisconsin. His father was a hard-working Sicilian fruit peddler, and it was Ray's job as a boy to tend to the horse and wagon. Ray was naturally curious, and the first time he saw a motorcar, he jumped off his father's fruit wagon and crawled underneath it to see how it worked. Thus began Ray's lifelong fascination with automobiles; he built his first car while he was still in high school in the 1920s.

Later as a young mechanic and owner of a Texaco station in Milwaukee, he built race cars for himself and his neighbors. By then, Ray had bought a house and garage on Van Buren Street in Milwaukee and married Grace Mielotz, the girl next door. Besasie and Grace where married for over 72 years and raised three sons and a daughter.

TURBOCHARGERS AND SUPERCHARGERS

It was while tuning a 1919 Cadillac, according to Ray's friend John Slusar, that Ray noticed the exhaust pulses came out of the tailpipe with some force. Ray thought it would be useful to put that energy back into the system, and when he ultimately launched Besasie Engineering, his chief product was an exhaust-driven turbocharger (although Ray called it a supercharger at the time).

Far-out tailfins and a sharp dorsal fin were part of the X-3's aero-inspired rear styling.
Linda Clark

Ray installed the turbocharger on his own 1948 Chevy, and to promote it, he and Grace toured the country, often racing prospective customers along the way and selling turbochargers to the losers.

Gottlieb Daimler had received a German patent for a supercharger in 1885, and Louis Renault patented his supercharger in France in 1902. But it was Swiss engineer Alfred Buchi who was granted the first patent for a turbocharger (or supercharger driven by exhaust-gas pulses). In 1916, Frenchman Auguste Rateau tested turbochargers in aircraft, and in 1918 General Electric produced a gain in horsepower with its turbocharged Liberty aircraft engine.

Over the next two decades, many different companies and industries in both Europe and America expressed more than a casual interest in both turbochargers and superchargers. According to Anthony Besasie, when General Motors began seminal research on turbos in 1946, they invited Ray to Detroit to share his drawings of his exhaust-driven supercharger with them. According to Slusar, when GM developed the turbocharged 1962 Corvair, an engineer visited Ray to seek his advice.

Interest in turbochargers waned after World War II with the arrival of the modern high-performance engine. It wasn't until smaller, fuel-efficient engines became fashionable in the late 1970s that there was a resurgence of interest in using turbos to boost performance in passenger cars.

Besasie's other passion was aeronautics, especially experimental aircraft, and in the 1930s he built two airplanes. Inspired by his young son Fred, he named one of them *Sunny Boy*, and because its wooden propeller had to be precisely balanced, he spent untold hours perfecting it. "My grandfather loved to build planes," his Ray's grandson Anthony recalls, "but he let others do the flying."

During World War II, Ray worked for the U.S. government fabricating airplane parts for American jet fighters and bombers. It was also in the 1940s that Ray began to work as the personal mechanic and sheet metal fabricator for famed industrial and automotive designer Brooks Stevens. A Wisconsin native, Stevens had opened his design shop in 1934 in Milwaukee, and by the 1940s had over 35 accounts.

LIKE FATHER, LIKE SONS

When the Korean War started in 1950, Ray and two of his sons, Ray Jr. and Joe, were drafted. Like his father, Ray Jr. was a master sheet metal fabricator whose skills were needed for aircraft building. Joe Besasie's talent as an illustrator landed him a job creating technical manuals. "My father has the ability to draw things to scale," Anthony notes, "and these perspective drawings were essential in military manuals."

Although Stevens had designed military sedans for Ford and the 1951 Paxton automobile, his first foray into building cars came in 1952 with the Excalibur J sports car, for which Ray Sr. formed the bodies. There were three J cars built, the last of which had a successful three-year racing career.

After Korea Ray Jr. and Joe also went to work for Brooks Stevens. Ray Jr. built and raced the Excalibur Formula Kart Experimental, a one-off kart designed by Stevens around 1960. According to *Hemmings Motor News*, the kart was powered by twin West Bend 820 two-cycle motors, each with dual carburetors ported to run methanol. The motors put out around 25 horsepower each, giving the kart a top speed of 130 miles per hour. Ray Jr. hand-built the twin collection tanks out of aluminum and welded them with oxyacetylene, a technique used during World War II on aircraft.

THE X-CARS

In his four-car garage behind his home in Milwaukee—not far from the neighborhood he was born and raised in—Ray Sr. and his sons had begun building the first of four experimental cars: the X-1 Barracuda. It was a two-seat sports car with a 1953 Corvette drivetrain and 235-cubic-inch Blue Flame six with sidedraft carburetors. The most conventional of the four cars, it had a traditional steering wheel. It passed through several owners over the years, and as recently as 2012 had a modified Pontiac 389 V-8, Borg Warner T-10 four-speed, and Pontiac rear end.

The more innovative X-2 was one of 28 nominees for *Motor Life*'s Top Custom of the Year. The rear-engined, aluminum-bodied X-2 featured a 365-cubic-inch Cadillac engine that, with a race cam and Besasie-made turbocharger, delivered 400 horsepower. Two radiators dispelled heat with dual fans that drew in air from scoops on each side of the body. The air was then expelled out of the large grille at the rear of the X-2, whose frame was made out of chrome moly tube.

Styled by Joe Besasie, the X-2 had a wraparound windshield and hydraulic sliding roof. The steering wheel was in the center of the seat, and the X-2 had no doors. You hopped in and out via recessed step plates on each side of the car. The fender-mounted running lights and seven-way taillights were advanced for their day. The pastel yellow body had a 4-foot-high dorsal fin.

The trio spent 5,200 hours and nearly $20,000 building the X-2, which reportedly went from 0 to 60 miles per hour in 6.5 seconds. Ray Sr. said he got around 22 miles per gallon on high-octane fuel while cruising at 62 miles per hour. *Mechanix Illustrated* featured the X-2 as a "Car of Tomorrow" in its February 1959 issue, and in the early 1960s, the X-2 appeared in a Clark gasoline commercial.

While on a road trip with the X-2, Ray Sr. sold it to Veda Schwartz, a florist from Phoenix, Arizona, who shipped the car to Barris Kustoms to be painted Candy Purple to match her shop's world-renowned orchids. The X-2 was last seen in sad shape in an abandoned yard near a railroad track in 1970.

The X-3, named the Explorer, was the most revolutionary X-car yet. Joe designed the car, and Ray Sr. and Ray Jr. built it. The car didn't have a steering wheel, and once again, step plates on each side of the body served in place of doors.

Instead of a steering wheel, the X-3 had a padded hydraulic lever in the center of the seat that enabled the driver to steer with either hands or knees. Ray's self-described tiller steering also had vertical handgrips on each side of the tiller and a tray between the grips that housed the controls. Various gauges, switches, knobs, and a couple levers were mounted on three separate instrument panels, with the gauges directly in front of the driver. Although some high-end luxury cars had padded dashboards, the X-3's padded dash was at least a decade ahead of Detroit's wide-spread promotion of them as a safety feature.

Built on a 1957 Chevy chassis, the X-3 had a Hydramatic transmission and Cadillac engine tuned to produce over 350 horsepower, a 0-to-60-miles-per-hour time of 6 seconds, and top speed of 140 miles per hour. Sporting huge tail fins and an airplane-like tail assembly, the X-3 had a chrome split bumper in front and four headlights.

According to a March 1961 *Mechanix Illustrated* story, the Besasies shelled out $5,000 for materials and another $15,000 worth of labor to produce the X-3. Ray Sr. didn't sell the car until the 1970s, and it is still in Wisconsin today.

Between X-cars, the Besasies helped Brooks Stevens launch the Excalibur SSK roadster in 1964, for which Stevens took his inspiration from the Mercedes-Benz SSK of the 1920s. Before work on the car began, Stevens asked staff designer Joe Besasie to develop a complete set of drawings from which the car would be built. Using Joe's drawings, the prototype was built in six weeks by William Stevens, metal fabricator Jules Mayeur, sheet metal fabricators Ray Sr. and Ray Jr., and machinist Frank Neuschwanger.

In the middle of their many projects, Brooks' sons, William and David, created the Excalibur Automobile Corporation in 1965. Ray Jr. was vice president of sales and marketing. But their attention soon turned to the next X-car.

Work on the Besasie X-4 began in the late 1960s, but Ray Sr. made changes to the car through the 1970s. It carried forward the tiller steering of the X-3 and much of the body styling of the X-2, but added new features. One was a turbo-like device Ray invented to improve the X-4's gas mileage.

"Another forward-looking feature on the X-4 was its passenger collision protection device or early stage airbag," Anthony recalls. "Passengers sat to the left and right of the driver. In front of them, the dash was constructed of aluminum that was trimmed and covered in leather. The dash top incorporated a three-inch foam pad that mounted to a hinge that was cocked in place under spring tension. If the X-4 was involved in a head-on collision, the driver could push a button on the tiller and the pads would hinge forward to protect the passengers from hitting the windshield."

The X-4 was powered by a supercharged Chrysler 440-cubic-inch engine (Ray later removed the supercharger) and rode on a Chrysler chassis with a steel frame. Ray formed and welded its all-aluminum body by hand with a hammer and torch.

Ray hung on to the X-4 for a few years, and friends and visitors to his shop recall getting rides in it. Bill Hebal brought a sports car to Ray for bodywork in the 1970s. "Not only did Ray give me a ride in the X-4, but he invited me into his home and showed me sketches of projects he was working on. Ray was a master with metal, especially when you consider that working with aluminum in the 1950s and 1960s was a lot harder than it is today," Bill remembers.

Somehow, between working at Brooks Stevens Associates and building his own cars, Ray found time to hand-form the nose cone on the jet-powered *Blue Flame* vehicle Gary Gabelich drove to a world land speed record on the Bonneville Salt Flats in Utah in 1970. The 37-foot-long *Blue Flame* had aluminum skin and, semi-monocoque aluminum frame with a welded tubular structure in the nose section. It was constructed by Reaction Dynamics in Milwaukee.

Ray showed off the X-3 and X-4 cars at Experimental Aircraft Association (EAA) Fly-Ins in Oshkosh. The annual week-long show attracts some 12,000 aircraft and 600,000 visitors each July. Car clubs often hold meets in conjunction with the show.

"As a kid with my grandfather at the EAA show in Oshkosh one summer," Anthony recalls. "I remember we were looking at a P-51 Mustang and he told me that if all the rivets on the wings were ground down and polished, it would improve drag coefficient. That was typical. He was always thinking about how things could be done better."

THE PORTUGUESE BARN FIND

BY LINDA CLARK

The scope of the collection is immense.
The makes range from Abarth, Alfa-Romeo,
Auburn, and Austin Healey to Volvo, Volkswagen,
Wolseley, and Wartburg. American manufacturers
include Chevys, Buicks, Cadillacs, Fords, Oldsmobiles,
Plymouths, Pontiacs, Lincoln Continentals,
Packards, and Studebakers.

THE GREATEST BARN FIND OF ALL TIME

THIS TALE REMINDS ME of those unsolicited letters you sometimes receive in the mail—the ones that invite you to a complimentary dinner in exchange for two hours of your time, during which you'll be captive to a sales pitch from a couple of guys trying to sell you land or mutual funds. In this case, the pitch may be secluded property in Portugal. Or a fund that invests in vineyards, cork, or Portugal's fertile agricultural land.

It is the kind of story that is picturesque and sweet, but too good to be true. But it *is* true, and it begins with a bunch of photographs of old cars.

The story and the photos appeared on the Internet. And the incredible pictures of vintage cars encrusted with decades of grime in a musty-looking cinderblock building were irresistible to car collectors.

Here's an aerial view of the nondescript, remote building that hid the cars for years. The doors were welded shut. Some of the cars inside were Alfa Romeo Giuliettas, a Lancia Aurelia B24, a Lancia Flaminia Coupe, a Porsche 356B, a Porsche 356C, and even a Volkswagen Beetle. *Manuel Menezes Morais*

One has to wonder how all these cars—check out the dusty, old Saab in the front— were parked so closely together, and then how they were subsequently removed! *Manuel Menezes Morais*

The doors finally opened to the huge collection of dusty cars.
Manuel Menezes Morais

You may have received the email yourself: there were several slightly different versions, but they all went something like this:

A New York man retired and wanted to use his retirement money wisely so it would last, so he decided to buy a home and a few acres in Portugal. The modest farmhouse had been vacant for 15 years. The owner and his wife both had died and there were no heirs. The house was sold to pay taxes.

There had been several lookers, but the large barn and steel doors had been welded shut. Nobody wanted to go to the extra expense to see what was in the barn, and it wasn't complimentary to the property anyway, so nobody made an offer on the place.

The New York guy bought it at just over half the property's worth, moved in, and set about to tear into the barn. Curiosity was killing him. So he and his wife bought a generator and a couple of grinders and cut through the welds. What was in the barn?

Now that your curiosity was piqued (as mine was), the email directed you to a link that provided photographic images of the barn's contents. Only a handful of the cars were highly valuable, but the sheer number of them and their dusty patina was captivating. They seemed to number in the hundreds, and although most were European, there were some American cars too. Looking at them, you couldn't help but feel that you had discovered something incredible.

But at the same time, a part of you knew that a car collection this big wouldn't have gone unnoticed. It couldn't have—someone, somewhere, would have heard about it, written about it, talked about it, or photographed it long ago. Why would it

A collection of late 1940s American cars, including a 1946 Ford gathering dust near the European cars. *Manuel Menezes Morais*

appear only now? After so many years and so many cars? It didn't make sense—this huge building full of slumbering, undisturbed cars didn't make sense.

Soon the Internet was hopping with all these questions and more. Some people even ventured answers, but most were too bizarre to be believable. And not long afterwards, a couple of websites concluded that the email was bogus, a hoax, a fraud, a trick. Of course, many car collectors had already figured that out for themselves.

Yet the photos had been made public for a reason, and no one was quicker to investigate their source than Tom Cotter in *Sports Car Market* magazine. About the time I was reading the suspicious story for the first time, Cotter was writing in his May 2007 column that the Portuguese barn find story was pure fiction. Being a lifelong car-in-the-barn finder, Cotter, (author of Motorbooks' *In the Barn* series) immediately did some digging, and he was able to ferret out some of the real story.

DIAMONDS IN THE ROUGH

A photographer named Manuel Menezes Morais, according to Cotter, had shot the car collection for its owner, a former car dealer who saved some of the cars he encountered in the course of business. At that time, the name of the owner and the collection's exact location were still undisclosed, but it was believed to be somewhere near Lisbon. Over the Internet, some collectors theorized the photos had been taken to catalog the collection for promotion or insurance purposes.

In the spring of 2009, German journalist and photographer Wolfgang Blaube traveled to Portugal, met with the owner and his son, and photographed many of the cars. His discovery was detailed in a two-part story in the French car enthusiast weekly *La Vie de L'Auto* on July 29 and August 5, 2009. Blaube actually found not one, but two large buildings, one containing around 189 cars and the other 103 cars.

The story revealed that the owner of the buildings and the cars, Antonio Ferreira de Almeida, had begun amassing the collection after Portugal's 1974 Carnation Revolution. It was not uncommon at that time for Portuguese collectors to store their cars in nearby Spain or sell them for a song. By the mid-1980s—and not yet 40 years old—Antonio had acquired over three hundred cars. He never missed a chance to buy one at a bargain price, and he ended up with cars of nearly every make, year, and country of origin. When his buying spree cooled in the mid-1990s, he had amassed about four hundred cars for his collection. It's estimated that about a hundred of them were in good-to-excellent condition.

Not surprisingly, because the photos had been circulated all over the Internet, the cars are for sale, but only the cars in the two huge buildings; according to Blaube another hundred or so cars are parked in underground garages in and around Lisbon. They contain Antonio's favorites, such as a Porsche 356 Carrera, a

Some of the most rare and valuable cars ever made were packed bumper to bumper in the building. *Manuel Menezes Morais*

Rare cars in dusty hibernation parked grille to trunk. *Manuel Menezes Morais*

A collection of Mercedes-Benz cars waited out the decades. *Manuel Menezes Morais*

Ferrari Dino 246 GT, Deutsch-Bonnet LeMans, and two early Citroen DS Chapron convertibles that are *not* for sale.

Antonio and his son, Antonio Jr., are savvy collectors who haven't priced the cars cheaply, said Blaube. The scope of the collection is immense. The makes range from Abarth, Alfa-Romeo, Auburn, and Austin Healey to Volvo, Volkswagen, Wolseley, and Wartburg. American manufacturers include Chevys, Buicks,

Cadillacs, Fords, Oldsmobiles, Plymouths, Pontiacs, Lincoln Continentals, Packards, and Studebakers.

There's also a 1932 Chrysler CD Roadster, 1968 Ford Mustang, 1967 Plymouth Barracuda, 1958 Nash Metropolitan, 1976 Cadillac Eldorado convertible, 1955 Chevrolet Bel Air, 1946 Willys Jeep, three 1950s Facel-Vegas, and a couple of Formula Fords, to cite a few models.

Some of the European models include a 1959 Alfa-Romeo Giulietta Spider, 1955 Jaguar XK-140 roadster, 1958 Austin-Healey Sprite MK1 roadster, 1962 MGB roadster, two 1955 MG Magnettes, 1966 Maserati Quattroporte, 1971 Opel 1900 coupe, 1957 Porsche 356A coupe, and 1967 Steyr-Puch 650 TR, to name a few.

There's even a 1973 Datsun 240Z and two 1960s Honda coupes. Although many have already sold, a comprehensive list of the cars as of the spring of 2009 can be found on the www.hagerty.com website. It doesn't include every car seen and photographed by Blaube, but it lists most of them. Blaube also recounts his Portugal barn find quest in greater detail in Tom Cotter's 2010 book, *The Corvette in the Barn.*

Exactly who invented the tale of the New York couple retiring to Portugal's countryside only to discover a long-forgotten building full of vintage cars remains unknown. But the accompanying photos turned out to be authentic, even if the story wasn't. And while it may have all been just a publicity ploy, it led to a fascinating true story in the end.

THE DEVIN-BODIED
FERRARI

BY LINDA CLARK

Shaughnessy says he can scan Ferrarri 340 virgin
bodies for the necessary data and precision to correctly
form the body. "Just to make a wooden body buck is a
twenty-five-thousand-dollar expense," he says.

A DEVIN BODY HIDES
A 1952 FERRARI 340 AMERICA

IN 2006 TOM SHAUGHNESSY of California won a vintage Devin Sports Spider on eBay for $26,912 that other bidders failed to discern was a 1952 Ferrari 340 America chassis. The precious Ferrari chassis had been concealed under the Devin fiberglass body since 1960.

This sale remains one of the most significant barn finds of all time.

Shaughnessy even thought he knew where the original V-12 engine was, and he hoped to convince the owner to trade for the engine. He estimated the cost for a 340 motor would be $200,000.

Shaughnessy made it happen. "It took six years, over a quarter-million dollars, and the help of a whole lot of people, but I got the original engine for the chassis," Shaughnessy said in 2012. "This 340 is probably the most important Ferrari found in the last twenty-five years."

Both he and the Devin's seller, Mike Sanfilippo of Illinois, were happy with the auction's outcome and plan to be on hand when the restoration is completed and the car is unveiled to the world. A retired drag racer, Sanfilippo bought the Devin for

$200 in 1991. He had planned to cut up the chassis to make a Hot Wheels dragster out of the body, but the project never materialized.

Shaughnessy, a Ferrari authority and seasoned car hunter, was prepared to bid as high as $264,000 if anyone else spotted the 340 chassis numbered 0202 A, but when the auction ended, he had won the car. Restored, it has an estimated value of nearly $3 million, according to Swiss-born Ferrari historian Marcel Massini.

Although the Devin body camouflaged its origins, the 340 was available to anyone willing to investigate. Sanfilippo thought it may have been a prototype Devin SS. Sanfilippo said many of the potential buyers planned to see the car during the eBay auction—but only one showed. Sanfilippo tore down the car for a series of photos and answered email queries from around the world.

Shaughnessy verified the 340 with the help of Ferrari expert Hillary Rabb, who examined the car. The duo unearthed the even-numbered 0202 A chassis, which meant it had been a factory competition car. It was one of around 475 built between 1948 and 1974, nearly all of which are accounted for. The numbers range from 0002-0896 and 1002-1050. Only a few of these rare cars are still missing, and they may be lost forever.

The chassis was originally built with a Spider body by Vignale. It's one of 25 340 Americas produced. Including this one, 11 were bodied by Vignale, 9 by Touring, and 5 by Ghia. Sister cars are 0196 A and 0204 A, according to Shaughnessy, and have helped with faithful reconstruction. Both underwent their own restorations.

A CAR OF MIXED PEDIGREE

Massini traced the remarkable history of 0202 A. The car competed in the 24 Hours of Le Mans in 1952 with French drivers Maurice Trintignant and Louis Rosier at the wheel, but it didn't finish. The factory then loaned it to Italian driver Piero Scotti, who campaigned the Ferrari in several notable races and won three major hill-climbs. Other racers borrowed it until American importer Luigi Chinetti bought it in 1953 and then reportedly sold it to California race car driver Ernie McAfee.

McAfee owned 0202 A until 1958, when he sold it to Paul Owens in Houston, who installed a Chevrolet V-8 engine in it. Like McAfee, Owens was both a racer and car collector. Following a crash in which the passenger was killed, 0202 A was refitted with a Devin body and advertised in *Sports Car* magazine for $4,250. The car passed through a Utah owner in 1963 before ending up in Chicago, where Sanfilippo bought it in 1990.

The Chicago owner's son had abandoned it in his garage, and Sanfilippo bought it for its Devin body. The Italian-inspired fiberglass body was the brainchild of Oklahoma-born Bill Devin who, after setting up business in California, designed and manufactured low-cost bodies to fit a variety of different chassis in the 1950s and early 1960s.

Shaughnessy's purchase price was merely a down payment on what it will cost to restore the preeminent Ferrari. Apart from a missing front spring, the front part of the chassis with the steering was intact. The center section and rear had been modified. But the brakes were complete and the axles and wheels were correct.

He believes a novice would have ended up paying a professional restoration shop seven figures—a huge sum, although still within reason given the completed car's estimated value of close to $3 million. An able restorer himself, Shaughnessy will still spend around $600,000.

In addition to the $250,000 for the engine, Shaughnessy estimated the transmission will cost $25,000, differential $20,000, chassis prep and repair $100,000, and a new body $200,000. But he had an edge, because he already had a transmission, rear end, pedal box, radiator, and oil cooler.

"The original motor was critical and now I have that," Shaughnessy says today. He had planned from the beginning to do a full restoration in cooperation with the Ferrari factory in Maranello, which had just formed a Classiche Division to authenticate vintage Ferraris.

"I'm still waiting for a decision from them," Shaughnessy says. "I'll work with them either in Italy or California. I'm thinking the factory could restore the chassis in Italy and I'll do the powertrain in California."

Shaughnessy says he can scan Ferrarri 340 virgin bodies for the necessary data and precision to correctly form the body. "Just to make a wooden body buck is a twenty-five-thousand-dollar expense," he says. In addition to the previously mentioned parts, within 90 days of buying the car, Shaughnessy also had the radiator, gauges, and steering wheel. But the body is obviously a more arduous challenge.

In addition to its attractive Vignale body, the 340 America rides on a 96.8-inch wheelbase and is powered with a 220 horsepower, 4.1-liter V-12. The transmission is a five-speed manual. The car weighs around 1,980 pounds and has a recorded top speed of 148 miles per hour.

And how did Sanfilippo react to the now famous eBay find? He felt elated that the car went to the right person. He told *Sports Car Market* in 2006 that he didn't have the knowledge, resources, or contacts to restore the Ferrari properly.

The car had been missing—and hiding under that Devin body—for over four decades. Now, at long last, it is back where it belongs.

THE LOST
AND FOUND
ASTON MARTIN DB4

BY LINDA CLARK

When the dust-covered DB4C/1104R awoke from its
32-year slumber in 2011, Blackman's 1970 St. John's College
parking pass was still affixed to the windshield. It read,
"Authority to park in the President's drive."

BOND. JAMES BOND.

YOU KNOW THE NAME. And if you know the name, then you certainly know the cars.

What you don't know is that 007 probably wouldn't have driven all those beautiful Aston Martins in the movies without the help of British tractor maker David Brown.

Unlike 007, the suave film spy, dapper industrialist Brown cut his teeth on the rough-riding agricultural machines that made him rich. It was Brown's passion for machinery that led to his acquisition of the famed but struggling Aston Martin company in 1947.

In 1948 Brown bought Lagonda, followed by the coachbuilder Tickford in 1955. The companies shared resources, and Brown eventually moved all of Aston Martin manufacturing to the Tickford site in Newport Pagnell. DB2 prototypes raced with honor in 1949, and in 1950 Brown brought out his production DB2 coupe, the first in the legendary series of cars that carried his DB initials.

Among them was the Silver Birch DB5 that provided Aston Martin's first link to the spy movie franchise, which continues even today. Bond's first stint behind the wheel of a DB5 happened in *Goldfinger* in 1964, and the car was later resurrected in five more 007 films, including *Skyfall*, which was an instant hit in late 2012.

Brown, considered the savior of Aston Martin, was born in 1904 and later joined the family gear-making company. By 1931, he was running it and teamed up with Irish inventor Harry Ferguson in 1936 to build tractors, which earned him a fortune during World War II.

After reading an ad in *The Times* of London offering a motor business for sale, Brown, a sportsman who played polo and raced cars and motorcycles, used profits from his tractor firm to buy Aston Martin. The car company, founded in 1913, built competition and road cars during the 1920s and 1930s that earned it accolades among motorsport enthusiasts, but sales never brought in enough money to make ends meet.

What Brown bought was a rented factory where aircraft parts had been made, a prototype saloon called the Atom, and the Aston Martin name. The Atom morphed into the open-topped DB1 of 1948, of which only 15 were built, but it was succeeded in 1950 by the twin-cam, inline-six-engined DB2, which formally ushered in the David Brown era.

UNVEILING A LEGEND

The rare 1963 Aston Martin DB4 convertible barn find of our story was unearthed in the United Kingdom in early 2011. It showed just 60,000 miles on its odometer. One of just 70 produced, it was missing for decades, never having been listed in the Aston Martin Owners Club Register. Amazingly, it had only two documented owners.

Its longtime second owner, who placed the car in storage in 1979, had bought the DB4 in 1978 from its original owner, 75-year-old agronomist Geoffrey Emett Blackman. Blackman came from a family of distinguished scientists and botanists. At Oxford University, he was the Sibthorpian Professor of Rural Economy and director of the Agricultural Research Council Unit of Experimental Agronomy there.

When the dust-covered DB4C/1104R awoke from its 32-year slumber in 2011, Blackman's 1970 St. John's College parking pass was still affixed to the windshield. It read, "Authority to park in the President's drive."

The original engine, number 370/1134, had been replaced by Blackman with what appeared to be another factory engine. In 1980 the second owner removed the replacement engine, number 370/472, with the intention of rebuilding it, but the project never happened. He put the engine, still not rebuilt, back in the car in 2011.

While the DB5 driven by James Bond in 1964 is the most recognizable Aston Martin from the David Brown period, the car actually had its roots in the previous decade, when development of the DB4 began. Work on the Aston Martin DB4 started in 1956, at the same time as the Aston Martin DB Mark III. The key people involved in its development were technical and general manager John Wyer, chassis engineer Harold Beach, and engine designer Tadek Marek, a former Austin engineer.

Every major component in the DB4 was new. Its four-seat aluminum coupe body was designed by Carrozzeria Touring of Milan, using their patented Superleggera (super-light) construction in which alloy panels were fixed to a tubular frame— designed by Harold Beach—built onto the DB4's strong steel platform chassis.

The Aston Martin DB4 debuted at the Paris Salon on October 12, 1958, and a week later at the London Motor Show to widespread acclaim. In London it shared a stand with the DB Mark III, which continued in production for almost a year.

All of the DB cars since 1948 had earned a racing pedigree for Aston Martin, but the DB4 was the key to establishing the company's road-car reputation. It was touted as the first production car capable of 0 to 100 miles per hour and back to zero in less than 30 seconds, claiming to reach 100 miles per hour in 21 seconds.

The DB4 was initially offered only as a two-door 2+2, although Britain's *The Autocar* didn't agree with the factory that four adults could fit comfortably in the car. "The body cannot be regarded as more than an occasional four-seater," the magazine said. "It would not be in the interest of a happy crew to embark on long journeys with more than three people in the car, as head and leg room in the back are very limited."

Such inconveniences were minor. The DB4's superb performance and flawless Italian styling made it an instant classic. But at 3,976 British pounds (nearly $12,000), the DB4 was anything but cheap. Nevertheless, sales remained brisk during its production life. A total of around 1,119 cars in all variants were built through 1963.

The DB4 had Dunlop Servo-assisted four-wheel disc brakes (a rarity in those days) and top-speed capabilities beyond 140 miles per hour, with a 0-to-60 time of

This 1963 Aston Martin DB4 convertible slept in the barn from 1979 to 2011, growing ever more valuable (even in its ramshackle, dirt-crusted condition). *Bonhams*

The shift lever is missing, the dirt is everywhere, but Aston Martin lovers see an original car just crying out for a sympathetic clean-up into a rolling time capsule. *Bonhams*

The famous Aston Martin twin-cam, 6-cylinder engine hadn't turned over in 32 years, but it was all there. The engine has to be completely rebuilt. *Bonhams*

around 9 seconds. In spite of its very fast speeds, interior appointments were plush, with leather everywhere, including a traditional wood-trimmed steering wheel.

Tadek Marek designed the DB4's 3.7-liter double overhead cam aluminum straight-six engine. Producing 240 horsepower at 5,000 rpm, it was mated to David Brown's in-house all-synchromesh four-speed manual gearbox with optional Laycock de Normanville electric overdrive. A Borg-Warner three-speed automatic was optional.

Underneath, the trailing link independent front suspension gave way to unequal length wishbones. At the rear, the DB4 had a live axle located by a Watts linkage instead of the Panhard rod used on earlier DB cars. Telescopic shock absorbers were used at the front of the DB4, with lever arm shocks at the rear.

The DB4 featured rack-and-pinion steering. There was a choice of final drive ratios, with the normal one for British and European use being 3.54:1. Cars destined for the United States got 3.77:1, unless customers intended to drive at extremely high speeds, for which a 3.31:1 ratio was available. Britain's *The Motor* magazine achieved a top speed of 139.3 miles per hour in a DB4 with the standard 3.54 final drive ratio.

Marek's straight-six engine was magnificent, as Aston Martin's late 1950s racing record attests. The racing versions won just about every victory possible in the sports car field, including Le Mans in 1959. These wins were even more impressive, according to race car drivers of the era, when you considered that the DB4's rear axle was a standard "live" de Dion type and not very sophisticated compared with other racers of the time.

The DB4 rode on a 98-inch wheelbase and weighed around 2,900 pounds. Avon Turbospeed tires were standard, but sports car racers of the day often fitted the DB4 with Dunlop R5 racing tires. The DB4 underwent five distinct series before it was replaced in 1963 by the DB5. Each series of DB4 was faster, better equipped, and more luxurious than the prior one.

A convertible version of the DB4 was unveiled in September 1961 at the London Motor Show. It was distinguished by a lower hood scoop and new seven vertical bar grille. It kept the DB4's basic body structure but had a strengthened floorpan, load-bearing hood well, and reinforced door sills.

There were no interior changes, except the convertible obviously offered passengers more head room than the coupe. Although styled in-house, the convertible retained the coupe's Italian overtones. The open-top cars cost about $750 more than the coupes. Just 70 convertibles were built.

The DB4 required high-test gasoline and got about 17 miles per gallon, according to *The Autocar*. Though classy and beautiful, the DB4 shared some irritations common to many British cars. They were prone to clutch slip, high oil consumption, cooling system faults, and brakes that pulled sporadically.

A LONG CAST OF CHARACTERS

It's hard not to think of James Bond when sliding behind the wheel of an Aston Martin DB4, but there were other famous fictional characters who shared the big screen with an Aston Martin. In the 1969 British caper film *The Italian Job* swindler Charlie Croker, played by actor Michael Caine, picks up his silver Aston Martin DB4 convertible from a garage after his release from prison. The actual car that got destroyed when Croker's DB4 got flipped into a gorge was a modified Fiat Spider convertible.

Peter Sellers drove the short wheelbase, two-seat derivative of the DB4, the DB4 GT coupe, in the 1963 black-and-white British comedy *The Wrong Arm of the Law*. Sellers played gang leader Pearly Gates, a robber who impersonates a fashion consultant to be near rich, gullible women. Who can forget the scene where Sellers and the Aston Martin DB4 GT became airborne on Cowley Mill Road in Uxbridge?

Decades of dust and neglect formed a real barn-find patina for this time machine of a DB4. *Bonhams*

Cleaning the grim off these beautiful wire wheels might be the easiest part of getting this petrified car back on the road. *Bonhams*

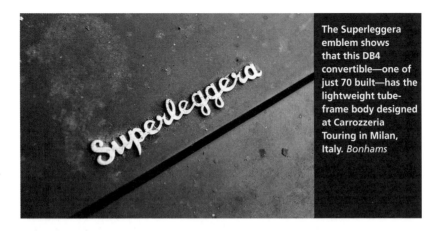

The Superleggera emblem shows that this DB4 convertible—one of just 70 built—has the lightweight tube-frame body designed at Carrozzeria Touring in Milan, Italy. *Bonhams*

It sounds strange, but this 1970 parking pass, which reads "Authority to park in the President's drive," added to the value of this car, which spent much of its driving life driving to and from the University of Oxford's St. John's College campus. *Bonhams*

The fate of this particular lost-and-found Aston Martin DB4 convertible was just as exciting. Once it was dusted off and the not-yet-rebuilt engine put back in it, the DB4 was offered for sale at the Bonhams Auction of Aston Martin sports cars and related automobilia on May 21, 2011. It was the 12th auction to be held at the Aston Martin Works Service Center in Newport Pagnell, birthplace of the DB4.

Showing the strength of Aston Martin's brand and the demand for cars from throughout the marque's nearly hundred-year history, the sale generated almost 6 million British pounds (around $9.6 million) from bidders around the globe. Only one of the 345 lots remained unsold. And yes, this Aston Martin DB4

The car was sold for $502,405 at Bonhams' Newport Pagnell auction on May 21, 2011, in this dilapidated, dusty condition. Barn-find cars are all the rage these days, and the dirt may have helped boost the price! *Bonhams*

convertible sold, in barn find condition, for $485,000, against a presale estimate of $130,000–$227,000.

Along with the barn find DB4 convertible, the new owner also received the instruction manual, workshop manual, and Swansea V5 registration document. Someday this rare convertible may surface again, only next time it will likely be in restored condition.

BURIED
IN A FERRARI

BY LINDA CLARK

West's body was temporarily entombed in a Texas mausoleum for two months while a court battle played out over her final request. The court ultimately ruled in her favor, after deciding that West's handwritten will was legal and that her car could be used as a coffin.

LEAVING IN STYLE

HERE THERE'S A WILL, there's a whim, and the peculiar 1977 burial of Texas oil and cattle heiress Sandra West in her vintage Ferrari shows that some whims go beyond life.

A crane lowered West and her Ferrari into the grave—but not before the story made national news. In the 2007 book *Death Lore, Texas Rituals, Superstitions and Legends of the Hereafter*, journalist Henry Wolff says that mortuary spokesman Peter Loring termed it the most unusual interment he had ever handled.

Even in Texas, where people have been buried with telephones, jugs of whiskey, and their favorite guns, Sandra West's unorthodox burial attracted attention. *The San Antonio Light* dubbed her an eccentric widow, and a teenage boy who attended her funeral called it a carnival. Journalist Ron Franscell described the $17,000 service as more festive than funereal.

It wasn't just that West wanted her blue Ferrari 330 America sports car to accompany her to the hereafter; her will also stipulated that she be buried "next to my husband, in my lace nightgown . . . in my Ferrari, with the seat slanted comfortably."

The rest of the story was just as weird. West's body was temporarily entombed in a Texas mausoleum for two months while a court battle played out over her final request. The court ultimately ruled in her favor, after deciding that West's handwritten will was legal and that her car could be used as a coffin. To complicate things, West died in California, but wanted to be buried in Texas.

Both places were a long way from New Jersey, where Sandra West was born Sandra Ilene Hara on January 2, 1939. While she was still a toddler, her parents moved to California, where they operated a small retail shop on Beverly Drive in Los Angeles.

West grew up on a quiet street in the shadow of the Beverly Hills Hotel and attended school in Beverly Hills and Los Angeles. A vivacious and dark-haired beauty, she never lacked suitors. In her early twenties, she met Texas oilman and rancher Ike West Jr., a descendant of the pioneer West family, in Vanderbilt, Texas.

After a two-year courtship, Sandra and Ike Jr. married in Las Vegas in 1965 and settled in Ike's Jr.'s restored 81-year-old colonial home in Texas. But the marriage was short-lived. After being discharged from a Los Angeles hospital, where he had undergone a crash weight-loss program, Ike Jr. was found dead in a room at the Las Vegas Flamingo Hotel in 1968.

Not long after, West fled the two-story colonial she and Ike Jr. had shared in San Antonio's historic King William district for the familiarity of Beverly Hills. Heir to Ike Jr.'s estimated $50 million fortune, she spent freely on real estate, sports cars, designer clothes, expensive jewelry, and rare stamps. She reportedly owned at least three Ferraris and a Stutz Blackhawk. Despite her flamboyant lifestyle, West was a serious philatelist and ardent student of ancient Egypt and its antiquities.

In early 1977 West suffered injuries in a traffic accident while driving her Ferrari 250 GTE. While recovering in her Beverly Hills home, she died on March 10, just a week after the crash. A coroner's inquest determined that West had died from an accidental overdose of prescription painkillers.

THE VROOM TOMB

West had been known to close friends as a practical joker, according to newspaper reports. However, friends said she had exhibited "bizarre behavior" in the months prior to her car accident.

Despite rumors of later versions, a handwritten will West created in 1972 was considered to be her last. And in a bequest worthy of the Egyptian pharaohs, she left the bulk of her multimillion-dollar estate to her brother-in-law, Sol West, on the condition that he have her buried in her blue Ferrari 330 America. Otherwise, he would receive only a pittance.

In addition to her cars, West's estate consisted of her Beverly Hills property, mineral rights, jewelry, a collection of rare stamps, and around $3 million in cash. Her unconventional burial request and her decision to leave nearly everything to Sol West triggered years of litigation among members of the Hara and West families—and even West's attorney—over validity of the will.

However, the more immediate issue was over jurisdiction—Texas versus California—and whether Sol had to carry out Sandra West's burial wishes. While a California court was deciding, West's body was allowed to be transported to San Antonio, Texas, for temporary burial.

On April 11, the Los Angeles Superior Court ruled that West's handwritten will was "unusual, but not illegal," thus allowing her Italian Ferrari to serve as a casket. The court instructed that it be placed inside a large wooden crate "to preserve the late Ms. West's dignity." An itemized budget for the funeral was included in the court order with an estimated cost of $15,000, which was $2,000 shy of the actual cost.

And so the millionaire widow of Texas oil and cattle heir Ike West Jr. was buried on May 19, 1977, in San Antonio's Masonic Cemetery, wearing a silver-colored lace nightgown, and seated as she requested at a comfortable angle behind the wheel of her blue Ferrari sports car.

The car and Sandra West were encased in a gray-painted wooden crate measuring 6 by 8 by 17 feet, according to the *San Antonio Express News*. The crate was hauled to the grave site on a flatbed truck, where a yellow crane lifted it from the truck and then lowered it into the burial ground. Standing by was a concrete mixing truck, which poured cement over and around the crate.

It was a burial fit for an Egyptian queen. It took place under the glare of television lights, and among cameras, microphones, reporters, and several hundred spectators. Television newscaster Harry Reasoner told his viewers about Sandra West's burial on the *ABC Evening News* that night, as did David Brinkley over at *NBC Nightly News*. West's burial made headlines in newspapers across America and was reported in the May 30, 1977, issue of *Time* magazine under the headline, "VVVroom Tomb."

Sandra was buried in the West family plot, adjacent to her late husband's grave. She had a simple, flat grave marker that read, "Sandra West, 1939–1977." More imposing were the large tombstones for some of the doyens of the West family, including the first-generation Texas brothers, Ike, Sol, and George, all of whom made their mark on the history of Texas cattle ranching.

It's speculated that West's other two Ferraris were sold at public auction in Los Angeles. Christie's auctioned her jewelry in 1979, and the collection sold for $885,000, which included a 4.97-carat diamond that fetched $305,000 alone.

Philatelic auctioneer Harmers International in London sold West's collection of rare stamps in 1980 for nearly $2 million. It contained early Germany and Bavaria stamps, many of which were the only known examples of their kind.

Controversy remains over which Ferrari Sandra West was buried in and whether it was the one she wanted to be buried in. It's speculated that Sol West may have substituted her wrecked 250 GTE model for her 330 America. Yet some say the California court instructed that she be buried in the wrecked one. Still others claim West wanted to be buried in her 365 GTB/4 Spyder.

In her will West requested that she be buried in her "favorite Ferrari" without specifying which one was her favorite. If she owned just one when she wrote her will in 1972, that would explain the omission. But since she owned three Ferraris at the time of her death, she took the secret of her favorite Ferrari to the grave.

THE PURLOINED 500K

BY JOHN DRANEAS

Some readers may wonder what RM Auction's liability might be here. In all likelihood, the answer is *not much*.

DIGGING INTO THE PAST

IN EARLY 2012, Frans van Haren and Tony Paalman, Dutch car collectors and business partners, proudly put their 1935 Mercedes-Benz 500K Roadster on display at the Techno Classica car show in Essen, Germany.

The two men had bought the car for $3,767,500 (including buyer's premium) at RM Auctions' 2011 sale in Monterey, California.

Life was good until the German police—executing a warrant issued by a local court—seized the 500K on the basis that it had been stolen from its rightful owner in 1945, right at the end of World War II.

The two men, who had millions invested in this car, were stunned.

The legal knots are plentiful and complicated. But let's first look at the long, strange journey of this very valuable car.

RM's 2010 Monterey catalog stated that this 500K, after being featured in the 1935 Berlin Motor Show, was sold to Hans Friedrich Prym in 1935. In the 1970s, according to the catalog, "it turned up in the collection of pioneer collector Russell Strauch." The almost four decades in between were inexplicable: "Its interim history," cited the catalog, "is unknown at this time."

That huge gap set Paalman to work. He began researching not only the car, but the owners behind it. He determined that Prym was a very wealthy man; Prym's family was an old-world industrialist powerhouse of descendants since the mid-1600s, champions of industry and entrepreneurships.

In 1935, the family company was doing extremely well—they had just invented the snap fastener used on clothing. But, according to Paalman, Prym had a dark side. "Although no one has proven that Prym was a member of the Nazi Party, he definitely did work for the Nazis," Paalman said. "The factory had been converted to manufacture airplane parts using about 600 slave laborers, many of whom died on the job."

The Prym family lost everything after the war. The final blow came in the form of approximately $30 million in damages they were forced to pay to the families of the slave laborers and fines from their convictions for cartel formation.

The family company survives today, but is no longer owned by the Pryms.

THE LEGAL CLAIMS

For this story's purposes, German law seems similar to U.S. law save for one important regard: in Germany, the owner of stolen property can have a court seize the property—to be held under court order—until the ownership can be resolved. In the U.S., the owner would have to provide strong evidence that he was likely to prevail in the litigation, and he would also have to post a bond to protect the interests of the other party.

Here, the property seizure resulted from a court filing from Prym's surviving son and grandson.

Their claim that the 500K was stolen is based upon their testimony that they had heard Prym say that "the car had been taken from them." and that the car "was stolen by the Americans."

To this day, Paalman believes the evidence was skimpy and didn't warrant the seizure of his car. He believes the filing for the warrant was made on a Saturday morning, and presented to a fill-in judge, one more sympathetic toward—or at least ignorant of—the proper seizure laws of Germany.

Paalman thinks the Pryms stand very little chance of success in the long run. He also believes the case raises very troubling issues—one being that some Germans very much want to forget everything about the grim Nazi years. Paalman also claims there has never been a case where the Americans were found to have stolen anything during their occupation of Germany.

"There are a few cases of Russians having done that, but never an American," Paalman said. "Every time the Americans confiscated any property, it was always done through proper legal means."

Let's consider some of the interesting legal issues this case raises. What would happen if the car is determined to have been stolen from Prym during the days just after World War II?

SELLER ON THE HOOK

There seems to be little doubt that the seller, which in this particular case was the Lyon Family Collection, would be liable. Under U.S. law, a seller of stolen property has no title to the property, and is therefore unable to pass good title to the innocent purchaser. Since passing legal title is of the essence of the sale, the seller would definitely owe the buyers a full refund.

The seller would then have full recourse against his seller, as he never had good title to the car either. However, that would be limited to the amount he paid for the car, not the amount he received for its sale.

That result comes from the theoretical nature of the legal action, which is "rescission." The innocent buyer is able to rescind (or unwind) the transaction, and revert each party to where they stood before the sale. That gets the buyer his purchase price back, and he just loses his profit.

And that legal concept is cumulative; that is, it channels through successive levels, from seller to seller (seven in this case), and each are entitled to full refunds. But once the chain is broken—which happens when a buyer cannot find or recover from his seller for any reason—the music stops, and he is left holding the bag. He cannot skip over his seller to reach the previous seller because he has no contractual relationship with him.

Some readers may wonder what RM's liability might be here. In all likelihood, the answer is *not much*. In an auction transaction, the auction company is not the seller, even though the buyer writes his check to them. Rather, the auction company is regarded as the seller's agent, merely assisting the seller in the transaction. The auction company may well be required to give up its commissions on the sale, but that is about it. Furthermore, all auction companies use seller and bidder contracts that make those terms clear.

Should the auction company have found out about this problem beforehand? RM, like all major auction companies, puts great effort into researching the cars

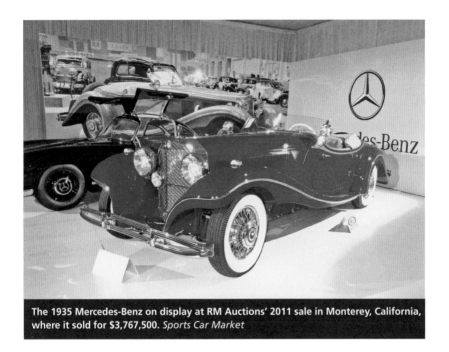

The 1935 Mercedes-Benz on display at RM Auctions' 2011 sale in Monterey, California, where it sold for $3,767,500. *Sports Car Market*

in its auctions. It doesn't want problems like this to arise, as its business models are focused on creating happy buyers. If its efforts fail, can it be held liable for its negligence?

Probably not.

Auction companies' bidder contracts make very clear that any efforts in this regard are made for their own protection. They do not assume any obligation to the bidder, who is required to perform his own investigation, if any. And that really makes perfect sense—the opposite rule would transform the auction company from a seller's agent to a seller or an insurer, which is not part of the deal.

But since we're getting into hypotheticals here, what if the auction company knew about this claim ahead of the auction? That makes things quite different.

Any sensible auction company would bring this to the attention of the seller and ask him to explain matters—after all, it's his car and therefore his problem. If the seller deals with the problem satisfactorily—or gives the auction company adequate assurances that the claim is unfounded—the auction company should be free to proceed, perhaps even without disclosure to bidders. But if the seller doesn't handle the situation adequately, then he and the auction company would be proceeding with a misrepresentation or fraud, and both parties would be liable.

In this case, German law seems similar to U.S. law—the rightful owner is protected, while the innocent purchaser is not. But in some countries, the innocent purchaser keeps the car and the rightful owner has to find and sue the thief.

Say, for example, van Haren and Paalman had purchased the car at an auction in Italy, where the law allows the innocent purchaser to keep the car. Would the German court apply the law of Italy, where they bought the car, and let them keep the 500K?

Or would the court apply German law and give it to the Pryms? And if van Haren and Paalman lost the car in the German court, what would happen when they went back to Italy to sue the seller? Would the Italian court apply Italian law to conclude that the seller gave them good title so he can't be sued, making it their problem they chose to take the car to Germany?

There's no easy answer. But enough about these hypothetical cases, as the actual case promises to be complicated enough: as of January 2013, the case was inching its way through the German courts.

Paalman and van Haren sought to have the case dismissed early in the process, as they claimed that the Prym family didn't have a legitimate claim. However, the German court ruled that the Prym family was able to prove the facts they asserted— that Hans Friedrich Prym owned the car, and that he claimed that American soldiers stole it after World War II.

The German court then ordered that the case proceed to a full trial. In the meantime, the car was placed in storage until the court determines the legal owner.

Will the Prym family get the car back or will van Haren and Paalman prove that the car is legally theirs? Only time will tell. Until then, the long, strange journey of this 1935 Mercedes-Benz 500K roadster continues.

LANCE MILLER'S QUEST

BY LINDA CLARK

There was no reason to believe it even still existed—race cars lead short, hard lives, and most end up on the scrap heap— but Miller knew that someday, somehow, he would own that car. The search for a 30-year-old race car had begun.

LEGENDARY RACERS, LEGENDARY RACETRACKS

IN THE SPRING OF 1960, three Corvettes crossed the Atlantic Ocean by ship with several tons of spare parts. They were white Corvettes, 1960-models. They disembarked at the port of Le Havre and were driven 200 miles to the town of Le Mans, France, to be prepped for the eponymous race, the world's oldest and most demanding endurance sports car race.

On June 25 and 26, 1960, this legendary race, long dominated by European cars such as Alfa Romeo and Jaguar, would for the first time feature four entries from a relatively young American brand—the Chevrolet Corvette.

Briggs Cunningham owned and entered three of those Corvettes. Painted white with blue racing stripes, the cars were identified as numbers 1, 2, and 3. When the entrants lined up for the start, biggest engines at the front, the Cunningham Corvettes occupied the first three spots.

Cunningham had given his drivers explicit instructions: "Don't take chances; finish the race!"

The number 2 car, driven by Dick Thompson and Fred Windridge, made a valiant effort. The first car out of the pits, Thompson's early lead lasted only half a lap, falling further behind when the car left the track and wound up in a sand pit. He eventually lurched free, but significant damage to the front end took hours to repair. Number 2 limped on, but frequent hard use of downshifts as the brakes began to fail blew up the engine, knocking it out of the race for good.

Number 1, driven by Briggs Cunningham and Bill Kimberly, was turned over to Kimberly, roughly two hours into the race. He lost control and the car crashed. Heavily damaged and on fire, it was out of the competition.

About this time, a hard rain moved onto the track. Most drivers slowed significantly, but John Fitch, in the number 3 Corvette, did not. The Corvette's narrow tires performed beautifully in the rain, and a switch to rain tires further boosted his confidence and traction. As other participants aquaplaned around the track, his uncanny ability to drive through the deluge allowed him to improve his position from 13th to 7th. Fitch found himself hoping it would rain for 24 hours straight!

Of course, it did not.

As co-driver Bob Grossman took over in the final stages, Fitch warned him that the car was overheating. Le Mans regulations prohibit the addition of fluids, such as coolant, except at specific intervals. Without coolant, it was unlikely the car could go on. With equal parts luck and ingenuity, the Cunningham team tiptoed their way around regulations, packing the engine and radiator with dry ice from a nearby ice cream cooler every few laps.

The crowd rallied behind the scrappy underdog Corvette throughout the final stages, and Grossman knew his job was simply to finish the race. And finish he did. Moments after crossing the line, the engine expired and the car had to be pushed back to the pits. But it was official: the Corvette was now a Le Mans competitor. A total of 55 cars had started the 24-hour race, but only 25 finished. The number 3 Corvette had finished eighth overall and even won its class.

A LIFELONG FAN

More than three thousand miles away, young Chip Miller—just 17 in 1960—was thrilled.

As cheering race fans bore witness to Cunningham's dream, the impact of the historic finish reverberated across the Atlantic and into the heart and mind of a teenaged Chip in Jenkintown, Pennsylvania.

The Number 3 Cunningham Corvette was returned to Le Mans during the summer of 2010. Here, it rests next to its automotive heirs in the Corvette racing series.
Richard Prince

As his son, Lance Miller, said years later, "I think my dad just followed that car ever since its victory. He very much knew all about it."

Chip fell in love with Corvettes early in life. All through high school and college he longed for one, and when he heard that a neighbor was selling a wrecked Corvette at a bargain price, Chip jumped at the chance. Forsaking a college education, he then took a job at a body shop to learn how to restore his prize—a white Corvette, model year 1960.

Two decades later, Chip Miller had gone from the body shop to co-founder of Carlisle Events, located in Carlisle, Pennsylvania. He and his partner Bill Miller were responsible for some of the largest and best known annual car events in the United States, including Corvettes at Carlisle.

Chip had built a life on what he loved and now had a custom-built garage filled with an impressive collection of historic Corvettes. One special example was still missing, and it was the one that inspired it all: The number 3 Le Mans Corvette.

There was no reason to believe it even still existed—race cars lead short, hard lives, and most end up on the scrap heap—but Miller knew that someday, somehow, he would own that car. The search for a 30-year-old race car had begun.

Lance Miller fulfills his father's dream at Le Mans—a small word and a firm handshake with John Fitch, the original driver of the Number 3 Corvette.
Richard Prince

In recent years Corvettes with significant racing history have sold in the neighborhood of $1 million. But back in the early 1960s, the 1960 Le Mans car, like most race cars of the day, wasn't considered anything special. Once Le Mans was over, the Cunningham Corvettes just disappeared.

Chip enlisted the aid of good friend and Corvette restorer Kevin Mackay, who took up the hunt for the Le Mans class winner. Leads were few and far between until inspiration rolled into Mackay's shop in the form of a 1967 Le Mans Corvette race car. While working on the 1967 car, Mackay noticed an inspection sheet from Le Mans that included the serial number for the car. He figured if they had the serial number for the 1967 car, why wouldn't they have one for the 1960 Corvettes?

It took six long months, but when the papers arrived at Corvette Repair, Mackay's world-famous shop in Valley Stream, New York, Mackay knew he had found the key to finding the famous 1960 Le Mans number 3 car. The inspection sheets showed the serial numbers of each Corvette raced at Le Mans that fabled year. Mackay ran the numbers and began to unravel the history of the number 3 car.

Shipped back to the United States after the race, number 3 had rattled around the country for a few years. The car eventually was parked in a Tampa warehouse until

1975, when a young Jim Ranahan stumbled across it while looking for a project car. Unpainted, with the body detached from the frame, the car didn't look like a famous, long-lost racer; it looked like a fixer-upper from a bygone era. Ranahan bought it for $300 and took it home.

Ranahan spent a year restoring it to drivable condition, and after owning it for just two years, he sold the 1960 Corvette—now red with white coves—to a man in Louisiana. The car changed hands twice more before James Walsh discovered it in a classic car showroom near the St. Louis airport in 1988. Walsh traded in his 1979 Corvette, paid the difference of $4,000, and drove it home that afternoon.

For the next five years, Walsh and his wife drove it around town, exhibiting it at area car shows. Then in 1993 he received a phone call from Kevin Mackay. Yes, Walsh still had the car, but no, he wasn't interested in selling. And Mackay wasn't the only shark circling.

Intrigued by the sudden burst of interest in his Corvette, Walsh made a short-lived attempt to track its history. He even briefly wondered if he had a Le Mans car, and he called Le Mans officials in France. He found the officials unhelpful at best and decided not to pursue it any further.

Mackay, meanwhile, was certain he'd found the prize. Without mentioning "Le Mans," "Cunningham," or even "race car," he simply kept in touch with Walsh, checking in every now and then, for the next seven years.

In August 2000 fate stepped in again. Mackay called to check in and Walsh, exhausted from a long day at work, said yes. In the end no money even changed hands—Walsh was willing to trade for a brand new, 2000 Lincoln Navigator. The arrangements were made, and after more than 40 years and seven oblivious owners later, Chip Miller had his prize.

McKay called Chip at 1:00 a.m. on a Sunday. When Chip heard his voice, he knew immediately what had happened. "Judy!" he yelled to his wife, "Judy! I got the car! We got the car!"

The red and white car was transported to Mackay's shop on Long Island, New York, where it would undergo an 18-month restoration back to its Le Mans race condition.

Miller and Mackay scheduled an autopsy of the Corvette, bringing together a panel of the most knowledgeable Corvette experts around, including both original drivers John Fitch and Bob Grossman. They all gathered at Mackay's shop on Chip Miller's 58th birthday.

The panel started by stripping away the red paint to see what lay beneath. Evidence of damage, or lack thereof, to the front right was a key factor in confirming that this was not only a Cunningham car, but the number 3 car. After eight hours of careful examination, they all agreed: this was, without a doubt, number 3.

As the day drew to a close, Chip Miller talked with the assembled team on the importance of the car and his attachment to it. This was a car he planned to keep for the rest of his life.

RESTORING A DREAM

After confirming that this was indeed the Le Mans car, the extensive restoration could now begin. To restore the car to its race-day state, which included numerous unique modifications, many custom parts had to be fabricated. It was the most extensive project Mackay's shop had ever tackled—in the end, nearly four thousand man hours, more than a year of work, and $300,000 went into Chip Miller's dream Corvette.

Forty two years after it raced at Le Mans, Chip Miller debuted his newly restored car at the Meadow Brook Concours, where it took honors for best in class. Chip's delight in the car was apparent as he happily showed it to anyone who asked.

The restored number 3 was soon featured in the Chip's Choice lineup of Special Corvettes at the August 2003 Corvettes at the Carlisle show where Chip put his dream in print in the show program:

"Dream: Take to Le Mans in June 2010 to celebrate the 50th Anniversary of its grandest race. I hope John Fitch (he'll be 92 years of age in June 2010) will be able to take some laps with me—sure, we'll take turns driving!" Unfortunately, Bob Grossman was not available—the number 3's second driver had died just three months before the car made its debut at the Meadow Brook Concours.

Chip—who so often proclaimed that "life is good"—had come within reach of fulfilling his dream of driving number 3 around Le Mans in 2010. But life is anything if predictable, and life was about to change for Chip.

Shortly after the 2003 Corvettes at Carlisle show, Chip started feeling sluggish. His legs became swollen, and he had trouble walking and breathing. The diagnosis came back: amyloidosis, a rare disease that strikes roughly three thousand people each year in the United States. This swift-moving disease is incurable, and on March 25, 2004, at 61 years of age, Chip Miller died.

From the moment he was forced to say an untimely goodbye to his father, Lance Miller knew what he had to do, even if he didn't know exactly how. Lance began emailing everyone he knew at GM and enlisting everyone he thought might be able to help to make certain his father's dream came true.

It was harder than Lance had even imagined, but in April 2010, after a year of details, arrangements, expenses, and frustrations, with the support of key players such as Mackay and Fitch, the pieces started falling into place. The number 3 Cunningham Corvette would once again board a boat bound for the Port of Le Havre.

From the moment it arrived in Le Mans, the number 3 car was treated as an honored guest.

Automotive photographer Richard Prince took photos of it on the track, flanked by the current Corvette racing vehicles, drivers, and crew. The car was then temporarily displayed in the automobile museum located at the Le Mans track before cruising 20 miles down the road to an annual British welcoming event where it was a guest of honor. A parade of the pilots saw number 3 rumbling through city streets lined with tens of thousands of cheering race fans.

John Fitch had arrived in France alongside Lance Miller. GM provided both with track credentials and unlimited access to their suite overlooking the pits. As Fitch, who had been spending his time signing autographs and enjoying the festivities, visited the pits, throngs of racing fans—most of whom had likely not even been born when Fitch last ran a lap around the track—chanted his name.

Through this unreal whirlwind of activity, race day finally arrived. Crowds swarmed around the number 3 car as it maneuvered into position for the ceremonial pre-race lap. As they waited for the signal to go, Lance asked Fitch to sign the dash of the car. Then, as he had done 50 years prior (albeit at a much slower pace), John Fitch pulled the number 3 Cunningham Corvette onto the track at Le Mans, leading 50 other Corvettes in a celebration of Corvette racing history.

In a post-lap interview, an emotional Lance Miller surveyed the cheering crowds, the pristine white, 1960 Corvette, and he knew what his father Chip would be thinking at that moment: "To be in that car and drive around that track and actually pull it off . . . life is good."

THE PONTIAC GHOST CARS

BY LINDA CLARK

Except for their glass-like coachwork, the Pontiac ghost cars, as they were more popularly known, were identical to their steel-bodied counterparts. "Complete in every detail, save for the insulating material normally applied to the inner surfaces of steel outer sheathing in production models," *Automobile Digest* noted, "it will be possible to drive the plastic Torpedo Eight car on the highway."

BIZARRE APPARITIONS

IMAGINE SEEING a transparent car on the road—in 1939.

Pontiac's drivable Plexiglas 1940 show car wasn't like anything else on the road. The first full-sized transparent car ever made in America, it bowed at General Motor's Highways and Horizons exhibit at the 1939–1940 New York World's Fair.

Pontiac's see-through body was originally styled as a 1939 Deluxe Six Four-Door Touring Sedan, but later updated with a 1940 clear Plexiglas nose clip. According to the July 1940 *Automobile Digest*, a second plastic car, a 1940 Torpedo Eight Four-Door Sedan, was built for the 1939–1940 Golden Gate International Exposition in San Francisco.

General Motors had used cutaway exhibits to dramatize new engineering and body construction features of its models over the years, and in 1930 a Cadillac

V-8 show chassis toured America. But nothing prepared World's Fair goers for the ghostly Pontiac that seemed to endow onlookers with X-ray vision.

Over 44 million people from around the globe visited the World of Tomorrow–themed World's Fair, which was billed as the biggest international event since World War I. America had hosted world fairs since the 1800s, but this was the first in the Big Apple. Conceived by a group of retired New York City policemen to lift the city and the country out of its Great Depression, it created a spectacular diversion from the crummy economy and the war clouds gathering over Europe.

Industrial designer Norman Bel Geddes fashioned the General Motors Pavilion, known as Futurama, which attempted to give fairgoers a glimpse of new products to come. It was prophetic in advancing concepts of the future, such as the nation's superhighways and its suburbs. A re-created auto dealership also let visitors see the entire line of new GM cars.

All of GM's divisions took part in the Previews of Progress. Electro-Motive Corporation displayed their then-new streamlined diesel-electric passenger locomotive. Frigidaire, which had introduced its first window-mounted room air-conditioner a year earlier, demonstrated its products.

The amazing plastic Pontiac, with its one-off body of Plexiglass instead of sheet metal, was constructed by GM's Fisher Body Division. Although it was a pioneering show car, it never spawned mass-production of plastic car bodies. *RM Auctions*

Nothing prepared World's Fair goers for the ghostly Pontiac that seemed to endow onlookers with X-ray vision. *RM Auctions*

The fair foretold much of what would become commonplace in prosperous post–World War II America. General Electric unveiled its patented fluorescent light bulb. DuPont demonstrated nylon and nylon stockings to the American public for the first time. View-Master made its debut, four years after the advent of Kodachrome color film made small photographic color images possible.

Sharing the limelight was the amazing plastic Pontiac, with its one-off body of Plexiglas instead of sheet metal. Both this transparent show car and its Torpedo Eight successor were constructed by GM's Fisher Body division. They were built to show the rigid interior bracing as well as other features, such as the working mechanism of the no-draft ventilation system used in the Uni-Steel Turret top Fisher bodies, according to *Automobile Digest*.

"The clear Plexiglas was chosen solely for its transparency," Pontiac historian John A. Gunnell said. "The strength and safety of all-steel bodies were really the point of this display—not just the 1939–1940 Pontiacs.

"The see-through cars also revealed GM's automatic door locking mechanisms, concealed door hinges, details of the independent front suspension, safety hood lock, new sealed beam headlights, improved deck lid supports, column gearshift controls and all the steering gear. Since most of these items were common to all GM cars, the Plexiglas Pontiacs were engineering showcases for the entire product range."

Except for their glass-like coachwork, the Pontiac ghost cars, as they were more popularly known, were identical to their steel-bodied counterparts. "Complete in every detail, save for the insulating material normally applied to the inner surfaces of steel outer sheathing in production models," *Automobile Digest* noted, "it will be possible to drive the plastic Torpedo Eight car on the highway."

Yet GM had never before considered using Plexiglas—a transparent, tough, flexible plastic substitute for glass—in regular production vehicles. This was in contrast to the soybean-derived plastic car Henry Ford patented in 1942. Ford hoped to make his plastic material a replacement for the metals used in cars. But World War II intervened, and when car production resumed after the war, Ford's experimental plastic endeavor diminished into oblivion.

Acrylic glass was developed by various laboratories in 1928 (variants date as far back as the mid-1800s), but in 1933 German chemist Otto Rohm trademarked his discovery as Plexiglas. Rohm and Hass Company (now part of the Dow Chemical Company) was the first to market the shatterproof plastic in 1933. Edmund Green, a former Rohm and Haas public relations man, told auto journalist Ken Gross in

Pontiac's incredible "Ghost Car" cost $25,000 to build, which is about $390,000 in inflation-adjusted dollars today. After the World's Fair closed on October 27, 1940, the Plexiglas show cars were displayed at Pontiac dealerships nationwide.
RM Auctions

Although it had acquired a few chips and cracks over the decades, the Plexiglas Pontiac had only 86 miles on it and was structurally sound when it sold at auction in 2011. *RM Auctions*

General Motors built the transparent show cars to display its new Uni-Steel Turret-top bodies. Despite their eerie ghost-like appearance, the Plexiglas Pontiacs were identical to their steel counterparts and could be driven on the highway. *RM Auctions*

1982 that R&H likely supplied Fisher Body with Plexiglas sections and the GM division did the rest.

No documentation exists that suggests a collaboration between GM and Rohm and Haas, but Green told Gross that he recalled seeing photos of the Plexiglas Pontiacs in old Rohm and Hass files, and remembered that R&H supplied GM with plastic panels for later show cars. *Automobile Digest* chronicled with lavish illustration the Fisher Body craftsmen heating, hand-sanding, molding, and shaping the clear plastic body panels, so there's little doubt that Fisher crafted the cars.

"And it's reasonable to assume that Rohm and Haas at least supplied the sheet stock to Fisher," historian Gunnell said.

Some clever detailing helped popularize the nickname "ghost car." In both show cars, all the hoses, grommets, mats, running boards—even the U.S. Royal tires—were molded in white rubber. The engine block, horns, air cleaner, and many mechanical parts were painted white. Glamorous touches included chrome plating of the instrument panel, window surrounds and all the nuts and bolts. The structural metal underneath was copper washed. All combined, it gave the cars an eerie look, especially at night.

The New York Times of May 4, 1939, showed the 1940 Plexiglas Pontiac Deluxe Six Touring Sedan on its way to the fair. Deluxe Six models used the GM B-body and sat on 120-inch wheelbases. The show car had Pontiac's 85-horsepower, 222.7-cubic-inch L-head six-cylinder engine, coil spring independent front suspension, live rear axle with semi-elliptic leaf springs, and four-wheel hydraulic drum brakes. Power was routed through a three-speed, column-mounted manual transmission. The ghost car cost around $25,000 to build, or almost $390,000 in inflation-adjusted dollars today.

Pontiac's second ghost car had the 1940 Torpedo Eight's larger GM C-body and rode on a longer 122-inch wheelbase. Power came from a 103-horsepower, 248.9-cubic-inch L-head eight-cylinder engine which featured a new-high-compression cylinder head. The drivetrain was identical to the Deluxe Six ghost car.

Although it was never used for mass-produced car bodies, Plexiglas found a market in military aircraft. Wind-, weather-, and shatter-resistant, it was the ideal replacement for glass in bomber and fighter noses, canopies and gun turrets. After World War II, Rohm and Haas developed countless civilian applications, including signs, lighting fixtures, submersibles, aquariums, sport stadiums, railroad cars, and automobiles. With the capability to custom-mold it into almost any shape—and

Pontiac's transparent "Ghost Car" still had its original all-white U.S. Royal tires and running boards when it sold to an anonymous bidder for $308,000, including buyer's premium, at an RM Auctions sale in Michigan in 2011. *RM Auctions*

also to cast it in countless colors with new dyes—Plexiglas remains a significant commercial, military, and medical material. Plexiglas is now used in everything from bone implants to dental fillings.

GHOSTLY REMINDERS OF THE PAST

After the World's Fair officially closed on October 27, 1940, both ghost cars were displayed at Pontiac dealerships nationwide, according to the GM Heritage Center. Then the original Deluxe Six ghost car was displayed at the Smithsonian Institution in Washington, DC, from 1942 to 1948. When its styling became outmoded, it was sold to H&H Pontiac of Gettysburg, Pennsylvania.

In 1962 another Pennsylvania Pontiac dealer, Arnold Motors in Carlisle, acquired the car and installed full seats to replace the temporary cutaway cushions used for display. It appeared at the first annual meet of the new Pontiac-Oakland Club International in 1973, where it was bought by Don Barlup, a restaurateur from Cumberland, Pennsylvania.

By that time the car's Plexiglas had become clouded with age—despite having just 70 miles on its odometer—so Barlup took it to S&H Pontiac in nearby Harrisburg for a spruce-up. The crew at the dealership removed each plastic panel, carefully cleaned and waxed both sides of each panel, and then put the car back together.

Barlup took the car to the Dutch Wonderland Classic Car Auction in Lancaster in 1979, where collector car dealer Leo Gephart bought it.

About a year later, Gephart sold it to car historian and collector Frank Kleptz of Indiana.

Kleptz owned the ghost car until he died in 2010. The Pontiac was drivable, but even Kleptz, who competed in the Great American Race 10 times and won its Spirit of the Event award, put fewer than a dozen miles on it. The sun tended to shine in and bake the car's occupants, and road stones easily damaged the Plexiglas panels.

In 2011 an anonymous bidder bought the Pontiac ghost car for $308,000, including buyer's premium, at the RM Auctions sale held in conjunction with the Concours d'Elegance of America in Plymouth, Michigan. "Even the family doesn't know who bought the car," said David Kleptz, Frank's son, in 2012.

According to the auction catalog, the ghost car had only 86 miles on it. Although it had acquired a few chips and cracks over the decades, it was structurally sound and cosmetically clear. It still had its original, all-white U.S. Royal tires and white rubber running boards. The only recent mechanical work had been replacing the fuel lines.

The fate of the second ghost car remains a mystery. It seems that its last documented sighting was its 1940 appearance at the Golden Gate Exposition.

THE GREEN BAY PARTS PACKER

BY LINDA CLARK

Some of the trailers hadn't been unsealed in over 25 years. The dramatic opening of those trailers was chronicled by Angelo Van Bogart in *Old Cars Weekly*. Incredibly, the first trailer Fisette opened had two 1970 Chevelle SS 454 hardtops in it.

TITLETOWN'S FINEST

"EVERYONE MUST LEAVE something behind when he dies. It doesn't matter what you do, so long as you change something from the way it was before you touched it," wrote Ray Bradbury in his 1953 classic, *Fahrenheit 451*. Five decades later, Don Schlag—known as the guy who left behind 21 semi-trailers of parts and cars—touched many lives and changed them.

Schlag's lifelong passion for collecting (and hoarding) Chevrolet performance parts ended up helping other hobbyists restore cars or even just keep them on the road. Around his hometown of Green Bay, Wisconsin, he was affectionately nicknamed "Dumpster Don" for his obsession with hoarding parts. His favored brand was General Motors because he was a dyed-in-the-wool Chevy guy.

Most of the parts Schlag put away were used, many were new old stock (NOS), and nearly all were rare. So were the unrestored, original low-mileage cars he saved. Some of these cars were Yenko Camaros, LS6 Chevelles, and ultra high-performance Corvettes.

Schlag began amassing his collection in the late 1950s while working for his father at the family's John Deere dealership in Green Bay. In addition to scouring local salvage yards and swap meets for parts, Schlag also bought brand-new ones from the local Chevy dealer, Broadway Chevrolet. He stored them in the basement of his father's implement store.

Corvettes were Schlag's first love, and he was known locally as a fuel-injection specialist. But he often convinced 'Vette owners who were having trouble with their injection units to swap them for a conventional induction system. Several hobbyists have speculated that this is how Schlag came to own so many fuel injection units.

Whatever his quirks, Schlag's single-minded determination to squirrel away Chevy muscle-car parts was awe-inspiring. He was frequently seen at swap meets in Milwaukee and Elkhart Lake, Wisconsin, as well as in Chicago. Schlag seldom drove one of his pristine high-performance cars though—people usually recall seeing him in either a beat-up station wagon or a rusted-out El Camino.

Schlag drove his recreational vehicle to California every year—with a trailer in tow—to search for parts. He was usually gone for several weeks and always returned home with a packed trailer. Schlag lived in a modest house adjacent to the Deere dealership that was crammed with Chevy parts. You couldn't step much farther than a few feet inside the front door without stumbling over crankshafts, camshafts, carburetors, and cylinder heads.

Larry Fisette, owner of DePere Auto Center in Wisconsin, stands among the 21 semitrailers of Chevrolet muscle cars and parts he bought from the Don Schlag estate. Fisette, a 46-year veteran of the car business, spent months opening each trailer, sorting the parts, and organizing them in a warehouse. *Old Cars Weekly*

After his father passed away, and the Deere dealership was liquidated in the early 1970s, Schlag moved his collection of cars and parts into semi-trailers (ironically, an auto parts store went up where the former implement dealership had been). During the fuel shortages of the late 1970s and early 1980s, Schlag became the local go-to guy if you wanted to swap your Chevy's thirsty big-block for a smaller engine. Schlag was also known to exchange the big-blocks for thriftier small-blocks in his own Chevys.

Acquaintances described Schlag as quiet and self-contained—unless the subject was cars. Then he was both knowledgeable and animated when he spoke, especially about Chevy muscle cars. But it's hard to find anyone who remembers seeing Schlag driving any collector cars other than his Corvettes from the late 1950s to early 1970s. He became more secretive about his cars and stockpile of parts as he got older. This may have been due to a couple of unsettling incidents; there was a robbery at the implement store in the early 1970s, and someone tried to steal one of his Corvettes from a local parking lot a few years later.

Neither event stopped Schlag from buying cars or parts, but he began immediately hiding them in his growing fleet of trailers. Eventually, even the trailers disappeared from their customary parking spots in Green Bay. To thwart thieves, Schlag occasionally moved the trailers to new locations, all within just a few

In addition to15 vehicles, Don Schlag's inventory from five decades of collecting included over 100 complete engines, around 25 of which were big-blocks. Several of the big-blocks, like the ones in the forefront, were fuel-injected. *Old Cars Weekly*

miles of his home. In the early 1990s, after one of his trailers was broken into and some of its contents stolen, Schlag reportedly welded some of the doors shut, let the air out of the tires, and parked the trailers end-to-end to make entry that much harder.

CHANGING HANDS

By the time Schlag died on June 2, 2005, at age 67, he had salted away over 50 years' worth of parts and cars in 21 separate trailers. In addition to tons of parts, they contained 15 vehicles, 12 of which were Chevrolet muscle cars. The others were a 1979 International Scout Diesel, a dune buggy Schlag had built as a young man, and a 1972 Mercedes-Benz 280 SE 3.5-liter that had belonged to Schlag's father.

Schlag's sister, Joanne Stepien, was executor of his will. Schlag's two all-original first-generation Corvettes went to his nephews. One was a 1957 Corvette Fuelie with optional big fuel tank and large brakes, and the other a 1957 Corvette Dual Quad, also with factory racing brakes and fuel tank. It's unknown whether either of them had ever been raced.

The rest of Schlag's collection was purchased by Larry Fisette, who owns De Pere Auto Center and Riverside Auto Body in the town of De Pere, just six miles south of Green Bay. A 46-year veteran of the automotive business, Fisette bought the 21 trailers along with the cars and parts that were in Schlag's home and garage.

Fisette did yeoman's work over the next several months opening each trailer, sorting the parts, and organizing them in a warehouse.

Some of the trailers hadn't been unsealed in over 25 years. The dramatic opening of those trailers was chronicled by Angelo Van Bogart in *Old Cars Weekly*. Incredibly, the first trailer Fisette opened had two 1970 Chevelle SS 454 hardtops in it. Other trailers had only shelving in them, while others were stuffed from floor to ceiling with parts.

In addition to the cars, the inventory contained over a hundred complete engines (an estimated 25 big-block and the rest small-block) plus new Corvette side exhaust pipes and radios, Yenko Nova and Camaro parts, and a whole lot more. There were also fuel-injection units, transmissions, intake and exhaust manifolds, new Holley four-barrel carburetors, cylinder heads, wheels, racing Corvette gas tanks, oil filters and more.

Except for the 1967 Corvette 427 Tri-Power roadster and one of the Camaros, Fisette sold almost the entire treasure trove in early 2006 to another collector, Scott

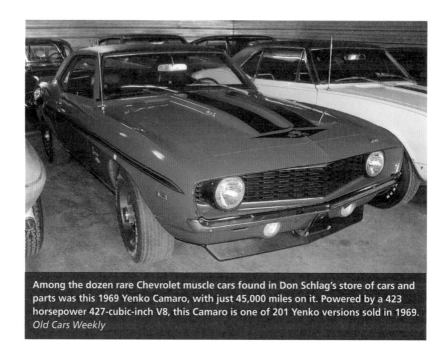

Among the dozen rare Chevrolet muscle cars found in Don Schlag's store of cars and parts was this 1969 Yenko Camaro, with just 45,000 miles on it. Powered by a 423 horsepower 427-cubic-inch V8, this Camaro is one of 201 Yenko versions sold in 1969. *Old Cars Weekly*

Milestone of Bethesda, Maryland. Milestone is known for his world-class General Motors muscle car and Cadillac dream car collection.

It took Milestone weeks of packing—with the help of five other hobbyists and several semis, trucks, and motor homes—to haul the huge inventory to his storage facility in Maryland in February 2006. He spent many more weeks just cataloging the parts and stocking them on shelves.

Milestone kept a few of the muscle cars and some of the spare parts that went with them before selling the remainder of the collection. Through various auctions, both traditional and online, the bulk of the cars and parts were sold to other hobbyists over the next three years. Thanks to Milestone's generosity, two of the Chevy muscle cars he kept were loaned to the Antique Automobile Club of America's (AACA) museum in Hershey, Pennsylvania.

One was an original, unrestored 1970 LS6 Chevelle SS hardtop, which became part of a permanent exhibit at the AACA museum in the spring of 2009. Still sporting its original blue paint with white stripes, the monster Chevelle is powered by Chevy's 450-horsepower, 454-cubic-inch V-8. In 1970, only 4,475 LS6 Chevelles were built. They also came in a convertible. The enormous weight of the engine and the comparatively weak frame of the car made it hard for Chevrolet to manufacture them on a large scale. Most were built to order and primarily bought by drag racers. This car was housed in the very first trailer Larry Fisette opened in late 2005, and it was last registered in 1975.

The other car loaned to the museum was a 1971 Camaro Z/28, also in original, unrestored condition. The car's 330-horsepower V-8 350-cubic-inch engine was part of the $786.75 optional Z/28 package that also included dual exhausts, Posi-Traction rear axle, sport suspension, heavy-duty radiator, rear deck spoiler, outside mirrors, plus special instrumentation, wheels, tires, grille, emblems, and paint. It's one of 4,862 Camaros with Z28 trim produced in 1971. Milestone's car is Burnt Orange with black stripes. It was part of a special Camaro and Firebird exhibit at the AACA museum from October 2009 to April 2010.

Collectors remain divided on whether Schlag was a man with a mission or a packrat without purpose. But no one denies that his stockpile of rare parts and cars has helped Chevy muscle-car fanatics and brought enjoyment to many others.

HEAVY ON CHEVY

Fifteen vehicles were found in the 21 semi-trailers of cars and parts accumulated over five decades by Don Schlag in Wisconsin. All were in unrestored, original condition. Here they are:

1. 1957 Corvette Fuelie with racing fuel tank and brakes.
2. 1957 Corvette Dual Quad with racing fuel tank and brakes.
3. 1963 Corvette fuel-injected coupe.
4. 1964 Corvette roadster, fuel injected four-speed with both tops.
5. 1967 Corvette roadster 427 Tri-Power, 37,000 miles.
6. 1974 Corvette coupe 454 big-block, 14,000 miles.
7. 1967 Camaro RS/SS coupe, four-speed 350-cubic-inch V-8.
8. 1969 Yenko Camaro, 45,000 miles.
9. 1971 Camaro Z/28 four-speed with 330 horsepower V-8.
10. 1970 Chevelle SS 454 automatic, bucket seats, color blue.
11. 1970 Chevelle SS 454 four-speed, bench seat, color gold.
12. 1970 or 1971 Monte Carlo V-8, junk condition.
13. 1972 Mercedes-Benz 280 SE 3.5-liter.
14. 1979 International Scout Diesel.
15. Dune buggy built by Don Schlag.

TRAINLOAD OF BUGATTIS

BY LINDA CLARK

When the truckloads of Bugattis arrived in Mulhouse that April, Schlumpf reportedly greeted them armed with a whip to chase away onlookers.

STEAL OF A DEAL

BUGATTI AUTOMOBILES are among the most coveted of collectibles. A 1936 Type 57SC Atlantic coupe sold in 2010 for over $28 million in a private sale brokered by the Gooding & Company auction firm. That sale blew away the $9.7 million paid for a 1931 Type 41 Royale at auction in 1987.

In a rare bargain, a 1925 Brescia Type 22 roadster that had been submerged in a Swiss lake for more than 70 years over a tax dispute sold to Peter Mullin of California at Bonhams's Retromobile in Paris for $345,000.

But collector Fritz Schlumpf of France scored the greatest Bugatti bargain of all time in 1964, when he bought 30 Bugattis—the largest collection in the United States at that time—from John W. Shakespeare of Illinois for just $85,000.

Shakespeare wanted to unload his collection because it was taking up so much of his time that he was getting out of shape. He was a wealthy amateur sports car racer, water skier, and skydiver from the small city of Centralia, about 60 miles east of St. Louis. His father was William Shakespeare, inventor of the level-winding fishing reel, who earned a fortune manufacturing tackle.

In addition to owning real estate, the younger Shakespeare was a partner in the Shakespeare Oil Company of Salem, Illinois. Born in 1905, he had been educated at Pittsburgh's Carnegie Institute of Technology and at Harvard.

Shakespeare had begun racing Porsches and Ferraris during the 1950s and bought an imported-car dealership that he renamed Shakespeare Motors. He was bitten by the Bugatti bug when he bought a Type 55 roadster by phone after seeing an ad in a sports car magazine.

In 1956 Shakespeare bought the crown jewel of his Bugatti collection, a 12.7-liter Type 41 Royale Park Ward limousine, for reportedly less than $10,000. Only six Royales were built, and the chassis alone sold for around $30,000 in 1927. Shakespeare bought his Royale from London Bugatti dealer and racer Jack Lemon Burton.

Dancing on its radiator cap was the prized symbol of all Royales—a silver elephant sculpted by Rembrandt Bugatti, brother of founder Ettore.

Schlumpf, a wealthy industrialist, had dreamed of owning a Bugatti since childhood. He purchased a Type 35B Grand Prix car just before World War II and added a Type 57 shortly after the war.

Schlumpf was a Swiss citizen born in Italy in 1906. After his mother was widowed, she moved the family to her hometown of Mulhouse in Alsace, France. Upon completing his education, Schlumpf found employment in the textile industry and later started his own business as a wool broker. In 1935 Schlumpf and his older brother Hans founded a wool products company and went on to earn their fortune through the acquisition of woolen mills in France's Alsace region. Schlumpf's assets grew in the postwar years to include an estate at Malmerspach.

In 1957 Schlumpf bought an unused textile mill in Mulhouse to house his growing—but secret—car collection, which he hoped to turn into a museum. He was especially enamored of the work of Ettore Bugatti, who had from 1909 to 1939 created the world's fastest and most stylish cars in his workshop in the Alsace town of Molsheim. Bugatti died in 1947, but the company lasted until 1956.

In 1962 alone, Schlump bought nearly 50 Bugattis. In the spring of 1963, he acquired 14 of Ettore Bugatti's personal cars, including his 14.7-liter Type 41 Royale Coupe Napoleon. The lot included many Bugatti engines, molds, and parts. And in 1964 Schlumpf bought John Shakespeare's 30 Bugattis.

Negotiations for Shakespeare's collection had begun in 1962 after Schlumpf obtained a copy of the Bugatti Register and sent letters to each owner expressing his interest in purchasing their cars. He also sent a personal letter to Bugatti historian Hugh Conway, the British publisher of the register, seeking his help in finding potential sellers. Schlump demanded "cars must be in perfect working order from mechanical and bodywork point of view" and noted he was prepared to pay well.

Shakespeare had previously expressed interest in selling his collection for $105,000, the amount he reportedly paid for it. Along with Hugh Conway, Bugatti club member Bob Shaw of Wheaton, Illinois, acted as liaison between Shakespeare and Schlumpf. Although he was interested in the collection, Schlumpf wanted to pay only $70,000 "if the cars are impeccable" and requested an inventory of serial numbers as well as photos of the cars.

Buyer and seller chose Shaw to inspect Shakespeare's collection in early 1963, and his report to Schlumpf was less than enthusiastic. Shakespeare's cars were stored in a converted foundry in the tiny village of Hoffman, about 7 miles west of Centralia. At the time of Shaw's visit, five of the Bugattis were in pieces for restoration. Shakespeare informed Shaw that Nevada casino owner and famous car collector Bill Harrah was interested in the Type 41 Royale limousine, but that he might accept a loss on his Bugattis if all 30 were kept together.

When the train finally arrived at its destination, collector Fritz Schlumpf greeted the authorities and other parties with a whip to scare off any motorsport vagabonds who might try anything fishy at the sight of 30 Bugattis.

Shaw told Schlumpf that most of Shakespeare's cars were parked on a dirt floor in a building with broken windows and a leaky roof. Many were in a state of disassembly and hadn't run for more than a year. But this didn't dishearten Schlumpf, who raised his offer to $85,000 and hoped the Bugattis could be shipped by spring.

WRONG SIDE OF THE TRACKS

What followed instead was a year of wrangling after Shakespeare informed Schlumpf that while readying the Bugattis for departure, he discovered a crack in the Royale's huge straight-eight engine block, for which Schlumpf recommended welding the iron casting. At one point, Shakespeare threatened to break up his collection. Schlumpf accused him of extortion and threatened to bring legal action.

Eventually buyer and seller came to terms. Shakespeare chose the Southern Railway System to transport the Bugattis to New Orleans for their ocean voyage to Le Havre, France, where the 30 Bugattis were trucked for the 430-mile drive to Mulhouse.

Cunningham outlined the route the cars would take. Otwell considered the height, length, and weight of each Bugatti to plan the loading order for the cars on three bi-level auto-rack cars. This required careful computation, as the Bugattis varied greatly in style, weight, and size, from a 7-foot electric carriage to the huge 18-feet-11-inch Royale limousine.

On March 30, 1964, the 30 Bugattis were carefully winched aboard the three open auto carriers parked on a rail siding next to Shakespeare's Hoffman, Illinois, shop. Loading began at 8:30 in the morning and it was 7:00 p.m. before the last of the tie-down chains was fastened. Southern Railway master mechanic R. R. Ray and one of Shakespeare's mechanics helped guide the Bugattis up the ramps of the auto carriers.

The 30 Bugattis arrived safely at Southern's Oliver Yard in New Orleans, where they were unloaded and hauled to dockside on flatbed trucks by the shipping firm of Dennis Sheen Company. They were then loaded aboard the Dutch freighter Grotedyk by Texas Transport and Terminal Company. The Grotedyk left New Orleans for Le Havre, France, on April 4.

When the truckloads of Bugattis arrived in Mulhouse that April, Schlumpf reportedly greeted them armed with a whip to chase away onlookers.

In 1965 Schlumpf transformed one of his mills into a restoration shop that employed seven mechanics, three bodywork specialists, five painters, and two upholsterers. Work on displaying his collection began in 1966, although converting his Mulhouse factory to the Schlumpf Museum took several years. Internal walls that had separated production areas were removed from the building. The newly created exhibition space was subdivided into districts of 10 to 20 cars each. They were surrounded by miles of wide, tiled walkways with names like Avenue Schlumpf and Rue Royale.

The money that fueled the car collection came from the Schlumpf brothers' textile mills. By the late 1960s the textile industry was moving to Asia and profits were falling. In 1971 Fritz Schlumpf was able to buy the mills of one of his struggling competitors. But in 1977, while his workers were on strike and occupying the mills, they discovered Schlumpf's hidden collection. By then it had grown to six hundred cars—including 123 Bugattis—three restaurants, and over eight hundred reproduction Pont Alexandre III lamp posts.

Fritz and Hans Schlumpf declared bankruptcy and fled to their native Switzerland, where they became permanent residents of a hotel in Basel. The strikers opened the collection to the public, but in 1979 a bankruptcy liquidator ordered the building closed and sold it to a group that included the city of Mulhouse, the Alsace region, the Paris Auto Show and the Automobile Club of France. Today the museum is considered a National Heritage by the French government and the collection cannot be exported or dispersed.

The two brothers were tried in absentia for tax evasion and convicted. Fritz was able to visit his beloved collection once more before he died in 1992 at age 86. There were two so-called reserve collections. One was located in the Mulhouse museum and contained some unrestored cars, chassis, and spare parts. Most of those cars have been restored by the French government and put on display.

A second reserve was stored in villages in Malmerspach and contained 62 cars, among them about 16 Bugattis, that never belonged to the Mulhouse museum and thus were not protected. But they had been seized by the bankruptcy court to cover Schlumpf's bills. They were awarded to Schlumpf's widow, Arlette, in 1999 to settle a lawsuit Fritz had filed against the French government in the late 1970s.

Arlette arranged for the sale of the Malmerspach collection, through collector car dealers Jaap Braam Ruben of the Netherlands and France's Bruno Vendiesse, before she died in 2008. Peter Mullin of California bought many of the cars, including six Shakespeare Bugattis, for his own museum in Oxnard, former site of Otis Chandler's museum of vintage cars and motorcycles. Mullin's extensively remodeled museum is dedicated to French cars of the art deco era.

The ill-fated Shakespeare was found murdered in the basement of his Illinois home in 1975. Although suspects in ten states and four countries were questioned, the case remains unsolved.

Although only 123 cars among the more than 500 in the Schlumpf Collection at the National Automobile Museum in Mulhouse are Bugattis, they were the object of Fritz Schlumpf's obsession.

Bugattis, some historians say, are not like other cars. They were the single-minded reflection of Ettore Bugatti's vision of sports, racing, and luxury cars. In that respect, Fritz Schlumpf and John Shakespeare's collections were two men's obsession with another man's obsession.

THE AMPHICAR

BY LINDA CLARK

"I've driven many types of cars and there's no automotive experience that compares to the thrill of driving an Amphicar into and out of the water," Mathiowetz said. "No matter how much you know about an Amphicar, and how much confidence you have in its abilities, the transition from land to water will make your heart race every time."

THE SPORTS CAR THAT SWIMS

FOR SHEER NOVELTY, few vehicles matched the Amphicar. It solved the Sunday afternoon dilemma of whether to take the car out for a drive or take the boat for a cruise on the lake.

The Amphicar did both, and it guaranteed to attract a crowd.

Billed as "The Sports Car that Swims," the diminutive-but-buoyant Amphicar was built in Germany from 1961 to 1968 and remains the world's only mass-produced amphibious passenger car.

The notion that a land vehicle could swim was not new. Amphibious carriages dated back to the 1700s, and Oliver Evans invented a steam-powered amphibious vehicle in 1805 to dredge Philadelphia's docks. But until the late1920s, most efforts to combine car and boat involved either putting wheels and axles on a boat or putting a boat on a modified car chassis.

Later, a broad range of amphibious recreation, expedition, and search & rescue vehicles emerged. But the most successful amphibians were military, the most familiar being the U.S. Army's DUKW—known among GIs as the Duck—a six-wheel-drive amphibious truck that saw combat during World War II and the

Korean War. General Motors built the vehicles, which the U.S. military originally rejected. The DUKW proved its worth during a rescue of stranded U.S. Coast Guard sailors during a heavy storm. A fleet of DUKWs are still in use as sightseeing boats at the Wisconsin Dells attraction in Wisconsin.

Sadly, the Amphicar was not nearly as seaworthy as the sturdy DUKW. The Amphicar's parents were German inventor Hans Trippel and wealthy German industrialist Harald Quandt. Trippel's nautically inspired Amphicar was the first marketable civilian floating car. Quandt, an Amphicar enthusiast, funded its launch.

Quandt's business empire included a 30 percent stake in Bavarian Motor Works (BMW) and nearly 10 percent in Daimler-Benz. As part owner of over two hundred companies, Quandt had no problem securing factory space for the Amphicar, negotiating the purchase of parts from other manufacturers and establishing a distribution network.

AN AMBITIOUS YOUNG MAN

At age 25, Trippel had put propellers on his race car, which led to the creation of his first amphibious car in 1932. His little front-drive two-seater swam, but not well. He went on to develop various four- and six-cylinder amphibious cars, some with four-wheel drive. In between amphibians, he designed several non-amphibious cars, including the Norwegian-built Troll.

Germany's armed forces used Trippel's floating four-wheel-drive passenger cars, and Germany's armed forces used amphibious sedans during World War II. Ferdinand Porsche's famed Volkswagen Schwimmwagen became a staple of the Wehrmacht and Waffen-SS's amphibious fleets, but even Dr. Porsche bought a Trippel amphibious car to study how it worked.

After the war, Tripple continued his pioneering work with amphibians and unveiled a civilian Eurocar with an Austin A35 engine at the 1959 Geneva Motor Show. It was marketed two years later as the Amphicar with a four-cylinder British Triumph Herald engine. Trippel wanted to base his Amphicar on the VW engine and chassis, but American marine laws prohibited air-cooled engines.

Working on a budget, the Quandt design team relied on existing parts. Engine ancillaries, taillights, and indicators came from England; the steel bodies, instruments, switches, and other electrical fittings, suspension system, and seaworthy gearbox from Germany. The nylon propellers came from Denmark, and the sealed-beam headlights from America. The wide whitewall tires came from Italy, Denmark, and Germany.

Amphicars were built by IWK, a Quandt subsidiary, in factories in Borsig, in West Berlin, and Lubeck, Trippel's hometown. Just 35 cars were built in 1960, and although a production run of 100,000 cars was IWK's break-even volume, only 3,878 Amphicars were ever built. All were four-passenger convertibles and were called the 770, named for the Amphicar's top speeds of 7 knots on water and 70 miles per hour on land.

Designed for the American and European leisure markets, Amphicars were offered in Regatta Red, Beach White, Lagoon Blue, and Fjord Green. All had white folding cloth tops, except for Beach White cars, which had black tops. Honoring its birthplace, the Amphicar's steering wheel hub depicted a rendering of Holstentor, the western entrance to Lubeck, a port city on the Baltic Sea.

THE BIG (APPLE) DEBUT

Amphicars debuted at the 1961 New York Auto Show and at the Miami, Florida, Boat Show. From 1964 Amphicars were sold in the United Kingdom. Advertised as a way to save marina fees, a total of 3,046 were sold in the United States, and the rest ended up in Europe. For use as a rescue vehicle, IWK offered an optional stretcher that was mounted to the rear of the Amphicar.

The 14-foot-long Amphicar had 9.5 inches of ground clearance for easy travel up and down the boat launch. Optional rear bumper guards shielded the propellers from running aground in shallow water. The rear-mounted 43-horsepower Triumph Herald engine drove the wheels through a two-part, four-speed Hermes gearbox. It delivered four speeds and reverse on land, and forward and reverse gears on water. The transfer lever sat next to the conventional gearshift on the center console.

Once on the launch pad, the Amphicar driver simply had to put the bilge plug in, secure the front luggage deck, flip up the lower locks to seal the doors and drive into the water.

Once afloat, the driver switched the water transmission into forward and the propellers took over. The front wheels then acted as rudders. The Amphicar had only 14 inches of freeboard, so avoiding wakes with the top down was a must if you didn't want to get wet.

To exit the water, the driver had only to steer the Amphicar toward land, engage first gear before the Amphicar hit the ground, and once the wheels were on land, disengage water drive.

If any water got into the car, the Amphicar's electric 6-gallon-per-minute bilge pump could be activated by a dashboard switch. Bilge water was ejected through an outlet at the rear. Amphicars were equipped with navigational lights, marine horn, engine fan, and a delayed starter, which could be overriden. Optional equipment included a radio, anchor, life preservers, distress flares, fire extinguisher, and paddle.

The Amphicar's steel body/hull was made watertight by continuous welds and lead seals of the joints. Doors had double locks and door openings were sealed with twin rubber strips. Because dual licensing was required in most states, Amphicars often sported Coast Guard registration numbers on their fenders. Whether used in salt water or fresh, Amphicars came with a six-month or 6,000-mile warranty.

Amphicars rode on an 82.7-inch wheelbase and had four-wheel independent coil-spring suspension. On land, the Herald inline four-cylinder engine required a bit of shifting, but the car cruised easily at 70 miles per hour. The high, aft-mounted engine gave the Amphicar a clumsy 40-60 weight distribution and chronic oversteer. The Amphicar's narrow 6.40 x 13 tires also contributed to the car's mediocre handling on land, but narrow tires made better rudders than wider tires.

Rust always threatened to put a damper on the Amphicar's fun, not only of the steel hull but of the linkages and cables inside it. Seals shrank over time, allowing tiny amounts of water to seep in and begin the corrosion process. Owners also had to dry their brakes after each swim and frequently grease brake linkages and universal joint bearings.

New Jersey–based Amphicar Corp. was IWK's American sales and distribution arm. Its president, Englishman Charles A. "Tony" Haigh, launched a multimedia ad blitz for the Amphicar. Radio and TV stations used Amphicars for disaster coverage. Sporting goods retailers and boating outfitters featured Amphicars among the rifles, fishing reels, and life jackets

In 1964 Amphicar joined Pepsi-Cola for a splash into the water in a "Come alive! You're in the Pepsi generation" TV ad. As part of the promotion, Pepsi bottlers were offered the chance to buy Amphicars at a $1,200 discount. Several bottlers took advantage of the offer and used Amphicars in various promotions. Afterward, they sold them to friends and employees. In 1965 British racing legend Stirling Moss was seen in print ads piloting an Amphicar down the Thames River in London.

Amphicar buyers included U.S. President Lyndon Johnson, who was often seen piloting his Lagoon Blue amphibian on the lake at his Texas ranch. Johnson reportedly liked to pile unsuspecting visitors into the car and then career into the lake (exclaiming to everyone that the brakes were broken). Johnson's press secretary, Pierre Salinger, also bought an Amphicar.

Mechanix Illustrated's Tom McCahill predicted the Amphicar owner would be the hit of the season at the local lake, while *Car and Driver* deemed the Amphicar a lousy car and even worse boat. A reviewer in the November 23, 1963, issue of *The New Yorker* was more impressed with the combination car-boat, calling it delightful.

In 1965 two Amphicars waddled down Alaska's Yukon River, and two others crossed the English Channel in 1968, miraculously surviving gale-force winds and 20-foot swells.

Amphicars were originally priced at around $3,300—not a cheap car in the early 1960s—but the price reduced in later years to about $2,800. Nevertheless, sales fell short of expectations, and the Amphicar didn't last long enough for the Quandt team to make improvements. Bigger engines, a fiberglass hull, four-wheel drive, flotation gear, more leg room, and chromed brass fittings never came to fruition. Smog and safety regulations in America ended the Amphicar's viability in late 1967, and when Harald Quandt died in a plane crash in September of that year, it lost its financial champion.

Often criticized for its drippy 1950s styling, there were two series of Amphicars. The 1961–1964 cars had a one-piece bumper and different sheet metal, axle shafts, and propellers. The 1965–1967 cars had better shafts and propellers, different body parts and a two-piece bumper.

THE AMPHICAR TODAY

Despite the Amphicar's high maintenance and corrosion-prone hulls, they have a devoted corps of owners who regularly gather for "swim-ins." One such fan, Keith Mathiowetz of Scandinavia, Wisconsin, has been obsessed with Amphicars since childhood and is a current member of the International Amphicar Owners Club.

"My interest in Amphicars began when I was about eight years old," he says. "Growing up in the late 1960s in Red Wing, Minnesota, a Mississippi River town, I saw a white Amphicar drive into the river while my family and I were at a local park. I already loved cars, so I was immediately attracted to the Amphicar's uniqueness and knew that someday I'd have one," he remembers.

Mathiowetz bought his complete—but extremely rough—1964 Lagoon Blue Amphicar in 1983. It was one of several remaining on the car lot of former Minneapolis Amphicar distributor Richard Holt. Holt was the largest Amphicar distributor in the Twin Cities area during the 1960s, and he still had a few leftover Amphicars well into the 1980s.

"He told me when I bought mine that he had sold it new to a man who later traded it in for a new 1967 Amphicar," Mathiowetz said. "After the trade-in, the blue car sat on the lot for over fifteen years. The engine had seized so the car was inoperable.

"After I bought the Amphicar, it languished in various garages. College and job relocations prevented me from doing a proper restoration. However, I did begin buying new old stock [NOS] and good used parts and storing them for future use. Restoration began in 2006 and is ongoing. The engine and transmission have been rebuilt, and the body has been repaired and repainted. I'm currently assembling the car."

Amphicars are a real restoration challenge, Mathiowetz said. Although they're considered a mass-produced car, they all have a hand-built, individual quality to them, which makes fitting and adjusting parts difficult. It's not like working on a Chevrolet or Ford.

Because this car is also a boat, special attention is needed to prevent water leaks. Every external hole in body/hull—for attaching bumpers, brake lines, headlights, taillights, steering gear, propeller shafts, and so on—must be sealed, usually with special gaskets. Generally, parts aren't difficult to obtain, but they are expensive.

"I've driven many types of cars and there's no automotive experience that compares to the thrill of driving an Amphicar into and out of the water," Mathiowetz said. "No matter how much you know about an Amphicar, and how much confidence you have in its abilities, the transition from land to water will make your heart race every time."

The final body and paint work of Mathiowetz's car was completed by fellow Amphicar enthusiast Tom Maruska of Duluth, Minnesota. Maruska broke a sales record when he sold his own restored 1964 Amphicar at the 2006 Barrett-Jackson Auction in Scottsdale for $115,000, plus an 8 percent buyer's commission. Typically, Amphicars sell for $45,000–$70,000, depending on rarity and condition.

At any price, the Amphicar continues to attract nautically minded collectors around the world. These hardy souls think nothing of venturing off terra firma in search of marine adventure, even if the going is slow and not without some peril.

Even with all of its compromises and drawbacks, the Amphicar makes people smile.

THE BUBBLE-SCREENED BOONDOGGLE

BY TOM COTTER

"Father Juliano was so far ahead of his time, he was considered weird. But I'm convinced he was a genius. The driver sits at least four-and-a-half feet from the windshield; there had never been a car built like that."

A HEAVEN-SENT HOBBY

NTHONY ALFRED JULIANO prayed he was making the right decision. The young man from Philadelphia was an enthusiast of cars and airplanes and had a knack for drawing.

In 1938, someone at General Motors was shown Juliano's car sketches. They were impressed enough with the 18-year-old lad's work to offer him enrollment in Harley Earl's newly opened school for automotive design students. But GM's offer came too late; Juliano had already decided to enter the priesthood.

Torn between two loves, Juliano was committed to becoming a man of the cloth.

Father Juliano attended the Holy Ghost seminary in Philadelphia from 1934 to 1940. He became an ordained priest in 1946, one year before graduating from Ferndale in Connecticut with dual degrees, a bachelor of arts and a degree in divinity. He joined the order of the Holy Ghost Fathers and began teaching at the Virginia Military Academy. Later, he became an art professor at Duquesne University in Pittsburgh.

In an attempt to get his doctorate in art and aerodynamics from Yale, Juliano was transferred to St. Mary's in Branford, Connecticut, where he was assistant pastor.

But he never forgot his first love—even as Father Juliano was reading the Bible and preparing for his doctorate, he was also reading technical manuals, *Mechanix Illustrated*, and every car magazine he could get his hands on. And as he pored over magazines and manuals, he thought about how to create the safest car on the road.

"He wanted to build the safest car in the world for his parishioners," said Andy Saunders, an auto restorer and custom car builder from Poole, England, and an authority on Father Juliano. Saunders owns the Juliano-built Aurora, seen on these pages.

"His thinking was so far ahead of his time. He was a genius."

A NEW DAWN

As opposed to today, where Volvo and Mercedes advertisements shout their companies' crash-test results as a marketing strategy, it was Juliano's belief that people cared more about style than safety.

Americans "won't pay for safety," he was quoted in a 1955 interview with Connecticut's *New Haven Register*. He sought to build a car that combined "unity and originality of design," that would have consumers flocking to buy his car for its beauty and acquiring the safety benefits as a bonus.

As can be seen from the accompanying photos of the Aurora, beauty is indeed in the eye of the beholder. Nonetheless, Father Juliano surged forward with his plans.

Selling the idea of car design to his superiors on the basis that it aided his thesis studies, he set up shop in an old horse stable in Branford and bought a wrecked 1953 Buick Roadmaster. He stripped the Buick's sheet metal, straightened the mangled frame, and spent the next four years designing and tinkering on what he hoped would be the safest, most beautiful car ever built. The Aurora was named for his young niece, Dawn; *aurora* is Latin for "dawn."

"Uncle Al was a part of our household during every holiday," said Father Juliano's niece Dawn O'Mara. "I can tell you that he definitely was not a hot rodder. He didn't know anything about the mechanical parts of cars. He was more of an artist and loved to paint in oil."

He began by building a clay scale model of his design, then used plywood and fiberglass to construct a body mold. According to O'Mara, her uncle worked with Owens/Corning in the development of the Aurora's body. The roof and gullwing-type

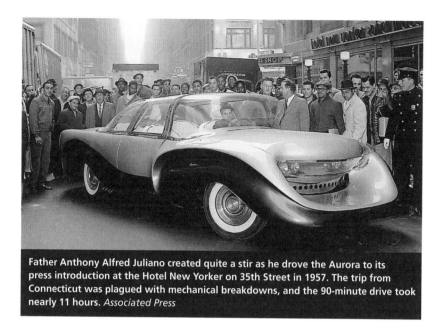

Father Anthony Alfred Juliano created quite a stir as he drove the Aurora to its press introduction at the Hotel New Yorker on 35th Street in 1957. The trip from Connecticut was plagued with mechanical breakdowns, and the 90-minute drive took nearly 11 hours. *Associated Press*

window canopy was constructed of shatterproof resin. Father Juliano worked tirelessly on the car, aided by sympathetic parishioners and a team of teenage boys eager to get their hands dirty working on cars.

Despite the Aurora's ungainly appearance, Father Juliano designed safety features into his car that were decades ahead of the automotive industry. Starting with the passenger compartment, one of the most obvious features is the car's bubble windshield. Father Juliano specified it be made of shatterproof resin so that it would be difficult for passengers to hit their heads on the windshield, a common injury at the time. Seat belts were also built into the car's design. He mounted the car's four "captain's chairs" high and toward the center of the car in order to give better protection in the event of a side impact. The four seats were also pedestal-mounted, allowing occupants to rotate up to 360 degrees prior to a crash for better protection.

The Aurora interior also featured a race car–type roll cage made of stainless steel, recessed gauges, and eight inches of padding on the dashboard. The car featured a collapsible steering column and side-impact protection bars.

The Aurora's exterior featured a front end with a huge foam-filled crush-zone that doubled as a "cowcatcher" to cradle errant pedestrians. The spare tire was located under the nose to assist in crash protection. Above the crush zone were six headlights, which were to be replaced with a light bar if the car were put into production.

The bubble windshield eliminated the need for windshield wipers, because like a jet plane, the car's speed would push rainwater to the sides. The Aurora also featured an automatic jacking system to aid in flat tire repair or other servicing.

Father Juliano wrote a sales brochure that claimed the Aurora was the World's Safest Car. The brochure noted that the car could be ordered with any type of power-plant: Cadillac, Lincoln, Imperial, Packard, Bugatti, or Mercedes-Benz. It also listed as options such items as fuel injection and supercharging, as well as a wide assortment of interior and exterior finishes.

The Custom Automobile Corporation of America, Father Juliano's enterprise, claimed that the Aurora's fiberglass styling was, "the most advanced in the world for a production automobile. It is built to last many years and will remain substantially the same year-in and year-out—a lifetime masterpiece of automotive engineering and design."

The promise was never fulfilled, however. The prototype cost $30,000 to construct, even though Father Juliano said he could manufacture models for $12,000 each and make a profit. But in 1957, the price was huge; even though it didn't include all the innovative safety features of the Aurora, a new Cadillac during the same period was less than $5,000.

The unfinished car was displayed at the 1956 Hartford (Connecticut) Autorama and was featured in the event program centerfold.

POISED TO FAIL

In 1957, en route to a press function to introduce the car to the New York media, it broke down at least 15 times on Father Juliano and needed to be towed to seven different service stations for repairs to unclog the fuel line. Apparently the Buick on which the Aurora was based had sat idle for all the years of design and construction, causing the gas tank to rust and clog the lines. That rust caused the fuel lines to clog repeatedly.

The trip from Branford, Connecticut, to Manhattan—which should have taken 90 minutes—took nearly 11 hours. At 3:00 p.m., Father Juliano once again called, saying that he was getting the Aurora's battery recharged in Harlem.

The media that had assembled at the Hotel New Yorker for the 8:00 a.m. press conference started to dissipate, and by the time the Aurora rolled up at 4:00 p.m., few media crews remained. The Associated Press, *New York Times*, and *Bridgeport Post* covered the car's arrival, but the media neglected to cover the car's safety features and instead mocked its voyage from Connecticut.

"Dream Car Arrives from Connecticut After Nightmare of Breakdowns," read the *Times* headline. The *Bridgeport Post* wrote, "Auto Built by Priest for Safety Perils Traffic," referring to the police request that Father Juliano move his car because of the rubbernecking traffic jam it had caused on 35th Street.

The Aurora's New York debut was supposed to kick off a 120-city tour around the United States, where Father Juliano had hoped to take orders from customers. Unfortunately the Aurora's styling didn't excite the public the way Father Juliano had hoped.

Additionally, questions began to arise about the funding for Father's automotive project. The car's development was at least partially funded by parishioners of St. Mary's church, and his superiors accused him of misappropriation of church donations. Others accused Father Juliano of spending parishioner donations not only for the Aurora project, but also for himself. Church officials met with Father Juliano, and he was summarily disciplined.

Father Juliano's niece, Dawn O'Mara, has her own opinion regarding the issue of her uncle's financial worries. "There were a lot of local folks who were impressed with Uncle Al's innovative ideas on safety features," said O'Mara. "You know, the seat belts, the windshield; they all wanted to get on the bandwagon because of all the positive hype.

"There was the intention of great profits."

O'Mara feels that many of the parishioners who invested their savings into the Custom Automotive Corporation's Aurora project began to have second thoughts

Father Juliano's project failed to attract investors or customers, so the car sat forlorn behind a Connecticut body shop for decades before being rescued by British car customizer Andy Saunders after he saw it in a magazine. *Vince Leto*

Because much of the car's body structure was constructed of wood, the 50 years it sat outdoors caused much of the car to disintegrate. This took years for Saunders to rebuild. *Andy Saunders*

once the shine started to wear off Father Juliano's dream. They sought their money returned or at least a way to save face.

Others suggest that General Motors was behind the accusations. These theories claim that the Aurora's safety features were so advanced that it threatened GM's own safety programs and the huge corporation's reputation. GM denied any involvement.

Regardless of blame, Father Juliano was drummed out of the Order of the Holy Ghost. He was investigated by the FBI and the Internal Revenue Service, but the investigations led nowhere.

Father Juliano compared himself to the late Preston Tucker, a manufacturer of the Torpedo, which was so advanced that he claims he was forced out of business in 1948 by the big Detroit automakers who didn't want to disturb the industry's status quo. Tucker also was accused of financial scandal, which was proved to be unfounded.

What wasn't publicized, though, was that Father Juliano had also put himself into deep personal debt financing the project to completion. He was bankrupt, and the Aurora was given as collateral to a repair shop for unpaid repair bills. The car went through several hands before landing in a field behind McPhee's Body Shop in Cheshire, Connecticut.

Juliano went on to live in Florida before moving back to Philadelphia, where he became involved in art restoration.

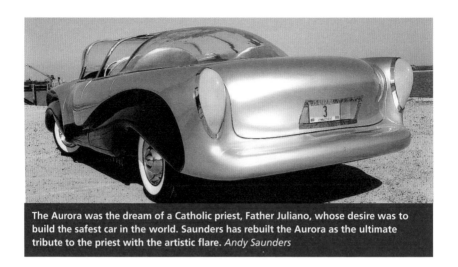

The Aurora was the dream of a Catholic priest, Father Juliano, whose desire was to build the safest car in the world. Saunders has rebuilt the Aurora as the ultimate tribute to the priest with the artistic flare. *Andy Saunders*

According to his niece, Father Juliano worked with Sotherby's and other art auction houses on painting and gold leaf frame restoration. "He was an artist in his own right," said O'Mara. "My brothers and I still own some of Uncle Al's paintings, and they are very, very good." O'Mara also said that her uncle planned to build another car and had sketches and plans for a new design, but he never went further than the planning stages.

In 1989, her uncle was doing art research in the Philadelphia Public Library when he suffered a massive heart attack. He was rushed to nearby Hahnemann Hospital, where he was put on life support and fell into a coma.

"The hospital didn't know who he was, because his car keys were in his pocket and his wallet was in his car in the library parking lot," she said. "My brother and I were called to identify him. Then, because my own father [Anthony Raymond Juliano] was in such bad condition, also in the hospital, my brother and I were asked to sign to take Uncle Al off life support." He died on March 2, 1989, and was buried in the Catholic cemetery in the Drexel Hill section of Philadelphia.

By the time Father Juliano was laid to rest, his Aurora safety car had already been resting in the field for more than 30 years. The body shop owner attempted to sell the car for $10,000 in 1978, but there were no interested parties.

THE UGLIEST CAR EVER SEEN

An issue of the British magazine *Thoroughbred & Classic Cars* featured the Aurora in their "Discovered" section, which highlights interesting classic cars that are found by readers.

Saunders, who builds custom show cars for a living, says the Aurora's restoration was the toughest job he has ever done. Even with its controversial styling, the car is quite dramatic in its newly restored condition. *Andy Saunders*

The car caught the attention of one interested reader—Andy Saunders. "I'd seen that car before in an old schoolbook," he said. Saunders showed the picture to his father, who said, "That's the ugliest car I've ever seen."

Saunders, who runs a custom auto fabrication shop called Andy Saunders Kustoms, Kampers, and Kars in Poole, England, has always dreamed of owning a prototype dream car. He felt this was his chance.

"I studied the picture in the magazine and saw the name of the body shop in the background and was able to read the phone number," he said. Saunders called the owner of the shop where the Aurora had now rested for at least 34 years.

"I paid one thousand five hundred dollars for it without ever seeing it in person," he said. "When it arrived in England, it was absolutely knocked. It was scrap. It was falling to pieces.

"All the door frames—the A-pillars, the B-pillars, firewall, wheel arches—they were all made of wood. Having sat in the field for so long, the water completely delaminated the wood."

But the fiberglass body was a different story. The wood would need to be fabricated and fitted piece-by-piece, meaning a tough manual labor chore for Saunders. The fiberglass had deteriorated so badly it was almost melted, according to Saunders.

"Father Juliano was so far ahead of his time, he was considered weird. But I'm convinced he was a genius. The driver sits at least four-and-a-half feet from the windshield; there had never been a car built like that."

When Saunders realized what he had bought, he became depressed. He dove in and spent virtually every night and weekend restoring, in some ways remanufacturing, the Aurora. He was able to retain the original chassis and running gear, front and rear fenders, and hood.

"Custom cars are a hobby for me," he said. "It's nothing for me to spend eighteen or nineteen hours a day working on cars. I can work 8:00 a.m. to 5:00 p.m. working on cars in my business, then work until 2:00 a.m. working on my own cars. I think they are the most exciting vehicles in the world.

"The roof structure held the whole [body] together, so we had to cut it in half to disassemble and reassemble the body," said Saunders, "or else the car would have fallen apart."

The largest challenge Saunders has faced is in replicating the unusual windshield.

"I can't get anyone to build a windshield like he [Father Juliano] did," he said. "The one we built turned yellow in five years, yet the original sat outside for more than thirty years and still was clear, but unfortunately unusable."

Saunders has copies of the original sales brochure from when the Aurora was displayed at the Hotel New Yorker in 1957, and every magazine the car was featured in, but unfortunately all the photos are in black and white. One cover photo, though, in *Motor Trend*, showed the car in black and silver, so that's how the car is finished.

"The picture looked to be 'color washed,' so I'm not quite sure of the exact colors of the Aurora," he said. "But I had nothing else to go with, and couldn't find a single chip of original paint on the car."

So far Saunders has spent US$12,000 working with aircraft manufacturers trying to copy that windshield.

"That car owes me," he said. "It's the most expensive car I've ever restored. The car cost me seventy-five to eighty thousand dollars, exclusive of the hours I've invested."

So far, Saunder's restored Aurora has been featured in a number of magazines and the prestigious Goodwood Festival of Speed in England. The Petersen Automotive Museum in Los Angeles also has granted a standing invitation for the car if it ever comes to America.

Saunders, though, doesn't pull any punches regarding his feelings for the finished product.

"I hate the bloody thing," he said. "I wish I'd never bought it.

"At least if I could register the bloody thing and drive it on the road, it would be different. But this bloody windshield!"

INDEX